American Heart
Association®

Fighting Heart Disease and Stroke

# Low-Fat, Low-Cholesterol

## cookbook

## ALSO BY THE AMERICAN HEART ASSOCIATION

American Heart Association®

Fighting Heart Disease and Stroke

# Low-Fat, Low-Cholesterol

## cookbook

second edition

heart-healthy, easy-to-make
recipes that taste great

Clarkson Potter/Publishers
New York

Your contribution to the American Heart Association supports research that helps make publications like this possible. For more information, call 1–800–AHA–USA1 (1–800–242–8721) or contact us online at *www.americanheart.org.*

Published by Clarkson Potter/Publishers, New York, New York.
Member of the Crown Publishing Group.

Random House, Inc. New York, Toronto, London, Sydney, Auckland
www.randomhouse.com

CLARKSON N. POTTER is a trademark and POTTER and colophon are registered trademarks of Random House, Inc.

Originally published in somewhat different form, in hardcover, by Times Books in 1989. This revised second edition was published by Times Books in 1997.

Printed in the United States of America

Art direction by Naomi Osnos
Book design by Maura Fadden Rosenthal/Mspace

Library of Congress Cataloging-in-Publication Data
American Heart Association low-fat, low-cholesterol cookbook : heart-healthy, easy-to-make recipes that taste great / American Heart Association.—2nd ed.
    Includes index.
    1. Low-fat diet—Recipes.  2. Low-cholesterol diet—Recipes.  I. American Heart Association.
RM237.7.A44  1997
641.5'6311—DC21                              97-17099

ISBN 0-609-80861-3

10 9 8 7 6 5

# PREFACE

Today the trend in trying to prevent heart disease in the United States is encouraging. Many people are replacing our country's traditional high-fat diet with foods low in saturated fat and cholesterol. In short, that means eating less fat and living to enjoy it more.

At the American Heart Association, we're delighted to see this trend. It shows you're heading in the right direction—toward healthier hearts and lives free from heart attack and stroke. One of the first steps in this direction is to reduce your blood cholesterol level by eating light, low-fat cuisine.

This second version of the *American Heart Association Low-Fat, Low-Cholesterol Cookbook* features some of the most creative low-fat cooking around. In it, you'll find everything you need to know about eating to lower your blood cholesterol level.

The star of the show is 194 appealing recipes, both old and new—each with a brand-new nutritional analysis. Many recipes from the original edition have been updated to take advantage of the new nonfat and low-fat products now available. You'll also find the tried-and-true Step I and Step II cholesterol-lowering diets. Plus, you'll get the full scoop on low-fat, low-cholesterol foods (including some new ones you may not know about) and how to cook them. You'll also find scientific information on how cholesterol affects your body, plus the latest on drugs to lower cholesterol.

At the American Heart Association, it's our goal to give you the tools you need to help keep your heart healthy. We know that changing your lifestyle to lower your cholesterol isn't easy. The payoff is enormous, however. We applaud your efforts, and we're here to help whenever you need us.

You have lots of good eating ahead of you on these pages. Go to it!

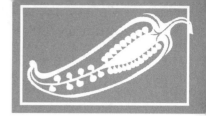

# ACKNOWLEDGMENTS

Volunteer Science Consultant: Scott M. Grundy, M.D., Ph.D.

American Heart Association Senior Science Consultant: Mary Winston, Ed.D., R.D.

American Heart Association Nutrition Science Consultant: Terry Bazzarre, Ph.D.

American Heart Association Director of Consumer Publications: Jane Anneken Ruehl

American Heart Association Senior Editor: Janice Roth Moss

Recipe Developers for Second Edition: Carol Ritchie
Linda Foley Woodrum

Recipe Developers for Original Edition: Laureen Mody, R.D.
Leni Reed, R.D.
Sherry Ferguson

Writer: Pat Harmon Naegele

Nutrient Analyses: Nutrition Coordinating Center, University of Minnesota

# CONTENTS

## APPENDIXES

# American Heart Association Low-Fat, Low-Cholesterol Cookbook

SECOND EDITION

# INTRODUCTION

Many Americans are lowering their cholesterol level, quitting smoking, watching their blood pressure, and becoming more active.

To us at the American Heart Association, this is gratifying because it means that many people are reducing their risk of heart attack and stroke. It means more Americans will have healthy hearts that last a lifetime.

Do you have high blood cholesterol? Has your doctor recommended that you eat less fat? If so, you've come to the right place. This new AHA *Low-Fat, Low-Cholesterol Cookbook* has it all. The recipes on these pages are simply scrumptious. Consider the bliss of sinking your teeth into Crab Spring Rolls with Peanut Dipping Sauce, Chicken Breasts Stuffed with Ricotta and Goat Cheese, and Mango Brûlée with Pine Nuts. You'll find they can all be part of healthful, low-fat eating.

You may want to start with our handy assessment tool designed to help you determine how much fat you're eating now (see "First, Look at the Way You're Eating Now," on page 9). Then you can easily see the changes you'll want to make so you can follow your doctor's advice. You'll also discover what foods to eat; how to shop for low-fat, low-cholesterol foods; and how to cook them in the heart-healthiest way. Plus, you'll find encouragement for your weight-loss efforts. We even have information on how to eat out in all kinds of restaurants, have fun, and *still* choose dishes that will do your heart good.

In the appendixes, you'll learn how your body handles cholesterol. You'll also see why a low-saturated-fat, low-cholesterol way of eating is so important. Check the updated chapter on cholesterol-lowering drugs for the latest scientific knowledge. Some of you won't be able to reduce your cholesterol to a safe level with diet alone. For you, this section will be vital.

If you're using this cookbook as an aid in developing a new help-your-heart eating plan, take a look at the Step I and Step II Diets on pages 12 and 13. On the other hand, if you just want to add to your repertoire of low-fat, low-cholesterol recipes, turn to page 26.

Whatever your goal, we hope this cookbook will give you many hours of delicious eating and many more years with a healthy heart.

# THE LOWDOWN ON HIGH CHOLESTEROL

Chances are you bought this cookbook because your doctor said you need to lower your cholesterol level. We think that's good advice. Why? Because research has shown clearly that too much cholesterol in your blood can lead to heart disease, America's number-one killer. Despite all our advances in preventing and treating heart disease, it still claims about 950,000 lives a year.

The fact is, about 12.4 million people currently living in the United States have coronary heart disease and about 4.5 million have had a stroke. Millions more are at risk of heart attack and stroke and don't even know it.

Now for the good news: You can cut your risk of heart disease dramatically by reducing your blood cholesterol level. You can do that by cutting down on saturated fat* and cholesterol in your diet. In fact, physicians and scientists say that the best ways to improve your heart health are to lower your cholesterol level and quit smoking.

In 1985, Oxford University's Richard Peto said, "We know two things about how to prevent death in middle age: smoking and cholesterol. Each of those two things is responsible for about one third of all deaths in middle age."

## WILL LOWERING MY CHOLESTEROL LEVEL REALLY HELP ME PREVENT HEART DISEASE?

Countless scientific studies have shown that high blood cholesterol plays a major role in heart disease. In fact, a number of large clinical trials show that high blood cholesterol is a direct cause of heart attack. For example, one National Heart, Lung, and Blood Institute study included 3,800 men with high cholesterol. Half were given a cholesterol-lowering drug called cholestyramine, and the other half were given a placebo. The men receiving the cholestyramine had significantly lower cholesterol levels and fewer heart attacks than the men receiving placebos. These results proved

---

* "Saturated fat" is popular shorthand for the more accurate term "saturated fatty acids." That's because what we call "saturated fat" is actually made up of lots of different varieties of saturated fatty acids. In fact, this is true for all fats, including polyunsaturated and monounsaturated. For easier reading, we'll generally use the shorthand versions of these terms.

that lowering blood cholesterol reduces both the risk of having a heart attack and the risk of dying from an attack. Other clinical trials using cholesterol-lowering drugs showed similar results. The results of more-recent trials show that reducing blood cholesterol can slow the formation of atherosclerosis in both men and women and can even bring about atherosclerosis regression in some people.

It's not just drug therapy that shows these results. A number of clinical trials have involved cholesterol-lowering diets. Several types of study have given us a large body of evidence that shows a powerful link between diet and heart disease. The evidence also proves beyond a doubt that to a large extent diet determines a person's blood cholesterol level. One study in Oslo, Norway, revealed that changing the diet to reduce blood cholesterol can definitely reduce the risk of heart attack. Similar trials reported from Los Angeles, Minneapolis, and Helsinki, Finland, agreed.

When the experts averaged the results of all these clinical trials, they were able to estimate how much lowering blood cholesterol will reduce the risk of heart attack. As a general rule, if you reduce your total cholesterol level by 1 percent, you reduce your heart attack risk by 2 percent. This means that if you reduced your blood cholesterol from 250 to 200 milligrams per deciliter (mg/dl), for example, you'd reduce your heart attack risk by 40 percent. That's quite a payoff. It's also why we wrote this cookbook: to help you reduce your cholesterol level—and one of your risks for heart attack—while enjoying delectable low-fat, low-cholesterol dishes.


## WHAT'S MY CHOLESTEROL LEVEL?

Your physician has probably measured your total blood cholesterol level along with your high-density lipoprotein (HDL) level. (HDLs are often called "good" cholesterol, the kind that's not likely to be deposited in your arteries and cause atherosclerosis.) If so, these blood cholesterol levels will show how you fit into one of the classifications on the following chart. This chart helps your doctor identify your risk of heart disease. In calculating your risk, he or she will also take into account your physical and medical history, as well as the presence of other risk factors (see appendix H, page 351).

## WHAT YOUR CHOLESTEROL NUMBERS MEAN

| Cholesterol (mg/dl) | Classification |
| --- | --- |
| Total less than 200 | Desirable |
| Total 200 to 239 | Borderline high risk |
| Total above 239 | High risk |
| HDL less than 35 | High risk |

## IF YOU'RE UNDER 200

As you can see on the chart above, if your total cholesterol level is less than 200 and your HDL level is 35 or more, high blood cholesterol is not a problem for you right now. Continue to eat a healthful diet that's low in fat, be physically active, and have your cholesterol level checked once every five years. Of course, if you have other major risk factors, such as smoking or high blood pressure, you're still at risk for heart disease and you'll want to follow the advice in this book. Even if you're totally healthy now, your best bet is to follow prudent dietary recommendations. The information in this cookbook can help you keep your cholesterol level—along with your risk of heart disease—low.

## IF YOU'RE 200 TO 239

If your cholesterol level is between 200 and 239, you're in a borderline zone. You face twice the risk of heart attack as people whose levels are well below 200. Don't feel alone: About 31 percent of American adults fall into this category. You shouldn't ignore this borderline status, especially if you have other risk factors. Start eating to lower your blood cholesterol using the Step I Diet, and have your cholesterol level checked again in a few months.

## IF YOU'RE 240 OR HIGHER

Finally, if your cholesterol level is 240 or higher, you could be at high risk of a heart attack. This is especially true if your HDL level is less than 35 mg/dl. Talk to your doctor, because it's likely you'll need further tests to determine the best treatment plan.

No matter what your classification, this cookbook can help you. These appetizing recipes were created to make low-fat, low-cholesterol eating a blissful experience and, in the process, protect you against America's number one killer, heart disease.

# HOW DO I EAT WITH MY HEART IN MIND?

Most cases of high blood cholesterol are caused by eating high-saturated-fat, high-cholesterol foods. It stands to reason, therefore, that most cases can be reversed by eating foods low in saturated fat and cholesterol. Usually, this is true. However, some people can't reduce their cholesterol level to below 200 without medication. (See "Drugs: When Diet Alone Won't Work," page 347, then talk with your doctor.)

If you've had a heart attack or have other major risk factors, lowering your cholesterol level to below 200 is extremely important. If you have heart disease, it's also important to reduce your low-density lipoprotein (LDL) cholesterol, the type that carries harmful cholesterol into your artery walls. You want to reduce your LDL level to below 100 mg/dl. If you don't have heart disease or risk factors, reduce it to below 130 mg/dl. (For more information about lipoproteins and how your body handles cholesterol, see page 344.)

If you have no other risk factors and haven't had a heart attack, you should aim—at the very least—to reduce your cholesterol level to below 240 and your LDL cholesterol level to below 160. Again, the closer you can come to a cholesterol level under 200, the better.

You may be wondering how much you'll have to change your diet to achieve these goals. That depends on a number of things. For many people, some relatively minor changes can reduce their cholesterol level significantly. Others need to make more extensive changes. The Step I and Step II Diets outlined beginning on page 9 help meet the needs of each of these groups. The Step I Diet will work for many people. It's recommended for everyone over the age of two. If you've had a heart attack or you need an extra boost to reach your goals, the Step II Diet can help you get there.

# THE STEP I AND STEP II CHOLESTEROL-LOWERING DIETS

## FIRST, LOOK AT THE WAY YOU'RE EATING NOW

Before you can change your eating habits to lower your cholesterol level, you need to know what you're eating now. The following checklist, from a questionnaire that's part of the National Cholesterol Education Program, will help you find out.

Think about the foods you eat each week. Then look at the food categories. Foods are listed in two groups under each category. When you see the foods you usually eat, follow the line out to the right under "Weekly Consumption" and "Serving Size." Check the circle that best describes the number of servings of those foods that you eat in one week. Then check the circle for your usual portion size. Do the same thing in each category. Add your scores, then check the total against the key on the bottom of page 11. Your score will tell you whether you need to make a few changes or whether you are already following the Step I or Step II Diet.

# MEDFICTS

In each food category for both **Group 1** and **Group 2** foods, check one circle from the **"Weekly Consumption"** column (number of servings eaten per week), then check one circle from the **"Serving Size"** column (size of the serving). If you check "Rarely/Never," do not check a serving-size circle. See bottom of next page for score.

## Food Category

| | Weekly Consumption | | | Serving Size | | | Score |
|---|---|---|---|---|---|---|---|
| | Rarely/Never | 3 or less | 4 or more | Small <6 oz | Average 6 oz per day | Large >6 oz | |

**Meats**
- Recommended amount per day: ≤6 oz (equal in size to two decks of playing cards).
- Base your estimate on the food you consume most often.
- Beef and lamb sections are trimmed to 1/8" fat.

**1** • 10 grams or more total fat in 3-oz cooked portion — Weekly: 3 pts, 7 pts — X — Serving: 1 pt, 2 pts, 3 pts = 

| Beef | Processed meats | Other Meat, Poultry, Seafood |
|---|---|---|
| Ground beef | 1/4-lb burger or large sandwich | Pork chops (center loin) |
| Ribs | Bacon | Pork roast (blade Boston sirloin) |
| Steak (T-bone, flank, porterhouse, tenderloin) | Lunch meat | Pork spareribs |
| Chuck blade roast | Sausage/knockwurst | Ground pork |
| Brisket | Hot dogs | Lamb chops |
| Meat loaf (with ground beef) | Ham (bone end) | Lamb (rib) |
| Corned beef | Ground turkey | Organ meats* |
| | | Chicken with skin |
| | | Eel, mackerel, pompano |

**2** • Less than 10 grams total fat in 3-oz cooked portion — 6 pts † =

| Lean beef | Low-fat Processed meats | Other Meat, Poultry, Seafood |
|---|---|---|
| Round steak (eye of round, top round) | Low-fat lunch meat | Chicken, turkey (without skin)‡ |
| Sirloin§ | Canadian bacon | Most seafood* |
| Tip and bottom round§ | "Lean" fast-food sandwich | Lamb (Leg shank) |
| Chuck arm pot roast§ | Boneless ham | Pork tenderloin |
| Top loin§ | | Pork sirloin, top loin |
| | | Veal cutlets, sirloin, shoulder |
| | | Ground veal, venison |
| | | Veal chops and ribs§ |
| | | Lamb (whole leg, loin, foreshank, sirloin)§ |

## Eggs
• Weekly consumption is the number of times you eat eggs each week.

Check the number of eggs eaten each time.

**1** Whole eggs, yolks — 3 pts, 7 pts — X — ≤1 (1 pt), 2 (2 pts), ≥3 (3 pts) =

**2** Egg whites, egg substitutes (1/2 cup = 2 eggs) =

## Dairy

**MILK** • Average serving: 1 cup

**1** Whole milk, 2% milk, 2% buttermilk, yogurt (whole milk) — 3 pts, 7 pts — X — 1 pt, 2 pts, 3 pts =

**2** Skim milk, 1% milk, skim-milk buttermilk, yogurt (nonfat and low-fat) =

**CHEESE** • Average serving: 1 oz

**1** Cream cheese, Cheddar, Monterey Jack, Colby, Swiss, American processed, blue cheese, regular cottage cheese (1/2 cup) and ricotta (1/4 cup) — 3 pts, 7 pts — X — 1 pt, 2 pts, 3 pts =

**2** Low-fat and fat-free cheeses, skim-milk mozzarella string cheese, low-fat, skim-milk and fat-free cottage cheese (1/2 cup) and ricotta (1/4 cup) =

**FROZEN DESSERTS** • Average serving: 1/2 cup

**1** Ice cream, milk shakes — 3 pts, 7 pts — X — 1 pt, 2 pts, 3 pts =

**2** Ice milk, frozen yogurt =

---

\* Organ meats, shrimp, abalone, and squid are low in fat but high in cholesterol.
† Score 6 points if this box checked.
‡ All parts not listed in Group 1 have <10 grams total fat.
§ Only lean cuts with all visible fat trimmed. If not trimmed of all visible fat, score as if in Group 1.

SUBTOTAL
(Add score from each category)

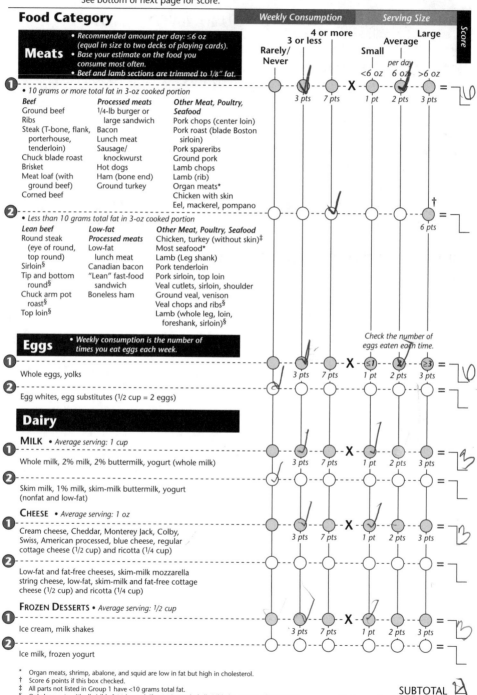

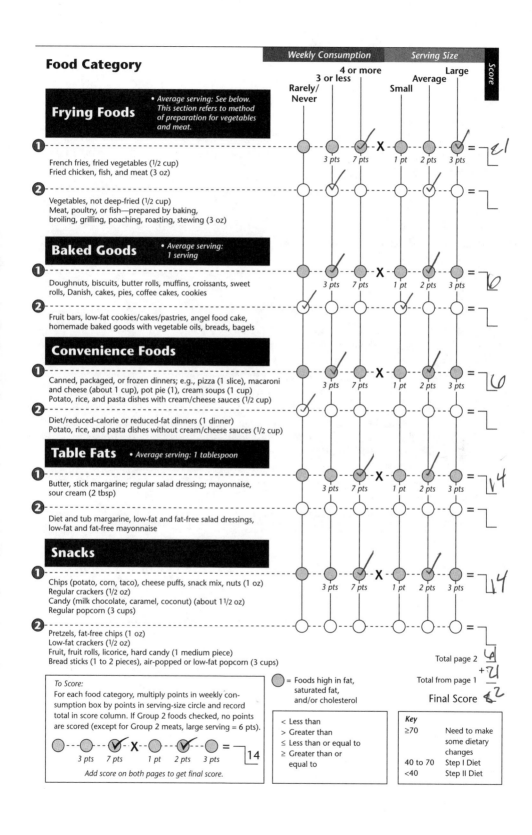

## Food Category

| | | Weekly Consumption | | | Serving Size | | | Score |
| | | Rarely/Never | 3 or less | 4 or more | Small | Average | Large | |

### Frying Foods
• Average serving: See below. This section refers to method of preparation for vegetables and meat.

**1** French fries, fried vegetables (1/2 cup)
Fried chicken, fish, and meat (3 oz)
— 3 pts | 7 pts — X — 1 pt | 2 pts | 3 pts = 21

**2** Vegetables, not deep-fried (1/2 cup)
Meat, poultry, or fish—prepared by baking, broiling, grilling, poaching, roasting, stewing (3 oz)
=

### Baked Goods
• Average serving: 1 serving

**1** Doughnuts, biscuits, butter rolls, muffins, croissants, sweet rolls, Danish, cakes, pies, coffee cakes, cookies
— 3 pts | 7 pts — X — 1 pt | 2 pts | 3 pts = 0

**2** Fruit bars, low-fat cookies/cakes/pastries, angel food cake, homemade baked goods with vegetable oils, breads, bagels
=

### Convenience Foods

**1** Canned, packaged, or frozen dinners; e.g., pizza (1 slice), macaroni and cheese (about 1 cup), pot pie (1), cream soups (1 cup)
Potato, rice, and pasta dishes with cream/cheese sauces (1/2 cup)
— 3 pts | 7 pts — X — 1 pt | 2 pts | 3 pts = 6

**2** Diet/reduced-calorie or reduced-fat dinners (1 dinner)
Potato, rice, and pasta dishes without cream/cheese sauces (1/2 cup)
=

### Table Fats
• Average serving: 1 tablespoon

**1** Butter, stick margarine; regular salad dressing; mayonnaise, sour cream (2 tbsp)
— 3 pts | 7 pts — X — 1 pt | 2 pts | 3 pts = 14

**2** Diet and tub margarine, low-fat and fat-free salad dressings, low-fat and fat-free mayonnaise
=

### Snacks

**1** Chips (potato, corn, taco), cheese puffs, snack mix, nuts (1 oz)
Regular crackers (1/2 oz)
Candy (milk chocolate, caramel, coconut) (about 1 1/2 oz)
Regular popcorn (3 cups)
— 3 pts | 7 pts — X — 1 pt | 2 pts | 3 pts = 14

**2** Pretzels, fat-free chips (1 oz)
Low-fat crackers (1/2 oz)
Fruit, fruit rolls, licorice, hard candy (1 medium piece)
Bread sticks (1 to 2 pieces), air-popped or low-fat popcorn (3 cups)
=

Total page 2 = 4

Total from page 1 + 21

Final Score 82

○ = Foods high in fat, saturated fat, and/or cholesterol

**To Score:**
For each food category, multiply points in weekly consumption box by points in serving-size circle and record total in score column. If Group 2 foods checked, no points are scored (except for Group 2 meats, large serving = 6 pts).

○ --- ○ --- ✓ X ○ --- ✓ --- ○ = 14
3 pts   7 pts   1 pt   2 pts   3 pts

*Add score on both pages to get final score.*

< Less than
> Greater than
≤ Less than or equal to
≥ Greater than or equal to

| Key | |
|---|---|
| ≥70 | Need to make some dietary changes |
| 40 to 70 | Step I Diet |
| <40 | Step II Diet |

# THE STEP I AND STEP II DIETS

If you want to reduce your blood cholesterol level, the Step I and Step II Diets are your good friends. Created jointly by the American Heart Association and the National Heart, Lung, and Blood Institute, these eating plans are designed to help you cut the fat, saturated fat, and cholesterol in your diet and lower your blood cholesterol level. If you're overweight, the plans can help you cut calories as well. All the recipes in this book are designed to fit in both diets.

The Step I Diet is recommended for the general public—it's the heart-healthiest way to eat for any healthy person over age two. It provides guidance for reducing saturated fat and cholesterol, and if you're overweight, cutting down on total calories. Take a look at the table below for an overview.

---

### THE STEP I DIET

- Eat at least five servings of fruits and vegetables daily.
- Eat at least six servings of grain products daily.
- Eat no more than 6 ounces (cooked weight) of lean meat, fish, or skinless poultry per day. Have at least two servings of fish per week.
- Balance food intake with physical activity to achieve and maintain a healthy weight.
- Choose a diet low in saturated fat, trans fat, and cholesterol and moderate in salt (sodium) and sugar. Eat less than 10 percent of your calories as saturated fat. Limit yourself to less than 300 milligrams (mg) of cholesterol and less than 2,400 mg of sodium daily.
- Include fat-free and low-fat dairy products, legumes, poultry, and lean meats in your eating plan.
- If you drink, limit yourself to one drink per day if you are a woman and two drinks per day if you are a man.

---

On this cholesterol-lowering plan, you'll want to know one thing right away: *How many grams of saturated fat can I safely eat every day?* When you know this, you can simply read the food labels and add up the number of saturated fat grams. All you have to do then is stay within the numbers allowed.

The table on page 13 shows the daily saturated fat limits for the Step I and Step II Diets based on calorie levels. First, determine the number of calories you need daily, depending on whether you want to lose, gain, or maintain your current weight at your present level of physical activity. Typical calorie levels for men are 2,000 to 2,500 calories to maintain weight and 1,600 to 2,000 to lose weight. For women, typical calorie levels are 1,600 to 2,000 to maintain weight and 1,200 to 1,600 to lose it.

Next, find the number of saturated fat grams recommended for your calorie level. That's the maximum number of grams you should eat in one day.

## COUNTING SATURATED FAT GRAMS

| Calories | Daily Saturated Fat Recommended,[*] | |
| | Step I | Step II |
| --- | --- | --- |
| 1,200 | 12 grams | 8 grams |
| 1,500 | 15 grams | 10 grams |
| 1,800[†] | 18 grams | 12 grams |
| 2,000 | 20 grams | 13 grams |
| 2,500[‡] | 25 grams | 17 grams |

[*]Amounts are equal to 9 percent of total calories for Step I and 6 percent of total calories for Step II. Remember that 1 gram of fat equals 9 calories.
[†]Average daily consumption for women.
[‡]Average daily consumption for men.

With this maximum in mind, you can read nutrition labels or pick up a copy of the American Heart Association's *Brand Name Fat and Cholesterol Counter* (or a similar guide) to find out the amount of saturated fat, cholesterol, sodium, and calories in what you eat. Then you can choose foods that fit your eating plan. Of course, you will occasionally slip and eat something that doesn't fit. Don't despair. Simply make up for the splurge by eating extra carefully for the rest of that day or the next.

After six months on the Step I Diet, your doctor should check your blood cholesterol again. If you've reached your target level for blood cholesterol, pat yourself on the back and adopt this way of eating permanently. It will help keep your cholesterol at a safe level for the rest of your life.

If you've followed the Step I Diet faithfully but your cholesterol hasn't dropped to your goal, your doctor will suggest that you move to the Step II Diet right away. It cuts the saturated fat and cholesterol in your diet a bit more to help you reach your goal. Your doctor may give you an individualized plan and may start you on a cholesterol-lowering drug.

## THE STEP II DIET

Follow the Step I Diet *except*:
- Eat less than 7 percent of your calories as saturated fat.
- Limit yourself to less than 200 milligrams of cholesterol daily.

As we outlined in the Step I Diet, you should figure the maximum number of grams of saturated fat you should eat every day, based on the number of calories you eat. (See the "Counting Saturated Fat Grams" chart on page 13.) The Step II Diet reduces the amount of saturated fat and cholesterol you eat more than the Step I Diet. As a result, it should lower your blood cholesterol more dramatically. That's why it's the plan recommended if you have heart disease.

To get the full benefits of the Step II Diet, it's a good idea to work with a registered dietitian or a qualified licensed nutritionist. After you've followed the Step II Diet for several months, ask your doctor to check your cholesterol level again. If you've reached your goal, good for you! It looks as if the Step II Diet is the one for you. If you haven't reached your goal, your doctor may make a change in your cholesterol-lowering drug along with watching your diet. (For information about drug therapy, see appendix G.)

## WHAT YOU NEED TO KNOW ABOUT CALORIES, CHOLESTEROL, AND FAT

Let's look at why these factors are important in lowering your blood cholesterol.

**Total Calories.** Being fat is no fun—for you or your heart. In addition to contributing to high blood cholesterol, obesity is a risk factor in its own right. That's why it's important for anyone carrying excess weight to cut calories and burn more calories in physical activity.

The fact is, many overweight Americans could lose weight by changing their sedentary lifestyles to include more exercise and controlling their calorie intake (see page 336). Exercise combined with cutting calories is more healthful for you than a severely restricted calorie intake. The eating plans in this book aren't weight-reducing diets. However, if you eat less fat without increasing your caloric intake, you'll naturally lose weight because fat contains a high concentration of calories. The American Heart Association recommends keeping your total fat intake below 30 percent of your total calories if you want to lose weight. Losing weight—even as little as 10 pounds—can help reduce low-density lipoproteins. Talk to your doctor about the best weight-loss program for you.

**Dietary Cholesterol.** Your body needs *some* cholesterol in order to function at its best. Most of the time, your liver manufactures all the cholesterol you need. The cholesterol in the foods you eat can add to the overall cholesterol level in your system. The Step I Diet suggests limiting the cholesterol you eat to fewer than 300 milligrams a day. The Step II Diet calls for eating no more than 200 milligrams of cholesterol a day.

**Saturated Fats.**   These fats are found in animal products and in some plant products. Some animal sources are cheese, butter, cream, whole milk, ice cream, fatty beef, pork, lamb, and poultry skin. Plant sources include coconut oil, palm kernel oil, palm oil, and cocoa butter.

The typical American diet contains about 13 percent of total calories from saturated fats. The Step I Diet recommends reducing saturated fats to 8 to 10 percent of your total calories; the Step II Diet, to less than 7 percent of total calories. That means most Americans should reduce their saturated fat intake by about one fourth to reach a healthful level.

**Trans Fats.**   When manufacturers add hydrogen to vegetable oil to make it solid, trans fats are created. These fats raise LDL. Some of the most significant sources of trans fats are margarine and commercially baked products such as cookies, crackers, and breads. Check ingredient labels so you can limit hydrogenated or partially hydrogenated oils. Select liquid or tub margarine when possible.

**Polyunsaturated Fats.**   As you eat less saturated fat, you may replace it with polyunsaturated fat—but only up to a point. An easy way to start is by cutting out butter and lard. Instead, substitute polyunsaturated vegetable oils, such as corn, safflower, and sunflower, or soft margarines that list a polyunsaturated vegetable oil as the primary ingredient.

**Monounsaturated Fats.**   For the obvious fats in your diet, such as salad dressings, spreads, and cooking oils, choose products made of polyunsaturated or monounsaturated fats. Olive oil and canola (rapeseed) oil are two major sources of monounsaturated fats.

for about 15 percent of your total daily calories. Olive oil and canola (rapeseed) oil are two major sources of monounsaturated fats.

**Carbohydrates.** For the best health, about 55 to 60 percent of your calories should come from carbohydrates. Most of these should be complex carbohydrates (starches and fibers), not simple sugars (cake and candy). The complex carbohydrates you get in fruits, vegetables, and whole grains are rich in vitamins, minerals, and fiber.

**Protein.** Most Americans eat much more protein than their bodies actually need. Both Step I and Step II recommend a protein intake that's just 15 percent of total calories. Remember, it's important to get your protein from a variety of foods, including dried peas and beans, meat, seafood, poultry, and soy products, such as tofu. Both plant and animal proteins give you a wide range of vitamins, minerals, fiber, and other nutrients.

# WHAT TO EAT

When you flip through the pages of this cookbook, you'll see mouthwatering recipes such as Spinach-Cheese Strudel, Pork with Corn-Cilantro Pesto, and Chocolate Custard Cake with Raspberries. Probably not what you expected on a low-fat, low-cholesterol diet, right?

The good news is that you can still eat most of your favorite foods—as long as you make a few key substitutions. You'll see that, with almost any dish, it's easy to reduce the fat and cholesterol but keep the flavor.

## DAIRY PRODUCTS AND EGGS

Hooray! You can have the dairy products you love and still lower your cholesterol. Check out your local supermarket for fat-free milk, nonfat and low-fat yogurts and frozen yogurts, and nonfat and low-fat cheeses.

If you normally use butter, which is high in saturated fat, substitute soft margarine. If you like cream in your coffee, try fat-free evaporated milk. It works just as well and contains almost no fat. Why are we recommending these changes? Because butterfat contains large amounts of saturated fat and cholesterol and tends to raise your blood cholesterol level. In the paragraphs below, take a look at the amount of fat you get in whole-milk dairy products.

**Whole, Low-Fat, and Fat-Free Milk.**   Did you know that almost half the calories in whole milk—a whopping 49 percent—comes from fat? Fat-free milk, on the other hand, gets only about .04 percent of its calories from fat. What a difference! Whole milk also contains a lot of cholesterol, plus most of its fat is highly saturated. Even 2 percent reduced-fat milk still gets an amazing 35 percent of its total calories from fat. That's why it's a good idea to choose low-fat or fat-free milk. Both are rich in protein, calcium, and other nutrients without having much fat. You'll see how switching to fat-free milk will dramatically help you cut your fat intake. Over time, many people come to prefer its lighter taste.

**Butter, Cream, and Ice Cream.**   These dairy products contain even more fat than whole milk. The good news is that you don't have to give up dairy foods to cut fat from your diet. Margarine, fat-free evaporated milk, and nonfat or low-fat frozen yogurt can give you the same tastes as the higher-fat alternatives. For example, margarine substitutes nicely for butter and is much lower in saturated fat. (It does contain the same total fat, though.) Although it can be tricky to bake with fat-free and reduced-fat margarines, you can put them to good use in sautéing, on vegetables, dotted on casseroles, and in many other ways. Another word to the wise—butter and cream are often "hidden" in foods, especially in baked goods and desserts. Read ingredient lists carefully to be sure you're not getting unwanted fat.

**Cheese.** For decades, people have considered cheese to be an acceptable high-protein substitute for meat. Unfortunately, they get a lot of fat in the process. Most cheeses contain large amounts of highly saturated fat. In fact, 60 to 70 percent of the calories in cheese comes from butterfat, about the same percentage as in ice cream. Fortunately, your supermarket has a nice selection of nonfat, low-fat, or part-skim cheeses. In the past, fat-free cheese was often criticized for not melting well. It's greatly improved, however, and a number of manufacturers now produce meltable fat-free cheese. (Do watch the sodium content, though.)

**Eggs.** One large egg yolk contains about 213 milligrams of cholesterol—almost your entire daily allowance. For that reason, you'll want to limit your consumption of egg yolks. A cautionary note: Egg yolk consumption isn't just the deviled egg you enjoyed at Saturday's picnic and the scrambled egg you had for Sunday breakfast. It also includes the yolks you may not be aware you're consuming. That's why we included the table below. Sometimes what you don't know *can* hurt you.

## HOW EGGS ADD UP

| Foods Containing Eggs | Approximate Portion of Whole Egg |
|---|---|
| **Beverages** | |
| Eggnog (½ cup) | ¼ |
| **Breads** | |
| Corn bread (⅑ of 9 × 9-inch pan) | ¼ |
| Muffin (1) | ¹⁄₁₀ |
| Pancakes, 4-inch (2) | ¼ |
| **Desserts** | |
| Baked custard or crème brûlée (6-ounce custard cup) | ½ |
| Chocolate, lemon meringue, or pumpkin pie (⅛ of 9-inch pie) | ⅓ |
| Pound cake (¹⁄₁₂ of loaf) | ¼ |
| Sponge cake (¹⁄₁₂ of 9 × 9-inch cake) | ½ |
| Tapioca pudding (½ cup) | ⅓ |
| Yellow or chocolate 2-layer cake (¹⁄₁₆ of 9-inch cake) | ⅛ |

| Foods Containing Eggs | Approximate Portion of Whole Egg |
|---|---|
| **Main Dishes** | |
| Cheese soufflé (1 cup) | ½ |
| Chicken salad (½ cup) | ⅓ |
| Corn pudding (½ cup) | ½ |
| Omelet (depends on size) | 1 to 3 |
| **Salad Dressings** | |
| Mayonnaise (¼ cup) | ¼ |
| Thousand Island (¼ cup) | ⅓ |

Egg whites, on the other hand, contain no fat or cholesterol at all and are a good source of protein. You can eat as many egg whites as you wish. You can even substitute two egg whites for one whole egg in most recipes. Also, many egg substitutes are available at your supermarket.

# MEAT PRODUCTS

When it comes to meat, aim for a total of 5 (Step II) to 6 (Step I) ounces per day, served in one or two portions. That's really all the poultry, seafood, or lean meat your body needs. Six ounces of lean meat contain between 500 and 600 calories. That's about one third of the total required daily calories for the average person, depending on how many calories you need for your size and activity level.

**Beef, Lamb, Pork, and Veal.** If you thought a cholesterol-lowering diet meant giving up meat, you'll be pleased to know it doesn't. A 3-ounce portion contains about 70 to 75 milligrams of cholesterol and an acceptable level of saturated fat—if you take certain precautions. Be sure the meat is lean, and before cooking the meat, trim all visible fat.

**Processed Meats.** Ordinary processed meats, including sausage, bologna, salami, and hot dogs, have lots of fat and calories. About 70 to 80 percent of their total calories is from fat, so steer clear of these foods. In general, you should eat processed meats sparingly. When you do include them, find the ones labeled "reduced fat," "low fat," or "nonfat." Read the nutrition labels, and choose those varieties with no more than 10 percent fat (by weight) or 3 grams of fat per ounce.

**Organ Meats.** Organ meats include liver, sweetbreads, kidney, brain, and heart. They are extremely high in cholesterol. If you can forgo organ meats, please do. Otherwise, save them for special occasions.

**Poultry.**   Almost all meat-eaters love poultry. It's in special demand by the health-conscious, who routinely substitute it for red meat. Of course, poultry is a good substitute only if it's eaten without the skin and visible fat. You'll want to remove the skin before cooking if you're using pieces or before eating if you're using a whole bird. In general, chicken and turkey are leaner than goose and duck.

## SEAFOOD

Fish contains less saturated fat than red meat. This gives fish a slight edge over lean red meat when you're eating to lower your cholesterol. The American Heart Association recommends eating fish at least twice a week. It particularly promotes those varieties of fish containing omega-3 fatty acids, which have been found to reduce triglyceride levels in people with markedly high triglycerides. Though scientists don't recommend fish oil supplements for most people, they do suggest eating these kinds of fish often. Some of the fish high in omega-3 fatty acids are Atlantic and coho salmon, albacore tuna, club mackerel, carp, lake whitefish, sweet smelt, and lake and brook trout.

Shrimp, lobster, crab, crayfish, and most other shellfish are very low in fat, although they do contain some cholesterol. Go ahead and add shellfish to your menu along with meat, poultry, and fish. Just remember to keep your combined servings of meat, poultry, and seafood at no more than 5 to 6 ounces per day.

## FRUITS, VEGETABLES, GRAINS, AND LEGUMES

These foods are the foundation of a low-fat eating plan. That's because they contain no cholesterol, are generally low in fat, and in many cases are high in fiber and vitamins. One of the few exceptions is coconut, which is high in saturated fat. Olives and avocados also are high in fat, but it's mostly unsaturated; watch your serving size so the calorie count doesn't creep up on you.

Be sure to check the ingredient labels of processed foods made from vegetables, grains, or legumes. You may find that fat or cholesterol was added during processing. (Breads and pastas made with egg yolks are examples, as are beans cooked with bacon.) Also, watch out for lots of sodium. When possible, buy the prepared foods (frozen and canned) without added sodium. In general, fresh produce is always an excellent choice. Fruits, vegetables, grains, and legumes will help you eat hearty, yet help your heart.

## NUTS AND SEEDS

Nuts and seeds contain lots of fat, but most of it is unsaturated. These tasty snacks also are loaded with calories.

Nuts and seeds contain no cholesterol. They're good sources of incomplete protein and, to some degree, can replace other high-protein foods. To get all the amino acids that make up a complete protein, you also need to eat plant foods that have complementary proteins. That is, the nuts and seeds with plant foods provide all eight essential amino acids. Examples of these combinations of complementary proteins are nuts with rice or whole-wheat bread with baked beans.

## BAKERY GOODS

Cakes, pies, doughnuts, cookies, and candy offer very little benefit to a cholesterol-lowering diet. They're typically high in calories and low in important nutrients. Plus, many baked goods are made with egg yolks and saturated fats, which will harm your cholesterol-lowering efforts. Commercially produced baked goods are usually the worst offenders. If you bake at home using unsaturated oils and substituting egg whites for whole eggs, you can at least control the fat. However, baked goods of any kind add lots of calories.

## FATS AND OILS

**Saturated, Monounsaturated, and Polyunsaturated Fats.** Fats and oils high in saturated fat tend to become hard at room temperature. These include butter, lard, and tallow from animals, as well as coconut, palm, and palm kernel oils from plants. These fats raise blood cholesterol, so you'll want to avoid them.

On the other hand, oils that stay liquid at room temperature are high in unsaturated fats. They include corn, safflower, sunflower, olive, and canola oils. All of these are low in saturated fat, and you can use them to help lower your blood cholesterol while keeping your meals tasty. Peanut oil has a somewhat higher level of saturated fat, but you can use it occasionally in cooking when you want a different taste.

**Hydrogenated Oils.** During food processing, fats become hydrogenated, changing from a liquid to a solid, more-saturated form. This process creates trans fatty acids, a type of fat that acts much like saturated fat in the body. Choose soft margarines that list liquid oil as the first ingredient. They're less hydrogenated than the harder, stick-type margarines.

## BEVERAGES

A cup or two of coffee or tea a day is fine for your cholesterol level as long as you don't add cream, whole milk, or creamers. Drink your coffee or tea in moderation and opt for fat-free milk or fat-free evaporated milk.

The latest scientific studies show that drinking one or two glasses of wine a day has a protective effect on your heart. But *only* one or two. If you drink more than that, you not only lose the protection, you also run many well-established risks, including negative effects on your heart. The bottom line? If you don't drink now, don't start. If you do drink, keep your alcohol intake to no more than two drinks a day for men and one drink a day for women. A drink is defined as 5 ounces of wine, 12 ounces of beer, or 1½ ounces of 80-proof liquor. It's a good idea to talk to your doctor before deciding what is best for you.

## A WORD ABOUT SODIUM

Your doctor may have told you to cut down on the amount of sodium in your food. The nutritional analysis of each recipe in this book shows how much sodium a serving contains. This lets you easily add up your daily sodium intake. We recommend eating no more than 2,400 milligrams of sodium a day.

The Step I and Step II Diets are not magic. They're based on a nutritious eating plan that emphasizes moderation in the amounts of total fat, saturated fat, and cholesterol you eat. Since fat is an acquired taste, many people who follow Step I or Step II never go back to their former way of eating. They come to prefer the lighter, fresher taste of low-fat dishes, such as the ones you'll find in this cookbook. We hope they'll become your new favorites.

# HOW TO USE THE NUTRIENT ANALYSES

Before we dig into some of the most delicious recipes on the planet, let's take a minute to learn how to use the nutrient analysis that accompanies each of them.

With each recipe, you'll find its nutritional breakdown—the calorie count and the amounts of protein, carbohydrate, total fat, saturated fat, polyunsaturated fat, monounsaturated fat, cholesterol, and sodium. This analysis will help you decide where the recipe fits into your eating plan. You'll find that the amount of each nutrient varies widely from one recipe to another. By reading these analyses carefully, you can choose recipes that best meet your needs. For example, if you're watching your sodium intake, pay particular attention to the sodium listings. Choose recipes in which the sodium content is low enough to fit into your daily eating plan.

Keep the following information in mind as you review the nutrient analyses of these recipes:

Each analysis is based on a single serving unless otherwise indicated.

Optional ingredients *were not included* in any nutrient analysis. The optional ingredients add flavor and perhaps texture but may also add sodium, saturated fat, or cholesterol. If you're trying to cut down on those categories, skip the optional ingredients or use them sparingly. The food will still taste great.

Ingredients with a weight range (a 2- to 3-pound chicken, for example) were analyzed at the average weight.

When a recipe lists two or more ingredient options (1 cup nonfat or low-fat yogurt, for example), the first was used in the nutrient analysis.

The specific amounts of the ingredients listed, not the amounts sometimes shown in parentheses, were analyzed. The amounts in parentheses are guidelines to help you decide how much of an ingredient to purchase to get at least what the recipe requires. For example, when a recipe calls for 3 tablespoons lime juice (2 limes), we analyzed the 3 tablespoons of juice, not the 2 limes. (We do not list the quantity in parentheses if only one, or part of one, item is needed.)

When a recipe calls for low-fat cheese, it was analyzed using cheese that has 33 percent less fat than regular cheese. If you want to reduce the fat even further, choose a fat-free cheese or one that has 50 percent less fat than regular cheese. If you're watching your sodium intake, be aware that the nonfat cheeses are typically higher in sodium than the low-fat cheeses.

The values for saturated, monounsaturated, and polyunsaturated fats may not add up precisely to the total fat in the recipe. That's because the total fat includes not only the fatty acids that are reflected in the analyses but also other fatty substances and glycerol that are not. It's also because all values are rounded to the nearest whole number.

When a recipe calls for acceptable margarine, remember to choose a margarine that lists liquid vegetable oil as the first ingredient. The margarine should contain no more than 2 grams of saturated fat per tablespoon. We used corn oil margarine for the analyses.

When a recipe calls for acceptable vegetable oil, we used corn oil. Other examples of acceptable vegetable oils are safflower, soybean, sunflower, sesame, canola, and olive. Use peanut oil only occasionally for a flavor change.

If a marinade was used for meat, poultry, or seafood, the nutrient analysis includes only the amount of marinade absorbed, based on U.S. Department of Agriculture (USDA) data on absorption. If the marinade is also used for basting or in a sauce or gravy, the nutrient analysis includes the full amounts of all ingredients.

Absorption data are not available for vegetable marinades, so we added in the total amount of marinade used in the recipe.

Feel free to make any creative substitutions that won't affect the recipe's nutritional profile. For example, you could use basil instead of thyme or try tarragon vinegar instead of white wine vinegar.

Also, be creative with garnishes, as we've done in the lovely photographs you'll see in this book. Just remember, if you eat them, count them, especially if they add saturated fat, cholesterol, or sodium.

We analyzed whole carrots with peel. Unless carrots are very old or the peel is discolored, simply scrub them and leave the peel on. That way, you'll get all the flavor and nutrients the carrots contain.

We analyzed the entire green onion unless only the white or only the green was specified. Use the part you like best—or the whole onion.

According to the USDA, there is virtually no difference in the nutritional values of fresh, frozen, and canned food when prepared for the table. When using frozen or canned foods, however, be sure to watch for added ingredients, such as salt, that may change the analysis.

The abbreviation for gram is "g"; the abbreviation for milligram is "mg."

# RECIPES

# APPETIZERS

Nectarine-Plum Chutney

Zucchini Spread

Hummus

Stuffed Chili Peppers

Toasted Ravioli with Italian Salsa

Crab Spring Rolls with Peanut
Dipping Sauce

Stuffed Mushrooms

Zesty Potato Skins

Chicken Triangles

Canapés with Roasted Garlic,
Artichoke, and Chèvre Spread

Melon Balls with Turkey and Ham

# NECTARINE-PLUM CHUTNEY

*Serves 8*

**COOK'S TIP ON ACIDIC FOODS:**

Vinegar and other acidic foods can react with aluminum, untreated carbon steel, and cast iron, possibly causing the food to taste metallic and the pot or pan to discolor.

*This sweet-and-sour condiment is versatile. Pour it over a block of nonfat or low-fat cream cheese and spread on crackers for an irresistible appetizer. Traditionally served with curried dishes, chutney also perks up almost any entrée from meat loaf to grilled chicken.*

3 small plums, pitted and diced

1 medium nectarine, pitted and diced

1 Granny Smith apple, peeled and diced

⅓ cup sugar

¼ small onion, diced

¼ red bell pepper, diced

¼ cup apple cider vinegar

2 tablespoons golden raisins

1 teaspoon grated orange rind

⅛ teaspoon salt

⅛ teaspoon ground nutmeg

Combine all ingredients in a 2-quart stainless steel, enameled steel, or nonstick saucepan. Bring mixture to a simmer over medium-high heat, stirring occasionally until sugar dissolves, about 3 to 4 minutes. Reduce heat and simmer, uncovered, stirring occasionally, for 40 to 45 minutes, or until fruit is tender. Cool and refrigerate until ready to use.

In an airtight container, chutney will keep for up to 7 days in the refrigerator.

**NUTRIENT ANALYSIS**

Calories 63
Protein 0 g
Carbohydrate 16 g
Total Fat 0 g
Saturated Fat 0 g
Polyunsaturated Fat 0 g
Monounsaturated Fat 0 g
Cholesterol 0 mg
Sodium 36 mg

# ZUCCHINI SPREAD

*Serves 8*

*A food processor makes preparation of this spread simple! Serve it with crackers, vegetable sticks, or rounds of crusty French bread, or use it as a sandwich spread: Lightly coat the inside of a pita half with the spread, then stuff the pita with your favorite vegetables.*

3½ cups unpeeled, shredded zucchini (about 1 to 1¼ pounds)

¼ cup finely chopped fresh parsley or cilantro

2 tablespoons red wine vinegar

1 tablespoon olive oil

1 clove garlic, minced, or ½ teaspoon bottled minced garlic

¼ teaspoon salt (optional)

Freshly ground pepper to taste

2 tablespoons finely chopped walnuts or pecans, preferably dry-roasted

Squeeze zucchini with fingers to remove excess water. Place zucchini and all other ingredients except nuts in a blender or food processor. Process until smooth, scraping sides as needed.

Spoon the mixture into a serving container and fold in nuts. Cover and chill before serving.

## COOK'S TIP ON DRY-ROASTING NUTS:

Stretch a few nuts into a lot of flavor by dry-roasting them. Heat nuts in an ungreased skillet over medium heat, stirring frequently, for 1 to 5 minutes, or until golden brown. Another method is to place nuts on a baking sheet and roast them in a 350° F oven for 10 to 15 minutes, stirring occasionally. If you prepare extra to freeze, you'll have a ready supply for future use.

## NUTRIENT ANALYSIS

Calories 37

Protein 1 g

Carbohydrate 2 g

Total Fat 3 g

Saturated Fat 0 g

Polyunsaturated Fat 1 g

Monounsaturated Fat 2 g

Cholesterol 0 mg

Sodium 3 mg

# HUMMUS

*Serves 8*

**COOK'S TIP
ON TAHINI:**

You can find tahini, a sesame seed paste, in health food stores and some supermarkets. If you prefer, you can make your own by blending ½ cup sesame seeds, 1 tablespoon water, 1 tablespoon fresh lemon juice, and a few drops of vegetable oil.

*Hummus is a Middle Eastern specialty traditionally served as a dip for raw vegetables or with flat Syrian bread or warm pita bread. An excellent source of protein because of the chick-peas, this recipe is lower in fat than the usual version. Hummus tastes best when refrigerated for about 24 hours before serving, which allows the flavors to blend.*

19-ounce can chick-peas, rinsed and drained

½ cup fresh lemon juice (about 3 medium lemons)

¼ cup tahini

¼ cup water

2 cloves garlic or 1 teaspoon bottled minced garlic

1 teaspoon olive oil

½ teaspoon ground cumin, or to taste

¼ teaspoon salt (optional)

⅛ teaspoon cayenne (optional)

Freshly ground pepper to taste

Water (optional)

½ cup finely chopped fresh parsley

In a blender or food processor, combine chick-peas, lemon juice, tahini, ¼ cup water, garlic, oil, cumin, salt, cayenne, and pepper. Process, scraping sides occasionally, until mixture is a smooth paste. If mixture is too thick, add more water, a few drops at a time. Stir in parsley.

**NUTRIENT ANALYSIS**

Calories 131
Protein 6 g
Carbohydrate 16 g
Total Fat 6 g
Saturated Fat 1 g
Polyunsaturated Fat 2 g
Monounsaturated Fat 2 g
Cholesterol 0 mg
Sodium 72 mg

# STUFFED CHILI PEPPERS

*Serves 14*

*Jalapeño peppers, the most popular and readily available chili peppers, range from hot to very hot. Lessen the intensity of these short green peppers by removing the ribs, or membranes, and the seeds.*

8 ounces nonfat or low-fat cottage cheese, rinsed and drained (1 cup)

2 tablespoons finely chopped red bell pepper

2 tablespoons snipped chives or finely chopped green onion (green part only)

1 clove garlic, minced, or ½ teaspoon bottled minced garlic

⅛ teaspoon salt

14 jalapeño peppers, halved lengthwise, seeded, and ribs removed*

Place cottage cheese in a blender or food processor. Process, scraping sides as necessary, until smooth.

Transfer cottage cheese to a small bowl and stir in remaining ingredients except jalapeños.

Spoon mixture into jalapeño pepper halves. (A small spoon, such as a baby spoon, works best.) Cover and chill until serving time.

* Hot chili peppers contain oils that can burn your skin, lips, and eyes. Wear rubber gloves or wash your hands thoroughly with warm, soapy water immediately after handling peppers.

**NUTRIENT ANALYSIS**

Calories 31
Protein 3 g
Carbohydrate 5 g
Total Fat 0 g
Saturated Fat 0 g
Polyunsaturated Fat 0 g
Monounsaturated Fat 0 g
Cholesterol 1 mg
Sodium 55 mg

# TOASTED RAVIOLI
# WITH ITALIAN SALSA

*Serves 10 as an appetizer*
*Serves 5 as an entrée*

*These tempting tidbits, traditionally deep-fried but baked in this recipe, boast an interesting fusion twist—a salsa flavored with herbs common to the Italian kitchen.*

16 ounces frozen beef ravioli (30 pieces)*

Vegetable oil spray

¼ cup nonfat or low-fat Italian salad dressing

½ cup dried bread crumbs

1½ teaspoons salt-free Italian herb seasoning

### ITALIAN SALSA

14.5-ounce can no-salt-added tomatoes with juice

½ small red onion, quartered

1 hot banana pepper or ½ green bell pepper, seeded and
   ribs removed

1 tablespoon chopped fresh oregano or 1 teaspoon dried

1 tablespoon chopped fresh basil or 1 teaspoon dried

1 clove garlic, halved, or ½ teaspoon bottled minced
   garlic

1 teaspoon balsamic vinegar or red wine vinegar

¼ teaspoon sugar

Vegetable oil spray

Cook ravioli according to package directions, omitting salt and oil. Drain and cool for at least 10 minutes.

Meanwhile, lightly spray 2 baking sheets with vegetable oil spray. Set aside.

Using a pastry brush, lightly coat top of each of the ravioli with dressing. Place on baking sheets.

Mix bread crumbs and herb seasoning. Sprinkle over ravioli. The ravioli can be refrigerated for up to 8 hours at this point.

**NUTRIENT ANALYSIS**
*(For appetizer serving)*

| | |
|---|---|
| Calories | 126 |
| Protein | 6 g |
| Carbohydrate | 20 g |
| Total Fat | 2 g |
| Saturated Fat | 1 g |
| Polyunsaturated Fat | 0 g |
| Monounsaturated Fat | 1 g |
| Cholesterol | 7 mg |
| Sodium | 220 mg |

Place all salsa ingredients in a blender or food processor and process for 15 to 20 seconds. Set aside. (Salsa will keep in the refrigerator for up to 4 days.)

Preheat oven to 400° F.

Lightly spray tops of ravioli with vegetable oil spray. Bake the ravioli for 9 to 11 minutes. Drizzle the salsa over the ravioli or use the salsa for dipping.

* Some prepared ravioli may be high in sodium and fat. When shopping, select the one with the lowest sodium and fat values.

## COOK'S TIP ON LEFTOVER FRESH HERBS:

Small amounts of fresh herbs, such as basil, oregano, cilantro, or a mixture, are the basis of easy herb cream cheese or herb margarine spread. Mix 2 tablespoons of chopped fresh herbs with 1 minced clove of garlic or ½ teaspoon bottled minced garlic and 8 ounces of nonfat or low-fat cream cheese or light margarine. Try a little herb cream cheese on a bagel or a dollop of herb margarine on a baked potato. You'll find lots of uses for these treats.

# CRAB SPRING ROLLS WITH PEANUT DIPPING SAUCE

*Serves 10*

*These golden-brown, crispy spring rolls are a treat in themselves—the sauce is a rich, fragrant bonus! Experiment with lean cooked chicken, ham, or beef instead of crab for variety. Find spring roll wrappers in an Asian grocery store (usually in the freezer section) or substitute egg roll wrappers.*

### SPRING ROLLS

Vegetable oil spray

4 cups shredded cabbage (about 1 pound)

1 medium carrot, shredded

½ cup bean sprouts (about 1 ounce)

2 green onions, thinly sliced

4 ounces nonfat imitation crabmeat, shredded

2 teaspoons rice vinegar

1 teaspoon reduced-sodium soy sauce

10 spring roll wrappers (8 × 8 inches)

White of 1 egg, lightly beaten

Vegetable oil spray

### DIPPING SAUCE

3 tablespoons reduced-fat peanut butter

3 tablespoons rice vinegar

2 tablespoons reduced-sodium soy sauce

2 tablespoons water

1 green onion, green part only, thinly sliced

½ teaspoon fragrant toasted sesame oil

Spray a large skillet with vegetable oil spray. Heat over medium-high heat for 1 to 2 minutes. Add the cabbage and cook, stirring occasionally, for 1 to 2 minutes.

Add the carrot, bean sprouts, and green onions and cook for 1 minute, stirring occasionally.

Add the crabmeat, vinegar, and soy sauce and cook until crabmeat is warmed through, about 30 seconds. Remove from heat and refrigerate for at least 30 minutes.

Preheat oven to 400° F.

To assemble spring rolls, place a spring roll wrapper on a flat surface, with one point of the wrapper pointing toward you. Spoon about ⅓ cup of the filling up the middle of the wrapper. Bring the bottom point of the wrapper over the filling. Lightly brush the two side points of the wrapper with egg white. Bring the side points into the center of the wrapper (wrapper will look like an unsealed envelope). Starting from the bottom, roll the wrapper up to the top point so the filling is enclosed. Lightly brush the top point with egg white and press to make sure the spring roll is sealed. Lightly spray outside of spring roll with vegetable oil spray and place on a baking sheet. Repeat with remaining wrappers.

Bake for 25 to 30 minutes, or until wrapper turns a light golden-brown.

While spring rolls are baking, place all dipping sauce ingredients except green onion in a medium bowl and whisk. Sprinkle dipping sauce with green onion and serve with the spring rolls.

**COOK'S TIP:**

You can assemble spring rolls and keep them in the refrigerator for up to 8 hours before baking or for up to 2 months in the freezer. (Do not thaw before baking.) The dipping sauce will keep for up to 2 days in the refrigerator, the filling for up to 4 days.

**COOK'S TIP ON SESAME OIL:**

Fragrant toasted sesame oil, also called toasted sesame oil or Asian sesame oil, is darker, stronger, and more fragrant than sesame oil. Fragrant toasted sesame oil is widely used in Asian and Indian foods. Because it is so flavorful, you get a lot of taste for just a little fat.

# STUFFED MUSHROOMS

*Serves 6*

*These hot appetizers are an ideal party food. Prepare them an hour in advance and pop them in the oven as your guests arrive. The aroma is mouthwatering!*

18 large mushrooms

1 teaspoon olive oil

¼ cup minced onion

¼ cup finely chopped walnuts (about 1 ounce)

1 clove garlic, minced, or ½ teaspoon bottled minced garlic

1 shredded wheat biscuit, crushed

1 tablespoon grated or shredded Parmesan cheese

½ teaspoon salt-free Italian herb seasoning

Freshly ground pepper to taste

½ teaspoon paprika

Preheat oven to 350° F.

Cut and discard a thin slice from end of each mushroom. Remove and finely chop remainder of stems.

Heat a nonstick skillet over medium-high heat. Add oil and swirl to coat bottom of skillet. When oil is hot, add chopped mushroom stems, onion, walnuts, and garlic. Sauté until onion is tender, 4 to 5 minutes. Remove from heat.

Stir in remaining ingredients except paprika.

Spoon stuffing into mushroom caps, packing mixture firmly. Arrange mushrooms in a shallow baking dish. Sprinkle tops lightly with paprika.

Bake for 20 to 25 minutes, or until mushrooms are tender and heated through.

**NUTRIENT ANALYSIS**

Calories 73
Protein 3 g
Carbohydrate 7 g
Total Fat 4 g
Saturated Fat 1 g
Polyunsaturated Fat 2 g
Monounsaturated Fat 1 g
Cholesterol 1 mg
Sodium 18 mg

# ZESTY POTATO SKINS

*Serves 8*

*Visually appealing and delicious, these are perfect for enter-taining or snacking.*

6 medium red potatoes, baked
   (about 1¼ pounds)

Vegetable oil spray

½ teaspoon garlic powder

½ teaspoon chili powder

½ teaspoon ground cumin

⅛ teaspoon pepper

1 cup nonfat or low-fat cottage cheese, undrained
   (8 ounces)

½ teaspoon grated lime rind

1½ tablespoons fresh lime juice

1 teaspoon dried chives

¼ teaspoon chili powder

24 slices black olives (4 large)

Preheat oven to 450° F.

Cut each potato in half. Scoop out the center, leaving about ¼ inch of potato on the inside of each skin. (Use leftover potato to make Shepherd's Pie, see page 160.) Cut skins into quarters. Lightly spray insides of skins with vegetable oil spray.

In a small bowl, combine garlic powder, ½ teaspoon chili powder, cumin, and pepper. Sprinkle mixture evenly on insides of potatoes.

Place skins, skin side down, on a baking sheet. Bake for 15 to 20 minutes, or until lightly browned.

Meanwhile, combine remaining ingredients except olives in a blender or food processor. Process until smooth.

Spoon about 1 teaspoon of the cottage cheese mixture on top of each potato skin and top with a slice of olive.

**NUTRIENT ANALYSIS**

| | |
|---|---|
| Calories | 50 |
| Protein | 4 g |
| Carbohydrate | 8 g |
| Total Fat | 0 g |
| Saturated Fat | 0 g |
| Polyunsaturated Fat | 0 g |
| Monounsaturated Fat | 0 g |
| Cholesterol | 0 mg |
| Sodium | 128 mg |

# CHICKEN TRIANGLES

*Serves 15*

**COOK'S TIP:**

For later use, place unbaked triangles on baking sheets. Place baking sheets in freezer. When triangles are frozen, store them in freezer in plastic bags. To bake, preheat oven to 400° F, place frozen triangles on baking sheets, and bake for 20 to 25 minutes, or until golden-brown.

*These little phyllo (fee´ low) triangles of garlicky chicken are great as nibbles, hors d'oeuvres, or a side dish. Phyllo is a paper-thin dough, available frozen in most large supermarkets and many specialty stores. Phyllo should be thawed in the refrigerator. Unopened, the thawed dough will keep for a month if refrigerated.*

1 pound boneless, skinless chicken breasts, all visible fat removed

2 tablespoons fresh lemon juice

1 tablespoon minced fresh parsley

1 tablespoon chopped fresh tarragon, oregano, or basil or 1 teaspoon dried, crumbled

2 cloves garlic, minced, or 1 teaspoon bottled minced garlic

1 teaspoon olive oil

¼ teaspoon salt (optional)

12 sheets phyllo

Butter-flavored vegetable oil spray

Rinse chicken breasts and pat dry with paper towels. Using a sharp knife or in the work bowl of a food processor fitted with a metal blade, finely chop chicken. Set aside.

In a medium bowl, combine lemon juice, parsley, tarragon, garlic, olive oil, and salt. Add chicken and toss to coat. Cover and refrigerate for at least 1 hour.

Preheat oven to 400° F.

Keeping unused dough covered with a damp tea towel to prevent drying, lightly spray a sheet of phyllo with vegetable oil spray. Stack a second sheet on top. With scissors or a sharp knife, cut the 2-layer sheet crosswise into 5 short strips.

Place a teaspoon of chicken filling on one of the 2-layer strips, leaving 1 inch at the bottom. Fold a corner across the filling and continue folding, corner to

**NUTRIENT ANALYSIS**

Calories 90

Protein 8 g

Carbohydrate 11 g

Total Fat 1 g

Saturated Fat 0 g

Polyunsaturated Fat 0 g

Monounsaturated Fat 0 g

Cholesterol 17 mg

Sodium 74 mg

corner (the way a flag is folded). The filling expands during cooking, so do not fold the dough too tightly. Tuck the excess dough under the triangle, then place on a baking sheet. Repeat with the remaining 10 sheets of phyllo and chicken.

Lightly spray the prepared triangles with vegetable oil spray.

Bake for 15 to 20 minutes, or until golden-brown.

# CANAPÉS WITH ROASTED GARLIC, ARTICHOKE, AND CHÈVRE SPREAD

*Serves 18*

**COOK'S TIP ON ROASTED GARLIC:**

Add roasted and peeled garlic cloves to your favorite spaghetti sauce or stew, mashed potatoes, or cold pasta salad. Puree roasted and peeled garlic and brush on toast, corn on the cob, or pizza dough before you add the sauce and toppings.

*You can make the spread for these canapés up to 3 days in advance. Planning is the secret to easy entertaining!*

6 7-inch pitas

6 cloves garlic, unpeeled

14-ounce can artichoke hearts, rinsed, drained, and chopped

½ cup fat-free, cholesterol-free mayonnaise

2 ounces chèvre (soft preferred)

⅛ teaspoon white pepper

2 tablespoons snipped fresh chives or thinly sliced green onion (green part only)

18 cherry tomatoes, cut in half

Preheat oven to 350° F.

Cut each pita into sixths. (Don't separate bottoms from tops.) Place pita pieces in a single layer on an ungreased baking sheet.

Place the garlic in a garlic roaster or any small oven-proof pan and place on the bottom oven rack. Bake for 5 minutes.

Place the bread on a rack in about the middle of the oven. Bake for 10 minutes. Remove the garlic and bread from the oven. (Leave oven on.) Let cool for 10 minutes.

Cut off stem ends of garlic. Squeeze garlic out onto a cutting board, discarding peel. Mince garlic.

In a medium bowl, combine garlic, artichokes, mayonnaise, chèvre, and pepper.

To assemble canapés, spread about 1 teaspoon of the artichoke mixture on each piece of pita. Sprinkle with chives. Press a cherry tomato half (cut side up) into the artichoke mixture.

Place canapés on an ungreased baking sheet. Bake for 5 minutes.

**NUTRIENT ANALYSIS**

Calories 91

Protein 3 g

Carbohydrate 17 g

Total Fat 1 g

Saturated Fat 1 g

Polyunsaturated Fat 0 g

Monounsaturated Fat 0 g

Cholesterol 3 mg

Sodium 228 mg

# MELON BALLS WITH TURKEY AND HAM

*Serves 15*

*This easy-to-fix appetizer combines fresh melons with ham, turkey, and a tangy-sweet, minted mustard dip.*

1 medium honeydew melon, cut in half and seeded

1 medium cantaloupe, cut in half and seeded

4 ounces thinly sliced, lean, low-sodium ham, all visible fat removed

4 ounces thinly sliced turkey, all visible fat removed

### DIPPING SAUCE

¼ cup spicy brown mustard

2 tablespoons honey

12 fresh mint leaves, chopped

Using the large side of a melon baller, cut balls from the melons; set aside.

Cut the ham and turkey into 4 × 1-inch strips.

Wrap each melon ball in a strip of ham or turkey and skewer with a toothpick.

In a small bowl, combine sauce ingredients. Serve with wrapped melon balls.

**NUTRIENT ANALYSIS**

Calories 80
Protein 4 g
Carbohydrate 16 g
Total Fat 1 g
Saturated Fat 0 g
Polyunsaturated Fat 0 g
Monounsaturated Fat 0 g
Cholesterol 7 mg
Sodium 202 mg

# SOUPS

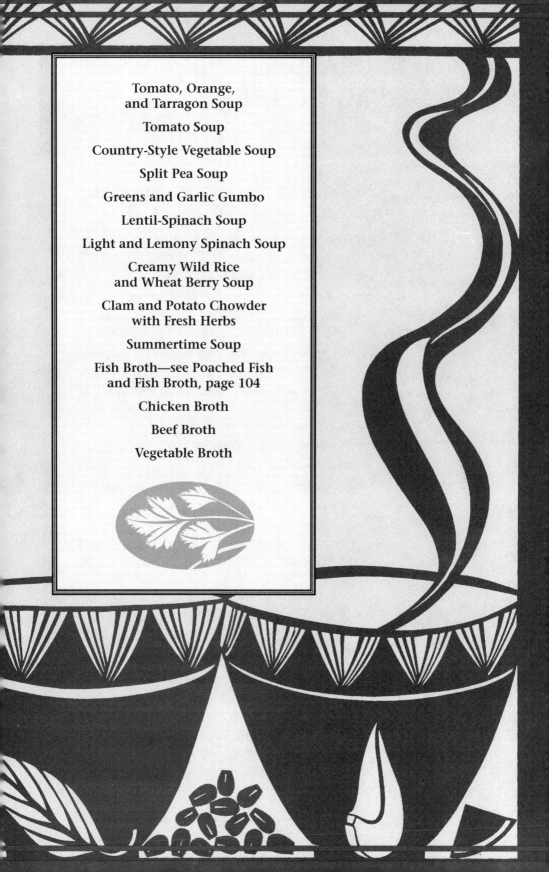

Tomato, Orange,
and Tarragon Soup

Tomato Soup

Country-Style Vegetable Soup

Split Pea Soup

Greens and Garlic Gumbo

Lentil-Spinach Soup

Light and Lemony Spinach Soup

Creamy Wild Rice
and Wheat Berry Soup

Clam and Potato Chowder
with Fresh Herbs

Summertime Soup

Fish Broth—see Poached Fish
and Fish Broth, page 104

Chicken Broth

Beef Broth

Vegetable Broth

# TOMATO, ORANGE, AND TARRAGON SOUP

*Serves 6*

*Establish your culinary reputation with this! A refreshing soup that can be served hot or cold, it's a sure winner.*

**COOK'S TIP ON GRATED ORANGE RIND:**

Use a tool called a zester or citrus zester to grate citrus rind easily. Be careful not to cut into the bitter pith, or white part, of the skin. An average medium orange yields 1 to 2 tablespoons of grated zest. Since this recipe uses only 1 teaspoon, you'll have some to freeze for another dish.

1 teaspoon acceptable vegetable oil

12 ounces white or red potatoes, peeled and diced

1 medium yellow or white onion, sliced

3 large tomatoes, chopped (about 1½ pounds)

2 cups low-sodium chicken broth (see page 55 or use commercial variety)

2 tablespoons chopped fresh tarragon or 2 teaspoons dried, crumbled

1 clove garlic, crushed, or ½ teaspoon bottled minced garlic

¼ teaspoon salt (optional)

Freshly ground pepper to taste

1 teaspoon grated orange rind

1 cup fresh orange juice (3 to 4 medium oranges)

Fresh tarragon or parsley sprigs (optional)

In a heavy nonstick saucepan, heat oil over medium-high heat. Sauté potatoes and onion for 2 to 3 minutes, or until onion is translucent.

Stir in tomatoes, broth, tarragon, garlic, salt, and pepper. Bring to a boil over high heat. Reduce heat and simmer, covered, for 20 to 25 minutes, or until vegetables are tender.

In a blender or food processor, process soup in small batches until liquefied. Pour through a sieve to remove coarse skins. Discard skins.

Stir orange rind and juice into strained soup. Reheat or serve chilled. Garnish with fresh tarragon.

**NUTRIENT ANALYSIS**

Calories 111
Protein 3 g
Carbohydrate 22 g
Total Fat 1 g
Saturated Fat 0 g
Polyunsaturated Fat 1 g
Monounsaturated Fat 0 g
Cholesterol 0 mg
Sodium 32 mg

# TOMATO SOUP

*Serves 6*

*Fresh-picked tomatoes and fresh dill are perfect partners for this soup.*

1 teaspoon olive oil

1 small white onion, chopped

4 green onions (green and white parts), chopped

2 tablespoons all-purpose flour

1 clove garlic, minced, or ½ teaspoon bottled minced garlic

4 cups low-sodium chicken broth (see page 55 or use commercial variety)

3 medium ripe tomatoes, chopped (about 1 pound)

2 tablespoons chopped fresh dill weed or 2 teaspoons dried

½ teaspoon sugar

½ teaspoon salt (optional)

Freshly ground pepper to taste

½ cup plain nonfat or low-fat yogurt, lightly beaten with a fork

2 tablespoons chopped fresh dill weed (optional)

Heat a large saucepan over medium-high heat. Add oil and swirl to coat bottom of skillet. When oil is hot, add white and green onions. Sauté for 2 to 3 minutes, or until white pieces are translucent.

Add flour and garlic; cook for 1 minute, stirring constantly.

Stir in broth. Bring to a boil over high heat.

Add tomatoes, dill weed, sugar, salt, and pepper. Reduce heat and simmer, covered, for 30 to 40 minutes, or until tomatoes are reduced to a pulp.

Allow soup to cool for a few minutes. Puree in small batches in a blender or food processor.

Reheat soup. Drizzle about 1 tablespoon of yogurt over each serving and sprinkle with dill weed.

**NUTRIENT ANALYSIS**

Calories 69
Protein 4 g
Carbohydrate 10 g
Total Fat 2 g
Saturated Fat 0 g
Polyunsaturated Fat 0 g
Monounsaturated Fat 1 g
Cholesterol 0 mg
Sodium 61 mg

# COUNTRY-STYLE VEGETABLE SOUP

*Serves 10*

**COOK'S TIP:**
If you like the crunch of celery, don't add it to the soup until about 10 minutes before serving.

*A great anytime dish, this hearty soup contains an abundance of fresh vegetables.*

1 pound white or red potatoes, chopped

4 large carrots, chopped

3 celery stalks with leaves, chopped

2 medium zucchini, chopped

1 medium onion, chopped

¼ cup finely chopped fresh parsley

2 bay leaves

¼ teaspoon salt (optional)

Freshly ground pepper to taste

6 cups low-sodium chicken broth (see page 55 or use commercial variety)

¾ cup shredded nonfat or low-fat Cheddar cheese (3 ounces)

In a large, heavy saucepan or Dutch oven, combine potatoes, carrots, celery, zucchini, onion, parsley, bay leaves, salt, and pepper.

Add broth. Bring to a boil over high heat. Reduce heat and simmer, covered, for 45 to 60 minutes, or until vegetables are very tender. Remove bay leaves.

Ladle soup into bowls and top with cheese.

**NUTRIENT ANALYSIS**

Calories 113

Protein 9 g

Carbohydrate 18 g

Total Fat 1 g

Saturated Fat 0 g

Polyunsaturated Fat 0 g

Monounsaturated Fat 0 g

Cholesterol 0 mg

Sodium 195 mg

# SPLIT PEA SOUP

*Serves 10*

*Recipes for split pea soup often call for salt pork. This recipe breaks with tradition and uses lean, low-sodium ham instead, giving you the taste without the fat. This soup freezes well.*

1 pound dried split green peas, rinsed and drained (about 2¼ cups)

8 cups water

2 medium yellow onions, cut into eighths

2 unpeeled carrots, cut into eighths

2 celery stalks with leaves, cut into eighths

4 ounces lean, low-sodium ham, all visible fat removed, cut into bite-size pieces

3 cloves garlic, crushed or minced, or 1½ teaspoons bottled minced garlic

3 tablespoons low-sodium soy sauce

1 teaspoon chopped fresh oregano or ¼ to ½ teaspoon dried, crumbled

½ teaspoon grated fresh gingerroot or ⅛ teaspoon ground ginger

3 dashes hot pepper sauce, or to taste

Freshly ground pepper to taste

In a large saucepan or Dutch oven, bring peas, water, onions, carrots, celery, ham, and garlic to a rapid boil over medium-high heat. Reduce heat and cook, covered, at a gently rolling boil for 1 to 1½ hours, or until peas are soft.

Add remaining ingredients. Simmer for 10 minutes to blend flavors.

In a blender or food processor, process 2 to 3 cups of soup at a time until smooth.

Return to saucepan and reheat if necessary.

**COOK'S TIP ON GINGERROOT:**

Select gingerroot with smooth skin and a spicy fragrance. You can keep leftover gingerroot, unpeeled, for about a week on the counter or wrap the gingerroot in a paper towel and refrigerate it in an airtight plastic bag for up to 3 weeks. For longer storage, place peeled gingerroot in a small jar with a tight-fitting lid and cover ginger with dry sherry, Madeira, or vodka. Refrigerate for up to 3 months. The liquid will be infused with flavor, making it great for cooking, as is the ginger.

**NUTRIENT ANALYSIS**

| | |
|---|---|
| Calories | 187 |
| Protein | 14 g |
| Carbohydrate | 32 g |
| Total Fat | 1 g |
| Saturated Fat | 0 g |
| Polyunsaturated Fat | 0 g |
| Monounsaturated Fat | 0 g |
| Cholesterol | 5 mg |
| Sodium | 294 mg |

# GREENS AND
# GARLIC GUMBO

*Serves 8*

**COOK'S TIP ON FRESH GREENS:**

Be sure to rinse the fresh greens well under running water to remove any dirt and sandy grit between the leaves.

*Gumbo typically starts with a high-fat roux that is made of oil and flour and cooked until it browns. We eliminated the oil but still browned the flour to give this southern soup an authentic Cajun taste.*

½ cup all-purpose flour

Vegetable oil spray

2 medium onions, chopped

2 stalks celery, chopped

1 medium yellow or green bell pepper, chopped

1 medium red bell pepper, chopped

6 cloves garlic, minced, or 1 tablespoon bottled minced garlic

6 ounces fresh collard greens, mustard greens, kale, or spinach, coarsely chopped (about 3 cups, loosely packed)

3 cups water

2 bunches watercress, coarsely chopped

1 bunch parsley, coarsely chopped

2 cups chopped lean, low-sodium ham (about 10 ounces)

½ teaspoon salt

¼ to ½ teaspoon ground black pepper

⅛ to ¼ teaspoon cayenne

4 cups cooked brown rice (1⅓ cups uncooked)

**NUTRIENT ANALYSIS**

Calories 211
Protein 11 g
Carbohydrate 37 g
Total Fat 2 g
Saturated Fat 1 g
Polyunsaturated Fat 1 g
Monounsaturated Fat 1 g
Cholesterol 16 g
Sodium 465 mg

In a Dutch oven, cook flour over medium-high heat for 5 minutes, stirring occasionally. Reduce heat to medium and cook, stirring constantly, for 5 to 7 minutes, or until flour is evenly browned. Remove flour from Dutch oven; set aside. Allow pot to cool.

Rinse and dry cooled Dutch oven, then spray with vegetable oil spray. Add onions, celery, bell peppers, and garlic. Cook over medium heat for 15 minutes, stirring occasionally.

Stir in browned flour and remaining ingredients except brown rice. Bring to a boil over high heat. Reduce heat and simmer, covered, for 30 minutes. Serve over brown rice.

# LENTIL-SPINACH SOUP

*Serves 8*

*The cheese or yogurt completes the protein in the lentils, making this delicious soup a nourishing main dish. This is a good recipe to double and freeze, but omit the cheese or yogurt until serving time.*

Vegetable oil spray

1 teaspoon olive oil

1 large onion, chopped

1 pound dried lentils, rinsed and drained (about 2¼ cups)

4 cups low-sodium chicken broth (see page 55 or use commercial variety)

4 cups water

1 pound fresh spinach, stemmed and torn into bite-size pieces (about 3 cups), or 10-ounce package frozen chopped spinach, defrosted and squeezed dry

½ teaspoon freshly ground pepper, or to taste

⅛ teaspoon ground allspice

Broth or water if needed

1 cup shredded nonfat or part-skim mozzarella cheese (4 ounces) or ½ cup plain nonfat or low-fat yogurt, lightly beaten with a fork (4 ounces)

## NUTRIENT ANALYSIS

Calories 249
Protein 23 g
Carbohydrate 38 g
Total Fat 2 g
Saturated Fat 0 g
Polyunsaturated Fat 1 g
Monounsaturated Fat 1 g
Cholesterol 0 mg
Sodium 165 mg

Spray a large stockpot or Dutch oven with vegetable oil spray. Heat over medium-high heat. Add oil and swirl to coat bottom of pot. When oil is hot, add onion. Sauté until golden-brown, 3 to 4 minutes.

Stir in lentils, broth, and water. Bring to a boil over high heat. Reduce heat and simmer, covered, stirring occasionally, for 45 to 60 minutes, or until lentils are tender.

Stir in spinach, pepper, and allspice. Simmer, covered, for 15 minutes. Thin the soup with additional broth or water if needed.

Ladle soup into bowls and top with cheese.

# LIGHT AND LEMONY
# SPINACH SOUP

*Serves 2*

*The unusual flavor combination makes this soup wonder-ful. And it's so easy to prepare!*

2 cups low-sodium chicken broth (see page 55 or use commercial variety)
2 teaspoons fresh lemon juice
¼ teaspoon dried thyme, crumbled
⅛ teaspoon salt (optional)
4 leaves spinach or other greens, such as escarole, torn
1 green onion (green part only), thinly sliced

In a 1-quart saucepan, combine broth, lemon juice, thyme, and salt. Bring to a boil over high heat.

Meanwhile, place spinach in bowls.

Pour hot soup over spinach. Top soup with green onion. Serve immediately.

**NUTRIENT ANALYSIS**

Calories 37
Protein 4 g
Carbohydrate 4 g
Total Fat 1 g
Saturated Fat 0 g
Polyunsaturated Fat 0 g
Monounsaturated Fat 0 g
Cholesterol 0 mg
Sodium 88 mg

# CREAMY WILD RICE AND WHEAT BERRY SOUP

*Serves 4*

**COOK'S TIP ON SPROUTED WHEAT BERRIES:**
Look for sprouted wheat berries in the produce section of large supermarkets or at health food stores. Use them instead of nuts for crunch in salads or sandwiches, or lightly sauté them and toss with cooked vegetables.

*Wild rice isn't a rice at all—it's the nutty-flavored seed of an annual marsh grass. If you can't locate wheat berries or millet, use an additional ¼ cup of wild rice instead.*

¼ cup wild rice

¼ cup wheat berries or millet

2 cups water

1 cup low-sodium chicken broth (see page 55 or use commercial variety)

1 cup chopped onion (about 2 medium)

1 cup chopped celery (about 3 stalks)

2 cloves garlic, minced, or 1 teaspoon bottled minced garlic

½ teaspoon curry powder

¼ teaspoon pepper

12-ounce can fat-free evaporated milk

2 tablespoons dry sherry (optional)

4 very thin lemon slices (optional)

2 tablespoons chopped fresh parsley (optional)

Place rice and wheat berries in a colander. Rinse under running water. Drain.

In a large saucepan, bring rice, wheat berries, water, broth, onion, celery, garlic, curry powder, and pepper to a boil over high heat. Reduce heat and simmer, covered, for 1 hour, or until rice is tender.

Stir in milk and sherry. Heat through.

Ladle soup into bowls and garnish with lemon slices and parsley.

**NUTRIENT ANALYSIS**

Calories 184
Protein 11 g
Carbohydrate 33 g
Total Fat 1 g
Saturated Fat 0 g
Polyunsaturated Fat 0 g
Monounsaturated Fat 0 g
Cholesterol 3 mg
Sodium 141 mg

SOUPS

# CLAM AND POTATO CHOWDER WITH FRESH HERBS

*Serves 4*

*Our heart-healthy chowder boasts an abundance of fresh herbs and tastes as rich as the New England original.*

½ pint shucked clams (8 ounces) or 6½-ounce can minced clams

Water if needed

1 medium white potato, peeled and finely chopped

1 medium turnip, peeled and finely chopped

½ cup chopped shallots or onion (about 4 medium shallots or 1 medium onion)

½ teaspoon instant low-sodium chicken bouillon granules

⅛ teaspoon pepper

2 12-ounce cans fat-free evaporated milk (divided use)

2 tablespoons all-purpose flour

2 teaspoons chopped fresh marjoram or oregano

1 teaspoon chopped fresh thyme

Chop shucked clams, reserving juice. Set clams aside. Strain clam juice to remove bits of shell. (Or drain canned clams, reserving juice.) If necessary, add water to clam juice to equal 1 cup.

In a medium saucepan, combine clam juice, potato, turnip, shallots, bouillon granules, and pepper. Bring to a boil over high heat. Reduce heat and simmer, covered, for about 10 minutes, or until vegetables are tender.

Stir in 2½ cups of milk. Increase heat to medium.

In a jar with a tight-fitting lid, combine remaining milk and flour. Cover and shake well to mix. Add to potato mixture in saucepan. Cook and stir over medium heat until thickened and bubbly, about 5 minutes.

Stir in clams. Cook and stir for 1 minute. Stir in marjoram and thyme just before serving.

**NUTRIENT ANALYSIS**

Calories 237
Protein 23 g
Carbohydrate 33 g
Total Fat 1 g
Saturated Fat 0 g
Polyunsaturated Fat 0 g
Monounsaturated Fat 0 g
Cholesterol 29 mg
Sodium 252 mg

# SUMMERTIME SOUP

*Serves 7*

**COOK'S TIP ON CUTTING MANGOES:**

Place the mango on its flattest side. Using a sharp knife, make a horizontal cut to slice off approximately the top half of the mango. (You won't be able to cut the fruit exactly in half because of the large pit.) Turn the mango over, pit side down. Slice off the top part of the second side. Remove the peel from all three pieces. Trim any remaining flesh from the pit.

*Soup made with melons? You bet! Serve this chilled creation in pretty bowls at your next summertime brunch—its delightful taste will please your guests.*

1 small ripe cantaloupe, peeled, seeded, and cubed

2 large ripe mangoes, peeled, pitted, and cubed

2 medium peaches, peeled, pitted, and cubed

3 cups fresh or frozen unsweetened strawberries (about 16 ounces)

½ cup plain nonfat or low-fat yogurt

⅓ cup frozen orange juice concentrate

⅓ cup port

2 tablespoons orange liqueur

1 tablespoon fresh lime juice

1½ teaspoons raspberry vinegar (see Herbed or Fruit Vinegar, page 86, or use commercial variety)

½ cup plain nonfat or low-fat yogurt, well chilled

Place all ingredients except ½ cup yogurt in a food processor. Process until thick and creamy. Pour into a serving bowl and freeze for about 20 minutes.

Spoon into individual bowls and top each serving with a heaping teaspoon of yogurt. Serve immediately.

**NUTRIENT ANALYSIS**

| | |
|---|---|
| Calories | 174 |
| Protein | 4 g |
| Carbohydrate | 37 g |
| Total Fat | 1 g |
| Saturated Fat | 0 g |
| Polyunsaturated Fat | 0 g |
| Monounsaturated Fat | 0 g |
| Cholesterol | 1 mg |
| Sodium | 38 mg |

# CHICKEN BROTH

*Makes 2½ quarts*

*Canned or frozen chicken broth is no match for homemade in flavor or cost. Because good broth is essential to so many recipes, prepare enough for now and later.*

3 pounds chicken pieces, skinned, all visible fat removed

3 quarts water

1 medium onion, unpeeled, coarsely chopped

2 celery stalks with leaves, chopped

2 large unpeeled carrots, chopped

1 teaspoon whole peppercorns, or to taste

½-inch piece fresh gingerroot, peeled and chopped (optional)

1 bay leaf

1 teaspoon dried thyme, crumbled

Place all ingredients in a large stockpot and bring to a boil over medium-high heat. Do not stir. Reduce heat and simmer, partially covered, for at least 1 hour, or until chicken is tender. Frequently skim the froth off the top. Remove chicken and strain broth.

To defat broth, cover and refrigerate until the fat hardens on the surface, then skim off and discard. The broth may gel during refrigeration; this is natural.

**COOK'S TIP ON BROTH:**

You don't have to use breasts and thighs for making broth. Keep a plastic bag in your freezer so you can collect chicken and turkey pieces such as wings, necks, and backs.

If you do cook the meatier pieces in your broth, remove the bones from the boiled chicken and use the meat in soups, salads, sandwiches, and casseroles.

Measure a tablespoonful of broth into each section of an ice cube tray, freeze, then transfer the cubes to plastic freezer bags. To add flavor, not fat, use 1 cube to sauté vegetables and other foods or thaw 4 cubes when you need ¼ cup of broth.

**NUTRIENT ANALYSIS**
*(For 1 cup)*

| | |
|---|---|
| Calories | 24 |
| Protein | 3 g |
| Carbohydrate | 1 g |
| Total Fat | 1 g |
| Saturated Fat | 0 g |
| Polyunsaturated Fat | 0 g |
| Monounsaturated Fat | 0 g |
| Cholesterol | 0 mg |
| Sodium | 56 mg |

# BEEF BROTH

*Makes 2 quarts*

**COOK'S TIP
ON BEEF OR
CHICKEN BROTH:**
The fewer times you stir
the broth, the clearer the
broth will be.

*For maximum flavor and color, roast the bones for this broth. Even if you skip this step and combine the unroasted bones with the remaining ingredients, you'll still get a good broth. (See the Cook's Tip on page 55 for a handy way to have homemade broth always available.)*

4 pounds beef or veal bones

3 quarts water

3 large unpeeled carrots, chopped

1 medium onion, unpeeled, coarsely chopped

6 fresh parsley sprigs

4 cloves garlic, halved

1 teaspoon whole peppercorns, or to taste

1 bay leaf

2 whole cloves

1 teaspoon dried thyme, crumbled

½ teaspoon celery seeds

Preheat oven to 400° F.

Place bones in a roasting pan and bake for 30 minutes, turning once. Discard accumulated fat.

Transfer bones and remaining ingredients to a large stockpot. Bring mixture to a boil over medium-high heat. Do not stir. Reduce heat and simmer gently, covered, for at least 4 hours. Frequently skim the froth off the top. Remove bones and strain broth.

To defat broth, cover and refrigerate until the fat hardens on the surface, then skim off and discard. The broth may gel during refrigeration; this is natural.

**NUTRIENT ANALYSIS**
*(For 1 cup)*

Calories 24

Protein 3 g

Carbohydrate 1 g

Total Fat 1 g

Saturated Fat 0 g

Polyunsaturated Fat 0 g

Monounsaturated Fat 0 g

Cholesterol 0 mg

Sodium 56 mg

# VEGETABLE BROTH

*Makes 2 quarts*

*Keep a plastic bag in your freezer to make it easy to accumulate vegetable trimmings for your broth. You can add carrot peels, the ends of asparagus, the leafy parts of celery, the green parts of leeks, and other "scraps" to enhance the flavor if you wish. Select just about any variety of vegetables and herbs for your broth—use your imagination! (See the Cook's Tip on page 55 for a handy way to have homemade broth always available.)*

9 cups cold water

2 medium white onions, unpeeled, coarsely chopped

3 large carrots, unpeeled, chopped

3 celery stalks with leaves, chopped

1 medium tomato, quartered

2 teaspoons dried thyme, crumbled

⅛ teaspoon black pepper

2 cups fresh spinach leaves (10 to 12 ounces)

Combine all ingredients except spinach in a large stockpot. Bring to a boil over high heat.

Reduce heat to low and simmer, partially covered, for 1 hour.

Add the spinach and cook for 5 minutes.

Remove vegetables with a slotted spoon, then pour broth through a fine strainer.

**NUTRIENT ANALYSIS**
*(For 1 cup)*

| | |
|---|---|
| Calories | 35 |
| Protein | 2 g |
| Carbohydrate | 8 g |
| Total Fat | 0 g |
| Saturated Fat | 0 g |
| Polyunsaturated Fat | 0 g |
| Monounsaturated Fat | 0 g |
| Cholesterol | 0 mg |
| Sodium | 54 mg |

# SALADS
## AND
# SALAD
# DRESSINGS

Salad with Creamy Mustard
Vinaigrette

Spinach Salad

Boston Citrus Salad

Warm Mushroom Salad

Jícama and Grapefruit Salad with
Ancho-Honey Salad Dressing

Cucumber-Melon Salad with
Raspberry Vinegar

Fresh Fruit Salad with Poppy Seed
and Yogurt Salad Dressing

Deviled Eggs

Lemon-Curried
Black-Eyed Pea Salad

Marinated Vegetable Salad

Potato Salad

Tabbouleh

Crispy Tortilla Salad

Salmon and Pasta Salad

Seafood Pasta Salad

Herbed Chicken Salad

Ham and Rice Salad

Feta Cheese Vinaigrette with
Dijon Mustard

Creamy Artichoke Vinaigrette

Creamy Herb Salad Dressing

Tomatillo-Avocado Puree

Gazpacho Salad Dressing

Parmesan-Peppercorn Ranch
Salad Dressing

Herbed or Fruit Vinegar

# SALAD WITH CREAMY MUSTARD VINAIGRETTE

*Serves 8*

*This recipe makes a double batch of dressing (about 10 tablespoons). Use half now and save the rest for another salad. In addition to providing iron and protein, tofu is what makes this dressing so creamy and rich.*

**4 teaspoons shelled sunflower seeds**

**DRESSING**

½ **cup soft or firm reduced-fat tofu, drained (4 ounces)**

½ **cup nonfat or low-fat vinaigrette**

**2 tablespoons water**

½ **teaspoon honey**

½ **teaspoon Dijon mustard**

**1 head leaf lettuce, torn into bite-size pieces, or about**
**½ pound mixed lettuce greens**

**3 dried apricot halves, slivered**

Preheat oven to 300° F.

Place sunflower seeds in a baking pan and bake for 12 minutes, or until very lightly browned. Remove from pan and let cool.

Meanwhile, pour liquid from tofu. Drain. Place tofu on a double layer of paper towels. Pat dry.

Meanwhile, in a blender or food processor, process dressing ingredients until creamy.

Toss lettuce with 5 tablespoons of dressing. (Refrigerate remainder of dressing for later use.) Top with apricots and sunflower seeds.

# SPINACH SALAD

*Serves 6*

*If you have a rotary grater, use the drum with the smallest holes to prepare the cooked egg whites. The finely grated whites will give a dressed-up look to this colorful salad.*

### DRESSING

½ cup nonfat or low-fat vinaigrette

1 tablespoon finely chopped fresh herbs or 1 teaspoon dried (parsley, basil, oregano, chives, tarragon, etc.)

1 to 2 teaspoons stone-ground mustard

### SALAD

1½ pounds fresh spinach

12 cherry tomatoes, quartered

1 small red onion, cut into thin rings

Freshly ground pepper to taste

2 hard-cooked eggs, whites only, grated or finely chopped

In a small bowl, combine dressing ingredients and mix well. For maximum flavor, cover and refrigerate for several hours.

Rinse spinach thoroughly in cold water. Drain well. Remove and discard stems and bruised or tough leaves. Tear spinach into bite-size pieces, placing them in a large salad bowl. Add remaining salad ingredients to spinach and toss.

Pour dressing over salad and toss. Sprinkle egg whites over salad. Serve immediately.

**NUTRIENT ANALYSIS**

Calories 66
Protein 5 g
Carbohydrate 12 g
Total Fat 1 g
Saturated Fat 0 g
Polyunsaturated Fat 0 g
Monounsaturated Fat 0 g
Cholesterol 0 mg
Sodium 328 mg

# BOSTON CITRUS SALAD

*Serves 6*

*Delicate, pale-green Boston lettuce is the perfect backdrop for juicy citrus fruit. The orange-flower water, found at Middle Eastern markets and most gourmet-type grocery stores, gives an aromatic touch to this salad. You can also use orange-flower water in cakes, cookies, puddings, and beverages.*

1 large head Boston, butter, or Bibb lettuce

2 large navel oranges

2 medium grapefruit

1 tablespoon fresh lemon juice

1 tablespoon honey

¼ teaspoon orange-flower water or orange liqueur (optional)

3 tablespoons slivered almonds, dry-roasted (about 1 ounce)

Tear lettuce leaves into bite-size pieces. Set aside.

Remove the peel and pith from the oranges. Cut oranges into ¼-inch slices. Cut slices in quarters. Set aside.

Peel and section grapefruit, collecting juice in a small bowl. Cut grapefruit into bite-size pieces. Set aside.

Add lemon juice, honey, and orange-flower water to reserved grapefruit juice. Pour juice mixture over lettuce. Stir to coat evenly.

Place lettuce on salad plates. Top each serving with grapefruit and orange pieces and a sprinkling of almonds.

**NUTRIENT ANALYSIS**

Calories 100

Protein 2 g

Carbohydrate 19 g

Total Fat 3 g

Saturated Fat 0 g

Polyunsaturated Fat 1 g

Monounsaturated Fat 2 g

Cholesterol 0 mg

Sodium 3 mg

# WARM MUSHROOM SALAD

*Serves 4*

*Balsamic vinegar gives mushrooms a deep, rich flavor. If you wish, you can use meaty-textured portobello mushrooms and serve your salad as part of a meatless meal.*

¼ cup port, sweet red wine, or frozen unsweetened
    apple juice concentrate

3 to 3½ tablespoons balsamic vinegar or rice vinegar

2 tablespoons water

3 cloves garlic, finely minced, or 1½ teaspoons bottled
    minced garlic

12 ounces fresh mushrooms, cut into ¼-inch-thick slices

1 teaspoon light margarine

⅛ teaspoon freshly ground pepper, or to taste

4 leaves Boston lettuce

1 teaspoon chopped fresh parsley

In a nonstick skillet, heat port, vinegar, water, and garlic over medium-high heat until small bubbles begin to form.

Add mushrooms and cook, stirring frequently, for 8 to 10 minutes, or until all liquid evaporates.

Add margarine and pepper. Stir to coat evenly.

Arrange mushrooms on lettuce leaves and sprinkle with parsley. Serve warm.

### NUTRIENT ANALYSIS

Calories 29

Protein 2 g

Carbohydrate 5 g

Total Fat 1 g

Saturated Fat 0 g

Polyunsaturated Fat 0 g

Monounsaturated Fat 0 g

Cholesterol 0 mg

Sodium 15 mg

# JÍCAMA AND GRAPEFRUIT SALAD WITH ANCHO-HONEY SALAD DRESSING

*Serves 4*

*Ancho chili peppers are dried poblano chili peppers. Wrinkled and dark reddish-brown, they add a medium-hot boost to the salad dressing.*

### DRESSING

½ cup water

2 ancho chili peppers, halved lengthwise and seeded*

2 cloves garlic, quartered

2 tablespoons white wine vinegar

2 tablespoons honey

1 tablespoon acceptable vegetable oil

1 tablespoon fresh lime juice

1 pound jícama, peeled and cut into very thin slices (about 3½ cups)

½ cup chopped red onion

¼ cup chopped fresh cilantro

2 medium red or pink grapefruit

In a small saucepan, combine water, chili peppers, and garlic. Bring to a boil over high heat. Reduce heat and simmer, uncovered, for 10 minutes.

Pour mixture into a blender or food processor. Process until smooth.

Add remaining dressing ingredients. Process until smooth.

In a medium bowl, combine jícama, onion, and cilantro. Pour dressing over jícama mixture, stirring to coat.

Cover and marinate in the refrigerator for 2 to 24 hours.

**NUTRIENT ANALYSIS**

Calories 167
Protein 2 g
Carbohydrate 34 g
Total Fat 4 g
Saturated Fat 0 g
Polyunsaturated Fat 2 g
Monounsaturated Fat 1 g
Cholesterol 0 mg
Sodium 9 mg

Shortly before serving, peel and section grapefruit. Drain. Gently stir grapefruit sections into jícama mixture.

* Hot chili peppers contain oils that can burn your skin, lips, and eyes. Wear rubber gloves or wash your hands thoroughly with warm, soapy water immediately after handling peppers.

## COOK'S TIP ON JÍCAMA:

Also called Mexican potato, this root vegetable has a thin brown skin and crunchy cream-colored flesh. Jícama has a sweet, nutty flavor and can be eaten raw or cooked. Use jícama as you would carrot and celery sticks, or chop or shred jícama to add to a fresh green salad. Choose bulbs that are firm and free of blemishes. Store whole jícama, unwrapped, in the refrigerator for up to 5 days. Peel the skin just before using. Wrap leftover jícama in plastic wrap and store for 2 to 3 days in the refrigerator.

# CUCUMBER-MELON SALAD WITH RASPBERRY VINEGAR

*Serves 4*

*Serve this refreshingly different dish as a salad, or turn it into a relish by finely chopping the ingredients.*

1 medium cucumber

½ large cantaloupe, seeded

1 bunch radishes

¼ cup raspberry vinegar (see Herbed or Fruit Vinegar, page 86, or use commercial variety)

Freshly ground pepper (optional)

4 lettuce leaves

Partially peel cucumber, leaving some of the dark green to add color. Cut cucumber into bite-size pieces and put them in a medium bowl.

Cut cantaloupe into cubes or use a melon baller to scoop out small balls. Add to cucumber pieces.

Thinly slice the radishes and combine with cucumber and cantaloupe.

Toss salad with vinegar and sprinkle with pepper. Refrigerate, covered, until chilled, about 30 minutes to 1 hour. Serve on individual plates lined with leaf lettuce.

**NUTRIENT ANALYSIS**

Calories 77

Protein 2 g

Carbohydrate 18 g

Total Fat 1 g

Saturated Fat 0 g

Polyunsaturated Fat 0 g

Monounsaturated Fat 0 g

Cholesterol 0 mg

Sodium 21 mg

# FRESH FRUIT SALAD WITH POPPY SEED AND YOGURT SALAD DRESSING

*Serves 6*

*Let your imagination run wild as you select a variety of fresh fruit for this salad. Aim for pleasing combinations of color and texture, as well as taste.*

3 medium oranges
3 cups assorted fresh fruit, cut into bite-size pieces
1 cup nonfat or low-fat lemon yogurt
¼ teaspoon poppy seeds
6 fresh mint sprigs or edible flowers

Cut each orange in half. Cut a thin slice from the bottom of each half so the oranges will sit upright. Remove the flesh from each half. Coarsely chop the flesh and place pieces in a large bowl.

Add other fruit to orange pieces. Stir to combine.

Place each orange "bowl" on a small plate. Place fruit in orange bowls, letting any extra fruit cascade onto the plate.

In a small bowl, whisk together yogurt and poppy seeds, then pour over fruit, using 2 to 3 tablespoons per serving. Top each serving with a sprig of mint or a flower.

## VARIATION

Replace yogurt and poppy seeds with 2 to 4 teaspoons of Fruit Vinegar (see page 86 or use commercial variety).

### NUTRIENT ANALYSIS

| | |
|---|---|
| Calories | 104 |
| Protein | 3 g |
| Carbohydrate | 25 g |
| Total Fat | 0 g |
| Saturated Fat | 0 g |
| Polyunsaturated Fat | 0 g |
| Monounsaturated Fat | 0 g |
| Cholesterol | 1 mg |
| Sodium | 18 mg |

# DEVILED EGGS

*Serves 12*

*To avoid the usual cholesterol of deviled eggs, this recipe uses tofu instead of egg yolks. Tofu is bland and takes on the flavors of the food mixed with it, so assertive flavorings (herbs, spices, marinades) pair well.*

1 dozen eggs, hard-cooked

10 ounces firm reduced-fat tofu, drained

2 tablespoons mustard

2 tablespoons sweet pickle relish

2 tablespoons chopped fresh chives or 2 teaspoons dried

1 teaspoon turmeric

1 teaspoon fresh lemon juice

¼ teaspoon salt

⅛ teaspoon pepper

Paprika (optional)

Remove shells from eggs. Slice eggs in half lengthwise; remove yolks and discard.

Pour liquid from tofu. Drain. Place tofu on a double layer of paper towels. Pat dry.

Place tofu in a large bowl. Using a fork, mash tofu into small bits.

Mix remaining ingredients except paprika in a small bowl. Add to tofu and stir to combine.

Spoon mixture into egg whites. Top with paprika, if desired. Serve chilled.

**NUTRIENT ANALYSIS**

Calories 31

Protein 5 g

Carbohydrate 2 g

Total Fat 0 g

Saturated Fat 0 g

Polyunsaturated Fat 0 g

Monounsaturated Fat 0 g

Cholesterol 0 mg

Sodium 167 mg

# LEMON-CURRIED BLACK-EYED PEA SALAD

*Serves 8*

This colorful salad comes together in a snap thanks to canned peas and corn. Rinsing the peas reduces their sodium content.

### SALAD

15-ounce can black-eyed peas, rinsed and drained

11-ounce can no-salt-added whole kernel corn, drained

½ cup chopped red onion

½ cup thinly sliced celery (1 to 2 stalks)

1 teaspoon finely shredded lemon peel

### DRESSING

2 tablespoons fresh lemon juice

1 tablespoon water

1 teaspoon olive oil

1 clove garlic, minced, or ½ teaspoon bottled minced garlic

½ teaspoon curry powder

½ teaspoon Dijon mustard

⅛ teaspoon pepper

**COOK'S TIP:**

If you want to use dried black-eyed peas, soak 1 cup of them overnight in enough water to cover. Drain and add 3 cups fresh water. Bring to a boil over high heat. Reduce heat and simmer, covered, for 50 to 60 minutes, or until just tender. Drain and continue with recipe.

In a medium bowl, combine salad ingredients. Set aside.

In a jar with a tight-fitting lid, combine dressing ingredients. Cover and shake well.

Pour dressing over black-eyed pea mixture. Stir until well coated.

Cover and refrigerate for 1 to 24 hours, or until serving time.

**NUTRIENT ANALYSIS**

Calories 80
Protein 4 g
Carbohydrate 15 g
Total Fat 1 g
Saturated Fat 0 g
Polyunsaturated Fat 0 g
Monounsaturated Fat 0 g
Cholesterol 0 mg
Sodium 62 mg

# MARINATED VEGETABLE SALAD

*Serves 8*

*For a delicious sandwich, drain any leftovers and use the vegetables to stuff a pita. Garnish with a little nonfat or low-fat Cheddar cheese and your favorite variety of lettuce.*

16-ounce bag frozen no-salt-added mixed vegetables, thawed

15-ounce can chick-peas, rinsed and drained

### MARINADE

⅓ cup nonfat or low-fat Italian salad dressing

¼ cup frozen unsweetened apple juice concentrate, thawed

2 tablespoons fresh lemon juice

1 tablespoon acceptable vegetable oil

1 tablespoon rice vinegar or white wine vinegar

2 cloves garlic, finely minced; 1 teaspoon bottled minced garlic; or ¼ teaspoon garlic powder

⅛ teaspoon freshly ground pepper, or to taste

8 lettuce leaves

Combine frozen vegetables and chick-peas in a large bowl.

In a jar with a tight-fitting lid, combine marinade ingredients. Shake well. Pour marinade over vegetable-bean mixture and stir to combine well.

Cover and marinate in refrigerator for several hours. Arrange salad over lettuce leaves.

## NUTRIENT ANALYSIS

Calories 136
Protein 5 g
Carbohydrate 24 g
Total Fat 3 g
Saturated Fat 0 g
Polyunsaturated Fat 1 g
Monounsaturated Fat 1 g
Cholesterol 0 mg
Sodium 169 mg

# POTATO SALAD

*Serves 8*

*A must for picnics, this salad is best if made at least a few hours in advance to allow the flavors to blend.*

2 pounds small red potatoes

Water

2 celery stalks, finely chopped

2 green onions (green and white parts), chopped

1 small red or green bell pepper, chopped

4 to 5 small radishes, minced

¼ cup finely chopped fresh parsley

## DRESSING

½ cup plain nonfat or low-fat yogurt

¼ cup fat-free, cholesterol-free mayonnaise

2 tablespoons cider vinegar or white wine vinegar

1 tablespoon fresh dill weed or 1 teaspoon dried

1 teaspoon Dijon mustard, or to taste

½ teaspoon celery seeds

½ teaspoon salt (optional)

Freshly ground pepper to taste

2 tablespoons finely chopped fresh parsley

½ teaspoon paprika

Place potatoes in a medium saucepan with enough water to cover. Bring to a boil over high heat. Cook, covered, until tender, about 30 minutes. Drain immediately. When potatoes are cool enough to handle, cut into ½-inch cubes and place in a large bowl.

Add celery, green onions, bell pepper, radishes, and ¼ cup parsley. Stir to combine.

In a small bowl, whisk together dressing ingredients and add to potato mixture. Mix gently.

Sprinkle with 2 tablespoons parsley and paprika. Cover and refrigerate for at least 2 hours before serving.

**NUTRIENT ANALYSIS**

Calories 114
Protein 3 g
Carbohydrate 26 g
Total Fat 0 g
Saturated Fat 0 g
Polyunsaturated Fat 0 g
Monounsaturated Fat 0 g
Cholesterol 0 mg
Sodium 87 mg

# TABBOULEH

*Serves 6*

*Make this dish well in advance—the flavors improve with age. Bulgur, a finely cracked wheat, is available at most supermarkets and at health food stores. To serve, place a scoop of the salad on a leaf of lettuce or use it to stuff hollowed-out tomatoes, zucchini halves, or bell peppers.*

2 cups water

2 cups low-sodium vegetable broth (see page 57 or use commercial variety)

1 cup bulgur (5 to 6 ounces)

¼ cup fresh lemon juice (1 to 2 lemons)

1 tablespoon olive oil

2 medium tomatoes, finely chopped

3 green onions (green and white parts), finely chopped

¼ cup finely chopped fresh mint or 1 tablespoon dried, crumbled

¼ cup finely chopped fresh parsley

Freshly ground pepper to taste

In a medium saucepan over high heat, bring water and broth to a boil.

Place bulgur in a large heatproof bowl. Stir in boiling water and broth. Cover and allow to stand for 1 hour, or until most of the liquid is absorbed.

Drain bulgur in a colander or sieve. Squeeze out excess moisture by using your hands or by placing bulgur in cheesecloth or a tea towel, gathering the ends together and squeezing.

Combine lemon juice and oil. Add to bulgur with remaining ingredients. Gently mix with a fork.

Cover and refrigerate for at least 1 hour. Serve chilled or at room temperature.

**NUTRIENT ANALYSIS**

Calories 118
Protein 4 g
Carbohydrate 22 g
Total Fat 3 g
Saturated Fat 0 g
Polyunsaturated Fat 0 g
Monounsaturated Fat 2 g
Cholesterol 0 mg
Sodium 97 mg

# CRISPY TORTILLA SALAD

*Serves 6*

*You can bake the tortillas and make the salsa for this crispy, light, Mexican-style salad in advance, then assemble the salad just before serving.*

6 6-inch corn tortillas

Vegetable oil spray

½ teaspoon chili powder

1 head iceberg lettuce, shredded (about 6 cups)

19-ounce can low-sodium kidney beans, drained

2 ounces nonfat or part-skim mozzarella cheese, grated (about ½ cup)

2 ounces nonfat or low-fat Cheddar cheese, grated (about ½ cup)

3 medium tomatoes, preferably 2 red and 1 yellow, chopped

6 tablespoons low-sodium salsa (see page 242 or use commercial variety)

Preheat oven to 350° F.

Spray both sides of each tortilla with vegetable oil spray. Sprinkle top side lightly with chili powder.

Bake tortillas in a single layer on a baking sheet for 10 to 15 minutes, or until crisp and lightly browned.

Top each tortilla with layers of remaining ingredients in the order listed.

## NUTRIENT ANALYSIS

| | |
|---|---|
| Calories | 211 |
| Protein | 18 g |
| Carbohydrate | 33 g |
| Total Fat | 2 g |
| Saturated Fat | 0 g |
| Polyunsaturated Fat | 1 g |
| Monounsaturated Fat | 0 g |
| Cholesterol | 0 mg |
| Sodium | 258 mg |

# SALMON AND PASTA SALAD

*Serves 5*

*This easy-to-fix salad is great for hot summer days, when tomatoes and cucumbers are at their best.*

### SALMON SALAD

1 cup uncooked elbow macaroni (4 ounces)

2½ tablespoons nonfat or low-fat Italian salad dressing

10-ounce package frozen no-salt-added asparagus

7⅔-ounce can salmon, drained, skin removed

1 large red bell pepper, diced

½ medium white onion, minced

1 tablespoon Worcestershire sauce

### DRESSING

1 cup nonfat or low-fat cottage cheese

2 tablespoons fresh lemon juice

2 to 3 dashes hot pepper sauce

1 to 2 tablespoons chopped fresh dill weed or 1 to
    2 teaspoons dried

15 cherry tomatoes, 5 Italian plum tomatoes, or 3 to
    4 tomatoes (optional)

3 medium cucumbers (optional)

Cook macaroni according to package directions, omitting salt and oil. Drain and return to saucepan.

Stir salad dressing into macaroni. Set aside.

Meanwhile, place a steamer basket in a medium saucepan. Add water to a depth of 1 to 2 inches. Be sure water does not touch the bottom of the basket. Bring water to a boil over high heat. Steam asparagus until tender-crisp, 3 to 5 minutes. Cut diagonally into bite-size pieces.

In a large bowl, mash salmon, including bones. Add remaining salad ingredients. Mix well.

**NUTRIENT ANALYSIS**

Calories 146

Protein 12 g

Carbohydrate 21 g

Total Fat 2 g

Saturated Fat 1 g

Polyunsaturated Fat 1 g

Monounsaturated Fat 0 g

Cholesterol 12 mg

Sodium 295 mg

In a blender or food processor, process dressing ingredients except dill weed until creamy.

Mix dill weed into dressing. Pour over the salmon salad mixture and stir. Cover and refrigerate.

Halve cherry tomatoes or slice other tomatoes; cut cucumbers into spears. Mound salmon salad in center of plates with tomato and cucumber pieces arranged around it.

# SEAFOOD PASTA SALAD

*Serves 6*

*Try poached fish (see Poached Fish and Fish Broth, page 104), tuna packed in spring water, canned salmon, fresh or frozen shrimp, nonfat imitation crab—the possibilities for this recipe go on and on.*

### SALAD

10-ounce package uncooked pasta shells

2 cups cooked seafood, skin and bones removed

1 small red onion, finely chopped

1 medium red, green, or yellow bell pepper, chopped

1 cup frozen no-salt-added green peas, thawed (about 5 ounces)

4 to 5 radishes, finely chopped

¼ cup minced fresh basil or 4 teaspoons dried, crumbled

¼ cup minced fresh parsley

### DRESSING

½ cup nonfat or low-fat Italian salad dressing

½ teaspoon Dijon mustard

1 small head romaine lettuce (optional)

2 small tomatoes, each cut into 6 wedges (optional)

Cook pasta according to package directions, omitting salt and oil. Drain and place in a large bowl.

Add remaining salad ingredients to pasta. Stir to combine.

In a small bowl, whisk together salad dressing and mustard. Gently stir into the pasta mixture.

Cover and refrigerate for several hours. Serve at room temperature or chilled.

For an attractive presentation, line a serving bowl or a platter with lettuce, fill with pasta, and top with tomato wedges.

**NUTRIENT ANALYSIS**

Calories 278

Protein 19 g

Carbohydrate 46 g

Total Fat 2 g

Saturated Fat 0 g

Polyunsaturated Fat 1 g

Monounsaturated Fat 0 g

Cholesterol 31 mg

Sodium 261 mg

# HERBED CHICKEN SALAD

*Serves 6*

*In addition to being an entrée salad, this dish is also good in pita pockets or on bread or whole-wheat crackers. It's excellent, too, when used as stuffing for tomatoes, bell peppers, or zucchini.*

### CHICKEN SALAD

2 cups cooked chicken, cut into bite-size pieces (about 12 ounces raw skinless, boneless breasts or half a 3- to 4-pound raw whole chicken)

¼ cup plain nonfat or low-fat yogurt

¼ cup fat-free, cholesterol-free mayonnaise

2 green onions (green and white parts), thinly sliced

1 small carrot, grated

2 radishes, grated

3 tablespoons chopped celery

2 tablespoons chopped green bell pepper

2 tablespoons chopped fresh parsley

1½ tablespoons tarragon vinegar or 1½ tablespoons rice vinegar or white wine vinegar and ⅛ teaspoon dried tarragon, crumbled

1 teaspoon Worcestershire sauce

1 teaspoon salt-free Italian herb seasoning

¼ teaspoon freshly ground pepper, or to taste

6 lettuce leaves

8-ounce can mandarin oranges in light syrup, drained, or 3 small tomatoes, sliced

In a large bowl, combine all chicken salad ingredients. Mix well.

Cover and refrigerate for at least 1 hour.

To serve, place a scoop of chicken salad on a lettuce leaf and top with mandarin orange segments.

**NUTRIENT ANALYSIS**

Calories 122
Protein 15 g
Carbohydrate 9 g
Total Fat 3 g
Saturated Fat 1 g
Polyunsaturated Fat 1 g
Monounsaturated Fat 1 g
Cholesterol 39 mg
Sodium 130 mg

# HAM AND RICE SALAD

*Serves 8*

*This makes a terrific entrée. Team it with a fresh fruit salad, such as either on page 67, and crusty bread.*

### HAM SALAD

1 cup brown or long-grain rice

1 cup low-sodium chicken broth (see page 55 or use commercial variety)

6 ounces lean, low-sodium ham, all visible fat removed, cut into ¼-inch cubes

1 cup fresh or frozen no-salt-added whole kernel corn, thawed (2 medium ears or 5 to 6 ounces frozen)

1 cup frozen no-salt-added green peas, thawed (about 5 ounces)

4 green onions (green and white parts), thinly sliced

1 medium red, yellow, or green bell pepper, finely chopped

4 to 5 radishes, finely chopped

¼ cup minced fresh parsley

1 tablespoon fresh dill weed or 1 teaspoon dried

### DRESSING

½ cup nonfat or low-fat Italian salad dressing

½ teaspoon Dijon mustard

1 small head lettuce, preferably red leaf

Fresh mint or parsley sprigs

Cook rice according to package instructions, substituting broth for 1 cup of the liquid and omitting salt. Allow to cool.

In a large bowl, combine rice with remaining ham salad ingredients.

In a small bowl, whisk together salad dressing and mustard. Stir dressing into rice mixture. Cover and refrigerate.

Serve at room temperature or chilled. Place a scoop of salad on a bed of lettuce and top with mint.

# FETA CHEESE VINAIGRETTE WITH DIJON MUSTARD

*Makes about 1 cup*

*This zesty vinaigrette will surprise you! Feta cheese mixed with honey provides tangy flavor to this dressing, which is especially delicious over crisp romaine lettuce.*

1 tablespoon cornstarch

¾ cup water

1 ounce feta cheese, crumbled

2 tablespoons white wine vinegar

2 tablespoons olive oil (extra-virgin preferred)

1 tablespoon Dijon mustard

2 teaspoons honey

1 clove garlic, minced, or ½ teaspoon bottled minced garlic

¼ teaspoon salt

⅛ teaspoon pepper

Place cornstarch in a small bowl. Stir in water. Pour mixture into a 1-quart saucepan. Bring to a boil over high heat, stirring occasionally, for about 2 to 3 minutes, or until thick and bubbly. Pour mixture into a medium bowl, cover, and refrigerate for at least 15 minutes.

Stir the remaining ingredients into the cornstarch mixture. You can refrigerate this vinaigrette, covered, for up to 5 days.

**COOK'S TIP:**

In most recipes that call for cornstarch, you can substitute an equal amount of arrowroot and use as directed in your recipe. In general, you should dissolve arrowroot and cornstarch in a cold liquid before heating the mixture or adding it to a hot liquid. Arrowroot is easily (and economically) available at health food stores and some supermarkets.

**NUTRIENT ANALYSIS**
*(For 2 tablespoons)*

| | |
|---|---|
| Calories | 51 |
| Protein | 1 g |
| Carbohydrate | 3 g |
| Total Fat | 4 g |
| Saturated Fat | 1 g |
| Polyunsaturated Fat | 0 g |
| Monounsaturated Fat | 3 g |
| Cholesterol | 3 mg |
| Sodium | 137 mg |

# CREAMY ARTICHOKE VINAIGRETTE

*Makes about ¾ cup*

*Pureeing the artichoke hearts makes this dressing wonderfully smooth. You can toss the remaining artichokes in with your salad.*

½ 14-ounce can artichoke hearts, rinsed and drained

¼ cup olive oil (extra-virgin preferred)

2 tablespoons fresh lemon juice

2 cloves garlic, minced, or 1 teaspoon bottled minced garlic

½ teaspoon Dijon mustard

¼ teaspoon freshly ground pepper

In a blender or food processor, process all ingredients until silky smooth.

Cover and refrigerate. Serve over salad greens.

**NUTRIENT ANALYSIS**

*(For 2 tablespoons)*

Calories 92
Protein 1 g
Carbohydrate 3 g
Total Fat 9 g
Saturated Fat 1 g
Polyunsaturated Fat 1 g
Monounsaturated Fat 7 g
Cholesterol 0 mg
Sodium 46 mg

# CREAMY HERB SALAD DRESSING

*Makes about 1¼ cups*

*Serve this dressing hot or cold. It can be used as a dip or on poultry, baked potatoes, or cold seafood. It keeps well when covered and refrigerated.*

½ cup plain nonfat or low-fat yogurt

½ cup nonfat or low-fat sour cream

1 green onion (green and white parts), minced

2 tablespoons minced fresh parsley or cilantro

½ teaspoon salt-free lemon-herb seasoning

½ teaspoon honey or sugar

¼ teaspoon salt-free Italian herb seasoning (optional)

Using a hand beater, whip together yogurt and sour cream in a small bowl.

Stir in remaining ingredients.

To serve cold, refrigerate, covered, until ready to use. To serve hot, gently warm over medium heat, stirring until heated through. Do not boil.

**NUTRIENT ANALYSIS**
*(For 2 tablespoons)*

| | |
|---|---|
| Calories | 17 |
| Protein | 2 g |
| Carbohydrate | 3 g |
| Total Fat | 0 g |
| Saturated Fat | 0 g |
| Polyunsaturated Fat | 0 g |
| Monounsaturated Fat | 0 g |
| Cholesterol | 1 mg |
| Sodium | 22 mg |

# TOMATILLO-AVOCADO PUREE

*Makes about 1 cup*

*Use this guacamole-like recipe as a salad dressing, condiment, or dip. Because avocados are high in fat, even though it's monounsaturated, use them sparingly. This recipe enhances the flavor of the avocado with broiled tomatillos, which look like small green tomatoes enclosed in thin, papery husks. They're available in Latin American markets and some supermarkets.*

Vegetable oil spray

6 tomatillos, husks removed (about 8 ounces), rinsed in cold water

1 medium ripe avocado, peeled, seeded, and chopped (about 1 cup)

1 green onion (green and white parts), chopped

2 cloves garlic, minced, or 1 teaspoon bottled minced garlic

½ fresh jalapeño pepper, seeded and chopped*

1 teaspoon sugar

1 teaspoon fresh lemon juice

½ teaspoon ground cumin

½ teaspoon chili powder

¼ teaspoon salt

⅛ teaspoon pepper

## NUTRIENT ANALYSIS

*(For 2 tablespoons)*

| | |
|---|---|
| Calories | 55 |
| Protein | 1 g |
| Carbohydrate | 6 g |
| Total Fat | 4 g |
| Saturated Fat | 1 g |
| Polyunsaturated Fat | 1 g |
| Monounsaturated Fat | 2 g |
| Cholesterol | 0 mg |
| Sodium | 78 mg |

Preheat broiler. Spray a broiler pan lightly with vegetable oil spray.

Cut tomatillos in half with a sharp knife. Place skin side up on prepared broiler pan. Broil 4 to 6 inches from heat for 5 minutes. Turn and broil for 2 to 3 minutes, or until tomatillos are slightly tender.

Place tomatillos in a covered container and refrigerate for at least 10 minutes. When tomatillos are cool, combine them with the remaining ingredients in a blender or food processor. Process for 1 minute, or until mixture is smooth.

* Hot chili peppers contain oils that can burn your skin, lips, and eyes. Wear rubber gloves or wash your hands thoroughly with warm, soapy water immediately after handling peppers.

# GAZPACHO SALAD DRESSING

*Makes about ¾ cup*

*Substituting other herbs, such as parsley, mint, oregano, or tarragon, or salt-free herb seasoning for the cilantro will give you a range of flavored salad dressings.*

6-ounce can low-sodium vegetable or tomato juice

1 tablespoon very finely chopped onion, any variety

1 tablespoon very finely chopped celery

1 tablespoon very finely chopped bell pepper, any variety

1 tablespoon grated carrot

1 tablespoon finely chopped fresh cilantro or 1 teaspoon dried, crumbled

1 teaspoon fresh lemon juice

½ teaspoon sugar

¼ teaspoon hot pepper sauce or ½ teaspoon Worcestershire sauce (optional)

Freshly ground pepper to taste

In a jar with a tight-fitting lid, combine all ingredients. Shake well and refrigerate for at least 2 hours, allowing flavors to blend.

## NUTRIENT ANALYSIS
*(For 2 tablespoons)*

| | |
|---|---|
| Calories | 9 |
| Protein | 0 g |
| Carbohydrate | 2 g |
| Total Fat | 0 g |
| Saturated Fat | 0 g |
| Polyunsaturated Fat | 0 g |
| Monounsaturated Fat | 0 g |
| Cholesterol | 0 mg |
| Sodium | 9 mg |

# PARMESAN-PEPPERCORN RANCH SALAD DRESSING

*Makes about 1 cup*

*Cool and creamy, this dressing puts the finishing touch on your salad masterpiece. Don't forget to pack some in a small airtight container along with some raw vegetables for lunchtime dipping!*

¾ cup low-fat buttermilk

¼ cup nonfat or low-fat sour cream

2 tablespoons fat-free, cholesterol-free mayonnaise

2 tablespoons grated or shredded Parmesan cheese

½ teaspoon dried parsley, crumbled

½ teaspoon dried chives

¼ teaspoon dried oregano, crumbled

¼ teaspoon garlic powder

⅛ teaspoon salt

⅛ teaspoon freshly ground black pepper

Combine all ingredients in a medium bowl, stirring gently with a whisk.

For the best flavor, refrigerate, covered, for at least 30 minutes before serving. Dressing can be refrigerated in an airtight container for up to 5 days.

**COOK'S TIP ON PEPPERCORNS:**

Peppercorns are berries that grow on pepper plant vines. The green peppercorn is mild and fresh flavored. The common black peppercorn tastes pungent, yet slightly sweet. For a mild-flavored pepper, try the white peppercorn. Pink peppercorns add a colorful and flavorful touch to sauces and other dishes. They aren't true peppercorns, but dried berries from a rose plant.

**NUTRIENT ANALYSIS**

*(For 2 tablespoons)*

| | |
|---|---|
| Calories | 24 |
| Protein | 2 g |
| Carbohydrate | 3 g |
| Total Fat | 1 g |
| Saturated Fat | 0 g |
| Polyunsaturated Fat | 0 g |
| Monounsaturated Fat | 0 g |
| Cholesterol | 2 mg |
| Sodium | 124 mg |

# HERBED OR FRUIT VINEGAR

*Makes about 1½ quarts*

*Herbed or fruit vinegars are simple-to-make, delicious substitutes for salt and high-fat salad dressings. They taste wonderful on vegetables as well as salads, or use them as marinades. Invent your own combinations and make several bottles of different flavors. Here are some ideas to get you started.*

1 quart red or white vinegar

2 tablespoons peppercorns, any color, crushed

1 to 2 cups fresh herbs, such as oregano, rosemary, tarragon, thyme, sage, or a combination of herbs; chopped shallots; or berries, such as blueberries, blackberries, raspberries, or a combination of berries

2 to 4 cloves garlic (optional)

2 tablespoons juniper berries (optional)

In a nonaluminum saucepan, bring vinegar and peppercorns to a boil. Remove from heat. Let vinegar cool until it reaches room temperature or slightly warmer.

While vinegar is cooling, thoroughly wash and dry bottles or jars with tight-fitting lids or corks.

Divide fresh herbs or berries among the bottles, adding garlic and/or juniper berries if desired. Add vinegar, leaving about 2 inches at the top of the bottle. Cap or cork the bottles tightly. If the seal is not tight or to add a decorative touch, use melted wax. Store bottles at room temperature or below in a cool, dry place for 2 to 6 weeks before using. This will allow the vinegar to develop flavor (the longer it stands, the stronger the flavor).

Strain vinegar once it has reached the desired flavor. For eye appeal, add a few sprigs of fresh herbs. Reseal bottles and store them at room temperature or in the refrigerator for up to 6 months.

If you don't have time to wait for the flavor of the vinegar to strengthen, try this quick method. Bring

**NUTRIENT ANALYSIS**

*(For 2 tablespoons)*

| | |
|---|---|
| Calories | 3 |
| Protein | 0 g |
| Carbohydrate | 1 g |
| Total Fat | 0 g |
| Saturated Fat | 0 g |
| Polyunsaturated Fat | 0 g |
| Monounsaturated Fat | 0 g |
| Cholesterol | 0 mg |
| Sodium | 0 mg |

vinegar to a boil, add peppercorns and herbs, and simmer for 20 minutes or longer, according to taste. Once vinegar has cooled, pour into bottles.

Some other good ingredient combinations include:

- White wine vinegar or white distilled vinegar, black pepper, tarragon, and shallots
- Red wine vinegar, white pepper, rosemary, and blueberries
- Red wine vinegar, black pepper, thyme, and juniper berries
- Cider vinegar, black pepper, tarragon, and garlic
- Balsamic vinegar, sage, and blackberries

# SEAFOOD

Bulgur-Stuffed Rainbow Trout

Stuffed Fish Fillets

Fish with Mustard Sauce over
Steamed Spinach

Fish in a Package

Poached Fish in Asian Broth

Grilled Cod with
Artichoke-Horseradish Sauce

Mesquite-Grilled Red Snapper
with Gingered Black Bean Salsa

Grilled Catfish with
Mustard-Lemon Sauce

Poached Fish and Fish Broth

Broiled Fish Steaks

Halibut Kebabs

Fish Stew

Tuna-Pasta Casserole

Tuna Salad Pita Sandwiches

Baked Crabmeat

Shrimp Remoulade

Seafood and Lemon Risotto

Cioppino

# BULGUR-STUFFED RAINBOW TROUT

*Serves 4*

*The clear, crisp waters of the Rocky Mountains are known for their abundance of trout. This version features these flavorful fish stuffed with a mixture of bulgur, vegetables, seasonings, and lemon.*

### STUFFING

½ cup boiling water

¼ cup bulgur

Vegetable oil spray

½ cup chopped onion or shallots (about 1 medium onion or 4 medium shallots)

½ cup chopped celery (1 to 2 stalks)

3 cloves garlic, minced, or 1½ teaspoons bottled minced garlic

¼ cup chopped fresh parsley or fresh basil

½ teaspoon finely shredded lemon peel

¼ teaspoon salt

⅛ teaspoon pepper

4 fresh or frozen dressed rainbow trout, thawed* (about 8 ounces each)

Freshly ground pepper

1 lemon, quartered

**NUTRIENT ANALYSIS**

| | |
|---|---|
| Calories | 367 |
| Protein | 50 g |
| Carbohydrate | 10 g |
| Total Fat | 13 g |
| Saturated Fat | 4 g |
| Polyunsaturated Fat | 4 g |
| Monounsaturated Fat | 4 g |
| Cholesterol | 149 mg |
| Sodium | 297 mg |

To prepare stuffing, combine boiling water and bulgur in a medium bowl. Let stand for 20 minutes, or until water is absorbed.

Preheat oven to 350° F.

Spray a medium saucepan with vegetable oil spray. Cook onion, celery, and garlic over medium-low heat for about 5 minutes, or until onion is tender. Remove from heat. Stir in bulgur, parsley, lemon peel, salt, and ⅛ teaspoon pepper.

Rinse fish and pat dry with paper towels. Spoon one fourth (about ¼ cup) of the bulgur mixture into each fish cavity. Arrange fish in a shallow baking pan.

Bake, uncovered, for 30 minutes, or until fish flakes easily when tested with a fork and filling is heated through. Remove skin from fish. Season fish with freshly ground pepper. Garnish with lemon.

## MICROWAVE DIRECTIONS

Prepare recipe as above, except after stuffing fish, place fish in a single layer in a 9 × 9 × 2-inch microwave-safe baking dish. Cover dish with vented plastic wrap. Cook on 100 percent power (high) for 5 minutes. Rotate dish a half-turn and cook for 5 minutes, or until fish flakes easily when tested with a fork and filling is heated through.

* Organs, scales, head, and tail have been removed; skin and bones remain.

# STUFFED FISH FILLETS

*Serves 6*

**COOK'S TIP ON MUFFIN PANS:**

If your muffin pan has chambers that you aren't using, spray only the ones you need (cleanup will be easier). Put about 2 tablespoons of water in the unused chambers to keep your muffin pan from warping.

*You can prepare this dish several hours before baking. Stuff the fillets, then cover and refrigerate them until shortly before baking time.*

6 fish fillets, such as sole or flounder (about 4 ounces each)

Vegetable oil spray

½ teaspoon white pepper

½ teaspoon paprika

1 teaspoon acceptable vegetable oil

6 ounces fresh mushrooms, finely chopped

4 green onions (green and white parts), finely chopped

¼ cup plain bread crumbs

¼ cup minced fresh parsley

3 tablespoons chopped almonds, preferably dry-roasted (1 to 1½ ounces)

1½ teaspoons acceptable vegetable oil

2 tablespoons minced fresh parsley

Preheat oven to 375° F.

Rinse fish and pat dry with paper towels.

Using vegetable oil spray, lightly spray six 6-ounce ovenproof custard cups or one 6-chamber muffin pan with 2½ × 1¼-inch cups. Curl each fillet inside a custard or muffin cup. Sprinkle with pepper and paprika.

Pour 1 teaspoon oil into a nonstick skillet over medium-high heat. Add mushrooms and onions and sauté until tender, about 2 minutes. Remove skillet from heat.

Stir in bread crumbs, ¼ cup parsley, and almonds. Spoon equal amounts of mixture into center of each container.

Brush tops with remaining oil. Bake for 15 minutes, or until fish is no longer translucent. Carefully remove each stuffed fillet from cup, spoon juice over top, and garnish with 2 tablespoons parsley.

# FISH WITH MUSTARD SAUCE
# OVER STEAMED SPINACH

*Serves 4*

*The golden mustard sauce, white fish, and dark green
spinach make a picture-perfect plate.*

4 sole or flounder fillets (about 4 ounces each)

¼ cup nonfat or low-fat ranch salad dressing

3 tablespoons plain nonfat or low-fat yogurt

1½ tablespoons prepared mustard

½ pound fresh spinach

Preheat oven to 400° F.

Rinse fish and pat dry with paper towels. Arrange in
an ovenproof glass baking dish.

Mix the dressing, yogurt, and mustard. Spoon evenly
over fish.

Bake until fish is no longer translucent, 8 to 10 minutes.

Meanwhile, remove tough stems from spinach. Rinse
spinach thoroughly. Drain.

Heat a nonstick skillet over medium-high heat.
When the skillet is hot, add the spinach and stir-fry just
to wilt the leaves, about 30 seconds.

Arrange spinach in a single layer on serving plates.
Top with baked fish. Serve immediately.

**NUTRIENT ANALYSIS**

| | |
|---|---|
| Calories | 130 |
| Protein | 21 g |
| Carbohydrate | 8 g |
| Total Fat | 2 g |
| Saturated Fat | 0 g |
| Polyunsaturated Fat | 1 g |
| Monounsaturated Fat | 0 g |
| Cholesterol | 53 mg |
| Sodium | 337 mg |

# FISH IN A PACKAGE

*Serves 10*

*Dazzle your guests by serving this entrée with a colorful slaw, Green Beans Almondine (see page 208), wild and white rice, and a fresh fruit dessert, such as Apple-Rhubarb Crisp (see page 284).*

10 thin fish fillets (about 4 ounces each), such as tilapia or flounder

STUFFING

1 teaspoon acceptable vegetable oil

1 small onion, chopped

8 ounces fresh mushrooms, sliced

½ cup plain bread crumbs

¼ cup minced fresh parsley

2 tablespoons chopped fresh dill weed or 2 teaspoons dried

½ teaspoon salt (optional)

Freshly ground pepper to taste

½ lemon

½ cup dry white wine or low-sodium chicken broth (see page 55 or use commercial variety)

1 lemon, sliced (optional)

Fresh parsley sprigs (optional)

**NUTRIENT ANALYSIS**

Calories 130
Protein 21 g
Carbohydrate 6 g
Total Fat 2 g
Saturated Fat 0 g
Polyunsaturated Fat 1 g
Monounsaturated Fat 0 g
Cholesterol 56 mg
Sodium 132 mg

Preheat oven to 350° F.

Rinse fish and pat dry with paper towels.

To prepare the stuffing, pour oil into a heavy nonstick skillet over medium-high heat. Add onion and sauté for 2 to 3 minutes, or until translucent.

Add mushrooms and sauté for 5 minutes. Remove skillet from heat.

Stir in remaining stuffing ingredients except ½ lemon.

Squeeze lemon over mixture. Set stuffing aside to cool and to allow bread crumbs to absorb the lemon juice.

Meanwhile, line a baking sheet with a piece of heavy-duty aluminum foil long enough to wrap and seal around the fish.

Just before baking, place 5 fish fillets, skin side down, in center of foil and spoon stuffing onto each. Place one of the remaining fillets, skin side up, on each "stuffed" fillet. Use toothpicks to secure fish.

Drizzle fish with wine. Wrap foil over fish and seal tightly to prevent steam and flavor from escaping.

Bake for about 45 minutes, or until fish flakes very easily with a fork. Open foil package carefully to prevent a steam burn. Slide fish onto serving platter and garnish with lemon slices and sprigs of parsley.

# POACHED FISH IN ASIAN BROTH

*Serves 4*

*Packed with spices and seasonings, this broth gives the fish a delicate flavor. The grated carrot confetti makes the dish pretty enough for company.*

BROTH

3 cups low-sodium chicken broth (see page 55 or use commercial variety)

2 tablespoons dry sherry

2 tablespoons low-sodium soy sauce

2 slices of lemon

3 thin slices fresh gingerroot

⅛ teaspoon cayenne

1 pound orange roughy or other thick, mild fish fillets

Water if needed

5 to 6 green onions (green part only), cut into 1-inch pieces

1 medium red bell pepper, cut into ¼ × 1-inch pieces

1 celery stalk, cut into ¼ × 1-inch pieces

½ teaspoon fragrant toasted sesame oil

1 carrot, grated

Freshly ground pepper to taste

**NUTRIENT ANALYSIS**

| | |
|---|---|
| Calories | 203 |
| Protein | 24 g |
| Carbohydrate | 7 g |
| Total Fat | 8 g |
| Saturated Fat | 2 g |
| Polyunsaturated Fat | 2 g |
| Monounsaturated Fat | 3 g |
| Cholesterol | 77 mg |
| Sodium | 418 mg |

In a nonaluminum fish poacher, a wok, or a large skillet, bring broth ingredients to a boil over high heat.

Rinse fish and pat dry with paper towels. Reduce heat and place fish in broth. Add small amount of water, if needed, to just cover fish. Simmer fish in broth for about 10 minutes per inch of thickness at the thickest point, or just until fish is no longer translucent. Do not overcook.

Remove fish with slotted spatulas and place equal portions in 4 soup bowls.

Return liquid to a boil. Add green onions, bell pepper, and celery. Cook 2 to 3 minutes, or until vegetables are tender-crisp. Remove and discard lemon and gingerroot. Using a slotted spoon, remove vegetables and place over fish.

Stir sesame oil into broth. Pour equal amounts of broth into soup bowls.

Sprinkle grated carrot and grind fresh pepper over each serving. Serve immediately.

# GRILLED COD WITH ARTICHOKE-HORSERADISH SAUCE

*Serves 4*

*California's artichoke industry started at the end of the nineteenth century. Today, this thistly plant is grown on about 12,000 acres in four counties. This recipe uses artichokes in a horseradish sauce that is served with grilled or broiled fish.*

14-ounce can artichoke hearts, rinsed and drained, or 9-ounce package frozen no-salt-added artichoke hearts, thawed and drained

Vegetable oil spray

1 tablespoon light margarine

½ cup chopped shallots or onion (about 4 medium shallots or 1 medium onion)

2 cloves garlic, minced, or 1 teaspoon bottled minced garlic

2 tablespoons all-purpose flour

⅛ teaspoon salt

⅛ teaspoon pepper

12-ounce can fat-free evaporated milk

1 to 2 tablespoons grated fresh or bottled horseradish

1 tablespoon chopped fresh oregano or 1 teaspoon dried, crumbled

4 small or 2 medium cod fillets or halibut steaks (about 1 pound)

Cut each artichoke heart into quarters. Set aside.

Prepare grill. Lightly spray grill rack with vegetable oil spray. Set aside.

In a medium saucepan, melt margarine over medium heat. Add shallots and garlic and cook for about 5 minutes, or until shallots are tender.

Stir in flour, salt, and pepper.

Add milk all at once. Cook and stir for 5 to 10 minutes, or until sauce is thickened and bubbly. Cook and stir 1 minute.

Stir in artichoke hearts, horseradish, and oregano. Cook and stir for 3 to 5 minutes, or until heated through. Keep warm.

Meanwhile, rinse fish and pat dry with paper towels. Place fish on prepared rack. Grill on an uncovered grill directly over medium-hot coals or over medium-high heat for 7 minutes. Turn and grill for 5 to 7 minutes, or until fish flakes easily when tested with a fork.

To serve, spoon artichoke sauce over cooked fish.

## BROILING DIRECTIONS

Prepare recipe as directed above except spray an unheated broiler rack with vegetable oil spray. Place fish on rack and broil 3 to 5 inches from heat for 7 minutes. Turn fish and broil 5 to 7 minutes, or until fish flakes easily when tested with a fork.

# MESQUITE-GRILLED RED SNAPPER WITH GINGERED BLACK BEAN SALSA

*Serves 4*

*Chunks of mesquite wood create the smoky taste in this grilled snapper recipe. Look for bags of mesquite chunks at your supermarket near the charcoal and lighter fluid.*

### SALSA

Vegetable oil spray

¼ cup chopped onion

¼ cup chopped carrot

1 to 2 jalapeño peppers, chopped*

2 tablespoons peeled and finely chopped gingerroot

2 to 3 cloves garlic, minced, or 1 to 1½ teaspoons bottled minced garlic

15-ounce can black beans, rinsed and drained, reserving 3 tablespoons liquid

¼ teaspoon salt

1 medium tomato, seeded and chopped

1 pound red snapper fillets (about ½ inch thick)

At least 1 hour before cooking, soak 4 to 6 mesquite wood chunks in enough water to cover. Lightly spray grill rack with vegetable oil spray. Set aside.

Prepare grill.

For salsa, spray a medium saucepan with vegetable oil spray. Cook onion, carrot, jalapeño peppers, gingerroot, and garlic over medium-low heat for about 5 minutes, or until onion is tender.

Stir black beans, reserved bean liquid, and salt into onion mixture. Cook over medium-low heat for 1 to 2 minutes, or until heated through.

Stir in tomato.

Drain wood chunks. Place wood chunks directly on medium-hot coals.

Rinse fish and pat dry with paper towels. Place fish on prepared rack. Grill on an uncovered grill directly over medium-hot coals for 5 minutes. Turn and grill for 5 to 7 minutes, or until fish flakes easily when tested with a fork.

Place fish on serving plates. Serve with salsa.

## BROILING DIRECTIONS

Prepare recipe as directed except spray an unheated broiler rack with vegetable oil spray. Place fish on rack and broil 3 to 5 inches from heat for 5 minutes. Turn fish and broil 5 to 7 minutes, or until fish flakes easily when tested with a fork.

* Hot chili peppers contain oils that can burn your skin, lips, and eyes. Wear rubber gloves or wash your hands thoroughly with warm, soapy water immediately after handling peppers.

# GRILLED CATFISH WITH MUSTARD-LEMON SAUCE

*Serves 4*

*This creamy mustard sauce is an easy way to dress up fish or chicken. You can substitute honey mustard for the Dijon mustard if you prefer.*

4 small catfish fillets (about 1 pound)
½ teaspoon pepper
Vegetable oil spray

SAUCE

Vegetable oil spray
2 cloves garlic, minced, or 1 teaspoon bottled minced garlic
1 tablespoon all-purpose flour
1¼ cups fat-free evaporated milk
1 tablespoon Dijon mustard
2 teaspoons finely shredded lemon rind
1 teaspoon chopped fresh basil, thyme, dill weed, parsley, or oregano or ¼ teaspoon dried herb
Fresh herbs (optional)

Prepare grill.

Rinse fish and pat dry with paper towels. Sprinkle both sides of fish with pepper. Lightly spray a grill basket or grill rack with vegetable oil spray. Place fish in basket or on rack.

Grill fish on uncovered grill directly over medium-hot coals for about 5 minutes per side, or until fish flakes easily when tested with a fork.

Meanwhile, for sauce, spray a small saucepan with vegetable oil spray. Cook garlic over medium heat for 2 minutes, stirring occasionally.

Stir in flour, then add milk all at once, stirring well (a whisk works well for this).

**NUTRIENT ANALYSIS**

Calories 195
Protein 31 g
Carbohydrate 12 g
Total Fat 2 g
Saturated Fat 0 g
Polyunsaturated Fat 1 g
Monounsaturated Fat 0 g
Cholesterol 72 mg
Sodium 249 mg

Add mustard and lemon peel. Cook and stir until thickened and bubbly, about 3 to 5 minutes.

Stir in chopped fresh herbs. Cook and stir 1 minute.

Serve grilled fish with sauce. Garnish with fresh herbs.

# POACHED FISH AND FISH BROTH

*Serves 4*

*Poaching is an excellent way to prepare fish—it's easy and requires little cleanup.*

### FISH BROTH

1 carrot, unpeeled, coarsely chopped

1 small onion, coarsely chopped

1 celery stalk with leaves, coarsely chopped

2 tablespoons rice vinegar or white wine vinegar

8 whole black peppercorns

1 bay leaf

1 pound fish fillets, fresh or frozen and thawed

Water

**NUTRIENT ANALYSIS**

Calories 103
Protein 21 g
Carbohydrate 0 g
Total Fat 1 g
Saturated Fat 0 g
Polyunsaturated Fat 1 g
Monounsaturated Fat 0 g
Cholesterol 60 mg
Sodium 93 mg

**NUTRIENT ANALYSIS**
*(For ½ cup broth)*
Calories 12
Protein 1 g
Carbohydrate 1 g
Total Fat 0 g
Saturated Fat 0 g
Polyunsaturated Fat 0 g
Monounsaturated Fat 0 g
Cholesterol 0 mg
Sodium 28 mg

In a large skillet, combine all fish broth ingredients.

Rinse fish and pat dry with paper towels. Lay fish on broth ingredients and add cool water just to cover.

Heat, uncovered, over medium heat until water begins to simmer; make sure the water does not boil. Simmer about 10 minutes per inch of thickness at the thickest point, or until flesh is firm and no longer translucent.

Carefully lifting fish with two large, slotted spatulas, remove fish to a serving platter. After a few minutes, drain off any excess liquid.

To serve chilled, refrigerate fish, then let it stand at room temperature for 10 to 15 minutes; this enhances its flavor.

Strain the poaching liquid to make fish broth for use in soups and sauces or for poaching other fish.

# BROILED FISH STEAKS

*Serves 6*

*Salmon steaks are particularly delicious fixed this easy way. Toss a salad and steam your favorite vegetables—dinner is ready in a flash!*

6 fish steaks, about ½ inch thick (about 4 ounces each)

2 tablespoons fat-free, cholesterol-free mayonnaise

1 tablespoon salt-free lemon-herb seasoning

Paprika to taste

1 lemon, thinly sliced

6 fresh parsley sprigs

Preheat broiler.

Rinse fish and pat dry with paper towels. Lightly coat both sides of each fish steak with mayonnaise. Place in a shallow broilerproof baking dish.

Sprinkle fish with half the lemon-herb seasoning and half the desired amount of paprika.

Broil for 3 to 4 minutes. Turn fish and sprinkle with remaining seasonings. Broil for 3 to 4 minutes, or until fish flakes easily when tested with a fork or is no longer translucent. Garnish with lemon slices and parsley. Serve immediately.

**NUTRIENT ANALYSIS**

| | |
|---|---|
| Calories | 108 |
| Protein | 21 g |
| Carbohydrate | 1 g |
| Total Fat | 1 g |
| Saturated Fat | 0 g |
| Polyunsaturated Fat | 1 g |
| Monounsaturated Fat | 0 g |
| Cholesterol | 60 mg |
| Sodium | 126 mg |

# HALIBUT KEBABS

*Serves 4*

*If you use wooden skewers for this easy-to-prepare main dish, soak them in water for at least 30 minutes to keep the wood from charring while broiling. Salt-free herb seasonings, such as the Italian herb variety used here, are handy for adding a dash of flavor in your cooking and at the table.*

1 pound halibut steak (about 1 inch thick)
¼ cup fresh lemon juice (1 to 2 medium lemons)
¼ cup olive oil
3 medium shallots, thinly sliced
1 teaspoon salt-free Italian herb seasoning
½ teaspoon dried thyme, crumbled
Vegetable oil spray
½ large red onion, cut lengthwise into thirds
1 lemon, cut into wedges

Preheat broiler.

Rinse fish and pat dry with paper towels. Remove skin.

Cut fish into 16 cubes and set aside.

In a large bowl, mix lemon juice, oil, shallots, herb seasoning, and thyme. Add fish and stir to coat. Cover and marinate in refrigerator for at least 5 minutes, but no more than 1 hour.

Meanwhile, spray broiler pan with vegetable oil spray.

Peel onion apart into single layers. Thread each skewer, alternating onion and fish, using 4 pieces of fish and 5 pieces of onion. Place kebabs on broiler pan. Broil kebabs 4 inches from heat for 2 to 2½ minutes on each side, or until fish is no longer translucent. Garnish with lemon wedges.

**NUTRIENT ANALYSIS**

| | |
|---|---|
| Calories | 111 |
| Protein | 22 g |
| Carbohydrate | 2 g |
| Total Fat | 1 g |
| Saturated Fat | 0 g |
| Polyunsaturated Fat | 1 g |
| Monounsaturated Fat | 0 g |
| Cholesterol | 60 mg |
| Sodium | 93 mg |

# FISH STEW

*Serves 6*

*A delicacy from the West Indies, this fragrant stew is a refreshing change from the usual baked fish. Serve it with a loaf of crusty bread and Salad with Creamy Mustard Vinaigrette (see page 60).*

1½ pounds fish fillets, at least ¾ inch thick, cut into 2-inch squares

¼ cup fresh lemon juice (1 to 2 medium lemons)

8 green onions (green and white parts), thinly sliced

1 cup chopped tomatoes (1 to 2)

1 pound red potatoes, with skin, cubed

1½ cups water

½ cup chopped fresh parsley

¼ cup low-sodium ketchup

3 cloves garlic, minced, or 1½ teaspoons bottled minced garlic

1½ teaspoons minced fresh gingerroot or ½ teaspoon ground ginger

Rinse fish and pat dry with paper towels. Sprinkle lemon juice over fish and mix well. Set aside.

In a 2½- to 3-quart saucepan over medium-high heat, cook green onions for 1 minute, or until wilted.

Add tomatoes and cook for 2 to 3 minutes, or until tomatoes are reduced almost to a pulp.

Add remaining ingredients except fish. Reduce heat and simmer, covered, for 10 minutes.

Add fish and simmer, covered, for 10 to 15 minutes, or until fish is almost cooked. Remove cover and simmer for 4 to 5 minutes to thicken sauce. Serve hot.

**NUTRIENT ANALYSIS**

Calories 199
Protein 24 g
Carbohydrate 22 g
Total Fat 2 g
Saturated Fat 0 g
Polyunsaturated Fat 1 g
Monounsaturated Fat 0 g
Cholesterol 60 mg
Sodium 111 mg

# TUNA-PASTA CASSEROLE

*Serves 6*

*This low-fat version of an old standby will please everyone in your family.*

8-ounce package linguine, vermicelli, spaghetti, or other thin pasta

1 teaspoon acceptable vegetable oil

1 small onion, chopped

1 clove garlic, minced, or ½ teaspoon bottled minced garlic

2 6½-ounce cans tuna in spring water, drained and rinsed

½ cup finely chopped carrot

⅓ cup finely chopped green bell pepper

¼ cup finely chopped fresh parsley

¼ teaspoon paprika, or to taste

1 cup nonfat or low-fat cottage cheese

½ cup nonfat or low-fat sour cream

½ cup plain nonfat or low-fat yogurt

Vegetable oil spray

½ cup plain bread crumbs, toasted

¼ cup grated or shredded Parmesan cheese (about 1 ounce)

Cook pasta according to package directions, omitting salt and oil. Drain.

Meanwhile, preheat oven to 350° F.

Pour oil into a nonstick skillet over medium-high heat. Add onion and garlic and sauté, stirring frequently, until onion is translucent, 2 to 3 minutes. Transfer onion and garlic to a large bowl.

Add tuna, carrot, bell pepper, parsley, and paprika to onion/garlic mixture and stir to combine. Set aside.

In a small bowl, blend cottage cheese, sour cream, and yogurt. Stir cottage cheese mixture and pasta into tuna mixture.

Spray a 9 × 11 × 2-inch casserole dish with vegetable oil spray. Pour tuna mixture into casserole dish.

In a small bowl, combine bread crumbs and Parmesan. Sprinkle over casserole.

Bake casserole for 30 to 45 minutes, or until top is lightly browned.

# TUNA SALAD PITA SANDWICHES

*Serves 6*

*Here is an old favorite served in a newfangled way.*

### TUNA SALAD

6½-ounce can tuna in spring water, drained and rinsed

1 medium carrot, shredded

3 green onions (green and white parts), finely chopped

3 tablespoons fat-free, cholesterol-free mayonnaise

2 tablespoons finely chopped celery

2 tablespoons finely chopped fresh parsley

2 tablespoons finely chopped green pepper

2 tablespoons low-sodium salsa (see page 242 or use commercial variety) or picante sauce

Freshly ground pepper to taste

3 7-inch whole-wheat pitas

6 lettuce leaves

1 medium tomato, cut into 6 slices

6 fresh medium mushrooms, sliced

½ cup fresh alfalfa or bean sprouts (optional)

6 fresh parsley sprigs (optional)

In a medium bowl, combine all tuna salad ingredients. Mix well. Cover and refrigerate for at least 1 hour.

Cut each pita in half. Line each half with a leaf of lettuce, a slice of tomato, mushroom slices, and sprouts. Spoon tuna salad into pitas and garnish each pita half with a sprig of parsley.

**NUTRIENT ANALYSIS**

Calories 158

Protein 12 g

Carbohydrate 26 g

Total Fat 1 g

Saturated Fat 0 g

Polyunsaturated Fat 1 g

Monounsaturated Fat 0 g

Cholesterol 8 mg

Sodium 277 mg

# BAKED CRABMEAT

*Serves 5 as an entrée*
*Serves 10 as an appetizer*

*This dish is a real treat—light, festive, and healthful.*

Vegetable oil spray
1 teaspoon light margarine
¼ cup finely chopped onion
1 pound crabmeat, all cartilage removed
2 tablespoons Dijon mustard
1 teaspoon Worcestershire sauce
Whites of 4 large eggs, stiffly beaten*
2 tablespoons grated or shredded Parmesan cheese

Preheat oven to 350° F.

Spray a 9 × 9-inch ovenproof casserole dish with vegetable oil spray. Set aside.

In a small saucepan, melt margarine over medium-high heat. Add onion and sauté for 2 to 3 minutes, or until soft.

Transfer onion to a medium bowl and stir in crabmeat, mustard, and Worcestershire sauce. Gently fold in beaten egg whites. Pour mixture into casserole dish and sprinkle with cheese.

Bake for 25 minutes, or until puffed and lightly browned. Remove from oven and cut into rectangles. Serve immediately.

* Even a single drop of egg yolk will prevent egg whites from rising, so separate eggs very carefully.

**NUTRIENT ANALYSIS**
*(For entrée serving)*

| | |
|---|---|
| Calories | 120 |
| Protein | 21 g |
| Carbohydrate | 2 g |
| Total Fat | 3 g |
| Saturated Fat | 1 g |
| Polyunsaturated Fat | 1 g |
| Monounsaturated Fat | 1 g |
| Cholesterol | 86 mg |
| Sodium | 411 mg |

# SHRIMP REMOULADE

**COOK'S TIP ON MUSTARD:**

Horseradish contributes to the heat and spiciness of Creole mustard. German mustard, spicy and a little sweet, ranges from mild to hot.

*Try this hot and spicy Cajun specialty as a cool main dish or make-ahead appetizer.*

6 cups water

1 lemon, quartered

2 cloves garlic, halved

2 bay leaves

¼ teaspoon salt

¼ teaspoon cayenne

### DRESSING

¼ cup finely chopped celery

¼ cup sliced green onions (about 2 or 3)

¼ cup chopped fresh parsley

3 tablespoons vinegar

2 tablespoons water

2 tablespoons Creole or German mustard

1 tablespoon grated fresh or bottled horseradish

1 teaspoon paprika

¼ teaspoon bottled hot pepper sauce

1 pound shrimp in shells, peeled and deveined

4 large lettuce leaves

**NUTRIENT ANALYSIS**

Calories 72
Protein 12 g
Carbohydrate 3 g
Total Fat 1 g
Saturated Fat 0 g
Polyunsaturated Fat 0 g
Monounsaturated Fat 0 g
Cholesterol 107 mg
Sodium 389 mg

In a medium saucepan, combine water, lemon, garlic, bay leaves, salt, and cayenne. Bring to a boil over high heat. Reduce heat and simmer, uncovered, for 10 minutes.

Meanwhile, in a medium bowl, stir together dressing ingredients. Set aside.

Increase heat under saucepan to high. Add shrimp and return to a boil. Reduce heat and simmer, uncovered, for 1 to 3 minutes, or until shrimp turn pink. Drain. Discard lemon, bay leaves, and garlic.

Add shrimp to dressing and stir until well combined. Cover and chill for 4 to 24 hours, stirring occasionally.

To serve, spoon chilled shrimp mixture onto lettuce leaves.

# SEAFOOD AND LEMON RISOTTO

*Serves 4*

**COOK'S TIP ON RISOTTO:**

For proper consistency, carefully regulate the cooking temperature so the risotto boils lightly, not vigorously. If the liquid is absorbed before the rice reaches the just-tender stage, add more broth, wine, or water, a little at a time. Arborio rice is usually used in risottos, but you can substitute a medium-grain rice if you prefer. It won't be quite as creamy, however.

*Creamy lemon-flavored rice joins scallops and shrimp in this hearty entrée, made colorful by snow peas and red bell pepper. This recipe uses a streamlined preparation method that lets you stir less than in most other risotto recipes.*

Vegetable oil spray

1 medium leek, sliced

2 cloves garlic, minced, or 1 teaspoon bottled minced garlic

1 cup Arborio rice (about 8 ounces)

1½ cups low-sodium chicken broth (see page 55 or use commercial variety)

½ cup low-sodium chicken broth

1 cup dry white wine or nonalcoholic white wine

8 ounces bay scallops, rinsed

8 ounces medium shrimp in shells, rinsed, peeled, and deveined

3 ounces fresh snow pea pods, trimmed and halved crosswise

½ medium red bell pepper, chopped

3 tablespoons grated or shredded Parmesan cheese

2 tablespoons chopped fresh basil or 2 teaspoons dried, crumbled

1½ to 2 tablespoons finely shredded lemon rind

Grated or shredded Parmesan cheese (optional)

**NUTRIENT ANALYSIS**

| | |
|---|---|
| Calories | 294 |
| Protein | 20 g |
| Carbohydrate | 44 g |
| Total Fat | 3 g |
| Saturated Fat | 1 g |
| Polyunsaturated Fat | 1 g |
| Monounsaturated Fat | 1 g |
| Cholesterol | 65 mg |
| Sodium | 243 mg |

Spray a medium saucepan with vegetable oil spray. Cook leek and garlic over medium-low heat for about 5 minutes, or until leek is tender.

Add rice. Stir well. Cook for 5 minutes, stirring often.

Add 1½ cups of broth. Bring to a boil over high heat, stirring occasionally. Reduce heat and simmer, uncovered, for 5 minutes, stirring occasionally.

Add remaining chicken broth and wine. Increase heat to medium and cook for 5 to 8 minutes, stirring constantly (a small amount of liquid should remain).

Add scallops, shrimp, pea pods, and bell pepper. Cook, stirring constantly, until liquid is almost absorbed, about 5 minutes (rice should be just tender and slightly creamy).

Stir in 3 tablespoons Parmesan, basil, and lemon peel. Heat through. Serve immediately. Serve with additional Parmesan, if desired.

# CIOPPINO

*Serves 6*

**COOK'S TIP:**

This dish freezes well; though the frozen fish will darken somewhat, the flavor won't suffer at all.

*Cioppino, a meal in a bowl, is great for entertaining because there is no last-minute cooking to worry about. Serve with crusty bread, salad, and fresh fruit for dessert.*

1 teaspoon acceptable vegetable oil

1 large carrot, thinly sliced

½ cup coarsely chopped celery (1 to 2 stalks)

1 medium green bell pepper, coarsely chopped

½ large yellow onion, coarsely chopped

1 pound halibut or shark steaks, skin removed, cut into 1-inch pieces

3 8-ounce bottles clam juice

1½ cups dry white wine, nonalcoholic white wine, or low-sodium chicken broth (see page 55 or use commercial variety)

6-ounce can tomato puree

1 bay leaf

8-ounce can baby clams, with juice

1 tablespoon chopped fresh basil or 1 teaspoon dried, crumbled

1½ teaspoons chopped fresh oregano or ½ teaspoon dried, crumbled

1½ teaspoons chopped fresh thyme or ½ teaspoon dried, crumbled

¼ cup finely chopped fresh parsley

6 crab claws

**NUTRIENT ANALYSIS**

Calories 184
Protein 27 g
Carbohydrate 10 g
Total Fat 3 g
Saturated Fat 1 g
Polyunsaturated Fat 1 g
Monounsaturated Fat 1 g
Cholesterol 80 mg
Sodium 375 mg

In a large nonstick skillet, heat oil over medium-high heat. Add carrot, celery, bell pepper, and onion and sauté until tender, 5 to 7 minutes.

Rinse fish and pat dry with paper towels. Set aside.

In a 4-quart saucepan, bring vegetable mixture, clam juice, wine, tomato puree, and bay leaf to a boil, covered.

Add remaining ingredients except crab claws and return mixture to a boil. Reduce heat and simmer, partially covered, for 15 minutes.

Add crab claws and heat for 2 minutes. Remove bay leaf. Serve immediately.

# POULTRY

Chicken Breasts Stuffed
with Ricotta and Goat Cheese

Cheese-Herb Chicken Medallions

Chicken Cordon Bleu

Garlic Chicken Fillets
in Balsamic Vinegar

Chicken with Mustard and Herbs

Chicken-Vegetable Stir-Fry

Thai Chicken
with Basil and Vegetables

Hearty Chicken Stew

Brunswick Stew

Chicken Fajitas

Cajun Tortilla Wrap

Asian Grilled Chicken

Crispy Oven-Fried Chicken

Chicken Ragout

Asparagus-Chicken à la King
with Roasted Peppers

Tandoori Cornish Hens

Roast Cornish Hens

Turkey Tetrazzini

Turkey and Vegetable Calzone

# CHICKEN BREASTS STUFFED WITH RICOTTA AND GOAT CHEESE

*Serves 4*

*This chicken dish is a snap to make and classy enough to serve for very special occasions. The tomato sauce keeps the chicken breasts moist.*

**Vegetable oil spray**

### STUFFING

**7 ounces nonfat or low-fat ricotta cheese**

**2 ounces goat cheese**

**2 tablespoons chopped fresh parsley or 2 teaspoons dried, crumbled**

**1 tablespoon chopped fresh chives or 1 teaspoon dried**

### SAUCE

**8-ounce can no-salt-added tomato sauce**

**2 teaspoons salt-free Italian herb seasoning**

**1½ teaspoons chopped fresh oregano or ½ teaspoon dried, crumbled**

**1 clove garlic, minced, or ½ teaspoon bottled minced garlic**

**¼ to ½ teaspoon salt**

**⅛ teaspoon pepper**

**4 boneless, skinless chicken breast halves (about 4 ounces each), all visible fat removed**

Preheat oven to 350° F. Spray a 1-quart casserole dish lightly with vegetable oil spray. Set aside.

In a small bowl, combine the stuffing ingredients. Set aside.

In another small bowl, combine the sauce ingredients. Set aside.

Rinse chicken breasts and pat dry with paper towels. Place breasts smooth side up between 2 sheets of plastic

**NUTRIENT ANALYSIS**

Calories 235
Protein 35 g
Carbohydrate 9 g
Total Fat 6 g
Saturated Fat 3 g
Polyunsaturated Fat 1 g
Monounsaturated Fat 2 g
Cholesterol 75 mg
Sodium 382 mg

wrap. Using a tortilla press or the smooth side of a meat mallet, lightly flatten the breasts, being careful not to tear the meat.

Spoon about one quarter of the stuffing lengthwise down the middle of each breast. Starting with the short end, roll up the breast jelly-roll style. Place the breast in the prepared casserole dish, seam side down (no need to secure with toothpicks). Repeat with the other breasts.

Spoon sauce over breasts. Bake, covered, for 40 to 45 minutes, or until chicken is cooked through.

# CHEESE-HERB CHICKEN MEDALLIONS

*Serves 6 as an entrée*
*Serves 12 as an appetizer*

**COOK'S TIP ON DRIED HERBS AND SPICES:**

Always store herbs and spices in airtight containers (glass jars recommended) away from heat and light. In general, whole spices and herbs will keep for about 1 year, though some may retain their flavor for as long as 3 to 4 years. Ground spices and herbs will keep for 6 months to 2 years. When the aroma becomes faint, use more of the spices and herbs to compensate for flavor loss.

*Although just about any fresh vegetable can be used to garnish this family favorite, carrots add a wonderful splash of color. Chilling the mozzarella beforehand keeps it from oozing when baking.*

6 boneless, skinless chicken breast halves (about 4 ounces each), all visible fat removed

1 tablespoon finely chopped fresh chives or 1 teaspoon dried

1 tablespoon finely chopped fresh basil or 1 teaspoon dried, crumbled

¼ teaspoon paprika

Freshly ground pepper to taste

3 ounces nonfat or part-skim mozzarella cheese, shredded, preferably chilled (about ⅔ cup)

2 carrots (optional)

Preheat oven to 400° F.

Rinse chicken breasts and pat dry with paper towels. Place breasts on a flat surface. Evenly sprinkle each breast with chives, basil, paprika, and pepper.

Form cheese into 6 loose balls and place one in the center of each breast. Roll chicken around cheese, making sure the ends are tucked in. Tie each breast with twine to retain cheese.

Place breasts in an ungreased baking dish. Bake for 15 to 20 minutes, or until chicken has turned white throughout. Allow chicken to cool for about 10 minutes before serving.

Meanwhile, prepare carrot curls. Using a potato peeler, pare carrots lengthwise into long, thin strips and soak in ice water for at least 10 minutes. Drain and pat dry.

To serve, cut each breast into ½-inch medallions. Arrange on a bed of carrot curls.

**NUTRIENT ANALYSIS**
*(For entrée serving)*

Calories 158
Protein 30 g
Carbohydrate 1 g
Total Fat 3 g
Saturated Fat 1 g
Polyunsaturated Fat 1 g
Monounsaturated Fat 1 g
Cholesterol 62 mg
Sodium 157 mg

# CHICKEN CORDON BLEU

*Serves 4*

*The good news is that ham may be leaner than you think. However, it is high in sodium, as is the nonfat mozzarella used here. You may want to balance your diet by watching your sodium intake the rest of the day.*

4 boneless, skinless chicken breast halves (about 4
   ounces each), all visible fat removed

2 slices nonfat or part-skim mozzarella cheese (about
   2 ounces)

4 slices lean, low-sodium ham (about 4 ounces), all
   visible fat removed

3 tablespoons whole-wheat or all-purpose flour

1 teaspoon dry mustard

½ teaspoon paprika

2 teaspoons olive oil

Rinse chicken breasts and pat dry with paper towels. Place breasts, smooth side up, between 2 sheets of plastic wrap. Using a tortilla press or the smooth side of a meat mallet, flatten breasts to half or less of their original thickness. Set aside.

Cut each slice of cheese in half and place half a slice on each slice of ham. Fold each ham slice over the cheese to form a packet that is about half as big as the piece of chicken. Place a packet on top of each breast. Fold the breast in half over the packet. If needed, use a wooden toothpick or small metal skewer to secure each breast.

On a medium plate, mix flour, mustard powder, and paprika. Coat each breast with flour mixture, then tap lightly to remove excess.

Heat a large nonstick skillet over medium-low heat. Add oil and swirl to coat bottom of skillet. When oil is hot, add chicken. Sauté on each side until chicken is golden-brown on the outside and no longer pink on the inside, 25 to 30 minutes. Sauté each seam side for about 20 seconds to seal.

| NUTRIENT ANALYSIS | |
| --- | --- |
| Calories | 230 |
| Protein | 35 g |
| Carbohydrate | 6 g |
| Total Fat | 7 g |
| Saturated Fat | 2 g |
| Polyunsaturated Fat | 1 g |
| Monounsaturated Fat | 3 g |
| Cholesterol | 76 mg |
| Sodium | 392 mg |

# GARLIC CHICKEN FILLETS IN BALSAMIC VINEGAR

*Serves 8*

*This entrée can be the center of an elegant meal that's easy to prepare quickly for unexpected company. Team it with Golden Rice (see page 229), add a steamed green vegetable or a tossed salad, and sit back and feast on the raves.*

8 boneless, skinless chicken breast halves (about 4 ounces each), all visible fat removed

½ cup all-purpose flour

2 teaspoons olive oil

6 to 8 cloves garlic, minced, or 3 to 4 teaspoons bottled minced garlic

Vegetable oil spray

1 cup low-sodium chicken broth (see page 55 or use commercial variety)

⅓ cup balsamic vinegar

Freshly ground pepper to taste

2 tablespoons water

1 tablespoon cornstarch

Rinse chicken breasts and pat dry with paper towels. Dredge breasts in flour; shake off excess.

Heat a large, heavy nonstick skillet over medium-high heat. Add oil and swirl to coat bottom of skillet. When oil is hot, add breasts. Cook on one side for 2 to 3 minutes, or until golden.

Add garlic to skillet. Spray top side of breasts with vegetable oil spray. Turn breasts and continue cooking about 2 to 3 minutes, or until golden.

Add broth, balsamic vinegar, and pepper. Reduce heat to medium-low and cook, covered, for 5 to 10 minutes, or until chicken is tender. (The timing depends on the thickness of the chicken breasts.) Remove chicken from skillet. Keep warm.

**NUTRIENT ANALYSIS**

Calories 183
Protein 26 g
Carbohydrate 9 g
Total Fat 4 g
Saturated Fat 1 g
Polyunsaturated Fat 1 g
Monounsaturated Fat 2 g
Cholesterol 62 mg
Sodium 65 mg

Pour water into a cup or small bowl. Add cornstarch, stirring until it dissolves.

Add cornstarch mixture to skillet and boil for 1 to 2 minutes, or until thick and smooth. Pour sauce over chicken and serve immediately.

# CHICKEN WITH MUSTARD AND HERBS

*Serves 4*

*Just because you don't have a lot of time to fix dinner doesn't mean you have to sacrifice flavor—or eat high-fat, high-sodium takeout food. With only a few ingredients, you can whip up an elegant entrée in minutes. Make extra to use for special sandwiches.*

Vegetable oil spray

4 boneless, skinless chicken breast halves (about 4 ounces each), all visible fat removed

1 tablespoon salt-free herb seasoning

1 teaspoon salt-free lemon-pepper seasoning

1 tablespoon fat-free, cholesterol-free mayonnaise

¼ cup spicy brown mustard

Preheat oven to 350° F. Spray a baking pan with vegetable oil spray.

Rinse chicken breasts and pat dry with paper towels. Place breasts in prepared pan.

Mix remaining ingredients to make a paste. Spread it thickly and evenly over the top of each breast.

Bake for 20 minutes, or just until meat is white throughout.

### NUTRIENT ANALYSIS

Calories 148
Protein 25 g
Carbohydrate 2 g
Total Fat 4 g
Saturated Fat 1 g
Polyunsaturated Fat 1 g
Monounsaturated Fat 1 g
Cholesterol 62 mg
Sodium 270 mg

# CHICKEN-VEGETABLE STIR-FRY

*Serves 6*

*A bed of rice or noodles pairs nicely with this stir-fry.*

1 pound boneless, skinless chicken breasts, all visible fat removed

1½ tablespoons low-sodium soy sauce

1 tablespoon grated fresh gingerroot or 1 teaspoon ground ginger

1 teaspoon acceptable vegetable oil

2 medium green, red, or yellow bell peppers, or any combination, cut into 1-inch strips

4 green onions (green and white parts), cut into 1-inch strips

¾ cup pineapple chunks, fresh or canned in their juice, ¼ cup of juice reserved

⅔ cup low-sodium chicken broth (see page 55 or use commercial variety)

¼ cup pineapple juice or juice reserved from canned pineapple

1½ tablespoons cornstarch

1 tablespoon sesame seeds, toasted

Rinse chicken breasts and pat dry with paper towels. Cut breasts into 1-inch cubes. Marinate in soy sauce and ginger for 30 to 45 minutes, stirring occasionally.

In a nonstick wok or skillet, heat oil over high heat. Add chicken and stir-fry for 2 minutes. Using a slotted spoon, remove chicken, leaving juices in the pan.

Add peppers and onions and stir-fry for 1 minute.

Add pineapple and chicken and stir-fry for 2 to 3 minutes. Vegetables should be tender-crisp.

Pour broth and pineapple juice into a small bowl. Add cornstarch, stirring to dissolve. Stir into chicken mixture. Boil for about 1 minute, or until thickened and smooth.

Put on serving dish and sprinkle with sesame seeds.

**NUTRIENT ANALYSIS**

Calories 147

Protein 18 g

Carbohydrate 9 g

Total Fat 4 g

Saturated Fat 1 g

Polyunsaturated Fat 1 g

Monounsaturated Fat 1 g

Cholesterol 41 mg

Sodium 477 mg

# THAI CHICKEN WITH BASIL AND VEGETABLES

*Serves 4*

**COOK'S TIP ON JASMINE RICE:**

Consider expanding your taste horizons by preparing jasmine rice from Thailand to accompany this dish. Jasmine rice is classified as an aromatic rice because of its perfumy fragrance and nutlike flavor.

**COOK'S TIP ON FISH SAUCE:**

Pungent and salty, fish sauce imparts a rich flavor to many Asian dishes. A little goes a long way, so purchase only a small bottle. Store fish sauce in a cool place for up to 6 months.

*Chicken stir-fried with colorful vegetables and flavored with fragrant basil makes a mouthwatering dish. Because this dish cooks quickly, have your ingredients gathered and prepped before you start cooking.*

SAUCE

2 tablespoons low-sodium chicken broth (see page 55 or use commercial variety) or water

2 teaspoons fish sauce

2 teaspoons sugar

1 teaspoon reduced-sodium soy sauce

1 pound boneless, skinless chicken breasts, all visible fat removed

1 teaspoon acceptable vegetable oil

2 cloves garlic, minced, or 1 teaspoon bottled minced garlic

1 serrano pepper, seeded and chopped (optional)

2 cups broccoli florets (about 4 ounces)

2 carrots, cut into very thin strips

4 green onions, cut into 1-inch pieces

¼ cup firmly packed fresh basil leaves

2 cups cooked rice, jasmine preferred

**NUTRIENT ANALYSIS**

| | |
|---|---|
| Calories | 290 |
| Protein | 29 g |
| Carbohydrate | 32 g |
| Total Fat | 5 g |
| Saturated Fat | 1 g |
| Polyunsaturated Fat | 2 g |
| Monounsaturated Fat | 1 g |
| Cholesterol | 62 mg |
| Sodium | 313 mg |

In a small bowl, combine sauce ingredients. Set aside.

Rinse chicken breasts and pat dry with paper towels. Thinly slice breasts. Set aside.

Heat a wok or large skillet over medium-high heat. Add oil and swirl to cover bottom of wok.

Add garlic and serrano pepper. Cook for 10 to 15 seconds.

Add chicken and stir-fry for 3 to 4 minutes, or until chicken is no longer pink in the center.

Add the broccoli, carrots, and green onions and stir-fry for 2 to 3 minutes, or until vegetables are tender-crisp.

Add the reserved sauce mixture and basil leaves. Stir-fry for 1 minute, or until mixture is warmed through. Serve over cooked rice.

# HEARTY CHICKEN STEW

*Serves 8*

*This is a good recipe to make ahead and refrigerate or freeze.*

2 pounds boneless, skinless chicken breasts, rinsed, patted dry with paper towels, and all visible fat removed

1 tablespoon acceptable vegetable oil

1 medium onion, finely chopped

1 tablespoon minced fresh gingerroot or 1 teaspoon ground ginger

3 cloves garlic, minced, or 1½ teaspoons bottled minced garlic

2 tablespoons all-purpose flour

2 medium tomatoes, diced

8 to 10 peppercorns, or to taste

6 whole cloves

1 cinnamon stick

2 cups water

1 tablespoon Worcestershire sauce

8 ounces small red or white potatoes, unpeeled and halved

12 ounces fresh or no-salt-added frozen baby carrots

6 ounces green peas, fresh or no-salt-added frozen (1 to 1¼ cup)

**NUTRIENT ANALYSIS**

Calories 228
Protein 27 g
Carbohydrate 18 g
Total Fat 5 g
Saturated Fat 1 g
Polyunsaturated Fat 2 g
Monounsaturated Fat 1 g
Cholesterol 62 mg
Sodium 123 mg

Cut chicken breasts into 1-inch cubes. Set aside.

In a deep skillet or Dutch oven, heat oil over medium-high heat. Sauté onion, gingerroot, and garlic until onion is soft, about 3 minutes.

Add flour and cook for 1 minute, stirring to prevent sticking. Stir in tomatoes and cook for 2 minutes.

Tie peppercorns, cloves, and cinnamon in a piece of cheesecloth. Add cheesecloth package, chicken, water, and Worcestershire sauce to onion mixture. Stir. Reduce heat and simmer, covered, for 20 minutes.

Add potatoes, carrots, and peas. Simmer, covered, until cooked, 20 to 25 minutes. Remove cheesecloth package.

# BRUNSWICK STEW

*Serves 6*

*You don't have to live in Brunswick County, Virginia, to enjoy this variation of its famous stew. Chicken chunks accented with vegetables and lima beans will warm you up on a cold day.*

Vegetable oil spray

1 teaspoon olive oil

1 medium onion, chopped

1 pound boneless, skinless chicken breasts, rinsed, patted dry with paper towels, and all visible fat removed

10 ounces baby lima beans, fresh or frozen with salt necessary for processing (1¼ to 1¾ cups)

10 ounces fresh or no-salt-added frozen whole kernel corn (about 2 cups)

3 cups low-sodium chicken broth (see page 55 or use commercial variety)

1½ cups chopped tomatoes

6-ounce can no-salt-added tomato paste

3 tablespoons fresh lemon juice

1 tablespoon Worcestershire sauce

Spray a deep skillet or Dutch oven with vegetable oil spray. Heat over medium-high heat. Add oil and swirl to coat bottom of skillet. When skillet is hot, add onion. Sauté until soft, about 3 minutes.

Meanwhile, cut chicken breasts into 1-inch cubes.

Add chicken and remaining ingredients to skillet. Reduce heat to low and simmer, covered, for 1 hour.

**NUTRIENT ANALYSIS**

Calories 238

Protein 24 g

Carbohydrate 29 g

Total Fat 4 g

Saturated Fat 1 g

Polyunsaturated Fat 1 g

Monounsaturated Fat 1 g

Cholesterol 41 mg

Sodium 144 mg

# CHICKEN FAJITAS

*Serves 4*

*Fun to make and fun to eat! Before rolling up the tortillas, add shredded lettuce, chopped tomatoes or salsa (see page 242), and nonfat or low-fat sour cream if you wish.*

1 pound boneless, skinless chicken breast halves, all visible fat removed

MARINADE

3 tablespoons Worcestershire sauce

1½ tablespoons fresh lemon or lime juice

1 tablespoon water

1 teaspoon acceptable vegetable oil

1 clove garlic, finely minced, or ½ teaspoon bottled minced garlic

⅛ teaspoon freshly ground black pepper, or to taste

1 large onion (any color)

1 large green bell pepper

1 teaspoon acceptable vegetable oil

8 6-inch corn tortillas or nonfat or low-fat flour tortillas*

Vegetable oil spray

Preheat oven to 350° F. Wrap tortillas in aluminum foil and set aside.

Rinse chicken breasts and pat dry with paper towels. Cut breasts lengthwise into ⅜-inch strips. Set aside.

In a large bowl, combine marinade ingredients.

Add chicken to marinade and stir to coat evenly. Cover and marinate in refrigerator for 10 to 20 minutes, stirring at least once.

Meanwhile, slice onion and bell pepper into ⅛-inch strips. Place vegetables in a small bowl. Stir 1 teaspoon oil into vegetable mixture. Set aside.

Heat tortillas in oven for 8 to 10 minutes.

**NUTRIENT ANALYSIS**

Calories 266
Protein 28 g
Carbohydrate 27 g
Total Fat 5 g
Saturated Fat 1 g
Polyunsaturated Fat 2 g
Monounsaturated Fat 1 g
Cholesterol 62 mg
Sodium 231 mg

Meanwhile, spray a nonstick skillet with vegetable oil spray. Add chicken and sauté over medium-high heat until no longer pink, about 4 minutes, stirring occasionally. Add onion and pepper slices. Sauté over medium-high heat, stirring constantly, for about 5 minutes, or until onion is slightly brown. Set aside.

To serve, place equal amounts of cooked chicken strips on each tortilla and top with onions and peppers. Roll tortilla around chicken strips and eat with fingers.

* Nonfat and low-fat flour tortillas can be high in sodium. When shopping, select the one with the lowest sodium value.

# CAJUN TORTILLA WRAP

*Serves 8*

*Cajun meets Mexican when you fill a warm tortilla with spicy strips of chicken breast, flavorful rice, fresh tomatoes, and colorful red onion slices. This recipe can be prepared ahead and reheated in the microwave, making it convenient for brown-bagging or for those hectic evenings when everyone's on a different schedule.*

### JAMBALAYA RICE

2 ounces light smoked sausage, cut into ¼-inch slices

½ medium onion, diced

½ green bell pepper, diced

1 celery stalk, diced

2 cloves garlic, minced, or 1 teaspoon bottled minced garlic

1 cup long-grain rice (6 to 8 ounces), rinsed in cold water and drained

1¼ cups water

8-ounce can no-salt-added tomato sauce

⅛ teaspoon cayenne

### SPICY CHICKEN STRIPS

2 boneless, skinless chicken breast halves (about 4 ounces each), all visible fat removed

Vegetable oil spray

½ teaspoon ground cumin

½ teaspoon chili powder

½ teaspoon garlic powder

⅛ teaspoon pepper

8 6-inch nonfat or low-fat flour tortillas*

2 Italian plum tomatoes, thinly sliced

½ medium red onion, thinly sliced

For the Jambalaya Rice, heat a medium nonstick saucepan over medium heat. Cook the sausage, onion, bell pepper, celery, and garlic for 2 to 3 minutes, stirring occasionally, until vegetables are tender.

Add the rice and cook for 2 minutes, stirring occasionally.

Stir in the remaining Jambalaya Rice ingredients. Bring mixture to a boil over high heat. Reduce heat to low and cook, covered, for 20 to 25 minutes, or until rice is tender. Set aside.

For the Spicy Chicken Strips, rinse chicken breasts and pat dry with paper towels. Cut breasts into 8 strips. Using vegetable oil spray, lightly spray one side of the chicken strips.

Combine the cumin, chili powder, garlic powder, and pepper in a small bowl. Sprinkle half the seasoning mixture on the sprayed side of chicken.

Heat a 10-inch nonstick or cast-iron skillet over medium-high heat. Place the chicken strips, seasoned side down, in the skillet. Lightly spray the tops of the chicken strips with vegetable oil spray. Sprinkle the remaining seasoning mixture over the top surface. Cook the chicken strips 2 to 3 minutes on each side, or until they are no longer pink in the center. Set aside.

If preparing wraps to eat right away, preheat oven to 350° F. Wrap tortillas completely in foil and warm for 10 minutes.

To assemble wraps, place a few slices of tomato and red onion in the middle of a tortilla (warm for eating right away or room temperature for later). Place a cooked chicken strip on top of the tomato and onion slices. Spoon about ⅓ cup of rice onto the chicken. Fold the right third of the tortilla to the center. Bring the bottom half up to the top. Roll the bottom edge up to the top. Serve immediately or keep in an airtight container or wrap individually in plastic wrap. To reheat, place 1 or 2 filled wraps on a microwave-safe plate. Microwave on 100 percent power (high) for 1½ to 2 minutes.

* Nonfat and low-fat flour tortillas can be high in sodium. When shopping, select the one with the lowest sodium value or substitute corn tortillas.

# ASIAN GRILLED CHICKEN

*Serves 6*

*The oil-free marinade and the slight barbecue taste make this chicken delicious.*

### MARINADE

¼ cup honey

3 tablespoons red wine vinegar

¼ cup low-sodium soy sauce

1 clove garlic, minced, or ½ teaspoon bottled minced garlic

2 tablespoons finely chopped fresh parsley

2 teaspoons grated fresh gingerroot or 1 teaspoon ground ginger

½ teaspoon freshly ground pepper

6 chicken breasts (about 3½ to 4 pounds), skinned, all visible fat removed

In a large bowl, combine all marinade ingredients and mix well.

Rinse chicken pieces and pat dry with paper towels. Add chicken to marinade and turn to coat all pieces. Cover and refrigerate for at least 2 hours, turning occasionally.

### GRILLING METHOD

Place chicken 6 inches from white-hot coals. Brushing pieces with marinade and turning them frequently, grill for 30 to 45 minutes, or until chicken is cooked through.

### BROILING METHOD

Preheat broiler. Arrange chicken pieces on baking sheet and place 5 inches from heat. Brushing pieces with marinade and turning them frequently, broil for 25 to 30 minutes, or until chicken is cooked through.

**NUTRIENT ANALYSIS**

Calories 142
Protein 26 g
Carbohydrate 0 g
Total Fat 3 g
Saturated Fat 1 g
Polyunsaturated Fat 1 g
Monounsaturated Fat 1 g
Cholesterol 66 mg
Sodium 93 mg

# CRISPY OVEN-FRIED CHICKEN

*Serves 6*

*This heart-healthy alternative to traditional fried chicken is spicy and easy to make. The ginger is a pleasant surprise for your taste buds.*

Vegetable oil spray

4 cups wheat-flake or corn-flake cereal, lightly crushed (4 to 5 ounces)

1 clove garlic, crushed, or ½ teaspoon bottled minced garlic (optional)

1 teaspoon ground ginger, or to taste

1 teaspoon paprika

¼ teaspoon salt (optional)

Freshly ground pepper to taste

12 pieces chicken (about 3½ pounds), skinned, all visible fat removed

Vegetable oil spray, butter-flavored or original

Preheat oven to 350° F. Spray a baking sheet with vegetable oil spray. Set aside.

Place cereal in a pie pan or on a piece of foil. Stir in garlic. Set aside.

Combine ginger, paprika, salt, and pepper in a small bowl.

Rinse chicken and pat dry with paper towels. Sprinkle seasonings on both sides of each piece.

Roll chicken in cereal crumbs to coat. Spray chicken lightly on all sides with vegetable oil spray. Place on prepared baking sheet.

Bake for 45 to 60 minutes, or until chicken is golden-brown and tender. Timing will vary according to the thickness of the chicken pieces.

**COOK'S TIP ON SKINNING POULTRY:**

You can dramatically reduce the amount of fat and cholesterol in poultry by discarding the skin. Due to its slippery nature, however, poultry skin can be a challenge to remove. Hold the poultry piece on a flat surface (a plastic cutting board is recommended), grasp the skin with a double thickness of paper towels, and pull firmly. Discard the paper towels. Use a knife or kitchen scissors to trim any remaining visible fat.

**NUTRIENT ANALYSIS**

| | |
|---|---|
| Calories | 235 |
| Protein | 28 g |
| Carbohydrate | 15 g |
| Total Fat | 6 g |
| Saturated Fat | 2 g |
| Polyunsaturated Fat | 2 g |
| Monounsaturated Fat | 2 g |
| Cholesterol | 77 mg |
| Sodium | 206 mg |

# CHICKEN RAGOUT

*Serves 6*

*This easy French stew is delicately flavored with thyme and tarragon. Using fresh instead of dried herbs will make it extra special. Served in your nicest casserole dish, it will be a favorite with guests. Have plenty of crusty French bread on hand to absorb the juices!*

12 pieces chicken (about 3½ pounds), skinned, all visible fat removed

⅓ cup all-purpose flour

½ teaspoon freshly ground pepper, or to taste

Vegetable oil spray

1 teaspoon olive oil

1 medium yellow or white onion, sliced

1 pound fresh mushrooms, sliced

1 cup low-sodium chicken broth (see page 55 or use commercial variety)

1 cup dry white wine, nonalcoholic white wine, or low-sodium chicken broth (see page 55 or use commercial variety)

¼ cup chopped fresh thyme or 1 tablespoon plus 1 teaspoon dried, crumbled

¼ cup chopped fresh tarragon or 1 tablespoon plus 1 teaspoon dried, crumbled

¼ cup finely chopped fresh parsley

2 cloves garlic, minced, or 1 teaspoon bottled minced garlic

¼ teaspoon salt (optional)

¼ cup cold water

2 tablespoons all-purpose flour

2 cups fresh or no-salt-added frozen green peas (14 to 16 ounces fresh or 10 ounces frozen)

Preheat oven to 400° F.

Rinse chicken pieces and pat dry with paper towels.

Combine ⅓ cup flour and pepper in a paper or plastic bag. Add chicken and shake well to coat pieces.

Spray a large nonstick skillet with vegetable oil spray. Heat skillet over medium-high heat. Add a few pieces of chicken and brown on all sides. Remove pieces to an ovenproof casserole dish or Dutch oven. Repeat process with remaining chicken.

Add oil to the same skillet; swirl oil to coat bottom of skillet. When oil is hot, add onion and cook for 2 to 3 minutes, or until onion is translucent.

Add mushrooms, broth, wine, thyme, tarragon, parsley, garlic, and salt; mix. Pour over chicken pieces.

Bake, covered, for 45 minutes.

In a small bowl, blend water and 2 tablespoons flour. Gradually add mixture to the liquid in the casserole, stirring gently.

Add peas to casserole and stir.

Bake, covered, for 15 to 20 minutes, or until chicken and peas are tender and sauce has thickened.

# ASPARAGUS-CHICKEN À LA KING WITH ROASTED PEPPERS

*Serves 4*

*Although this creamy chicken mixture is typically served over toast points, try it with cooked pasta, rice, couscous, or spaghetti squash strands for a change.*

Vegetable oil spray

2 medium red or green bell peppers

8 ounces fresh asparagus, bias-sliced in bite-size pieces, or 10-ounce package no-salt-added frozen cut asparagus

10½ ounces low-sodium chicken broth (see page 55 or use commercial variety)

¼ teaspoon dried tarragon or thyme, crumbled

⅛ teaspoon salt

⅛ teaspoon pepper

6 ounces fat-free evaporated milk

⅓ cup all-purpose flour

6 ounces fat-free evaporated milk

2 cups chopped cooked skinless chicken or turkey breast (about 12 ounces raw boneless, skinless breasts, 1½ pounds raw skinless breasts with bones, or 12 ounces raw turkey breast, all visible fat removed)

Preheat broiler.

Spray a broiling pan or baking sheet with vegetable oil spray. Cut peppers into quarters or halves. Remove stems, ribs, and seeds. Place peppers cut side down on prepared pan. Broil peppers 3 to 4 inches from heat for 3 to 5 minutes, or until skin is bubbly and black.

Place peppers in a plastic bag, a bowl covered with plastic wrap, or a clean paper sack. Seal and let stand for at least 15 minutes, or until cool enough to handle. Gently pull the skin off cooled peppers using your fingers or paper towels, or trim off charred skin with a paring knife. Discard skin. Rinse and chop peppers.

Meanwhile, in a large saucepan over high heat, combine asparagus, broth, tarragon, salt, and pepper. Bring to a boil. Reduce heat and simmer, covered, for 5 minutes.

In a screw-top jar, combine half the milk and all the flour. Cover and shake well. Stir into asparagus mixture.

Stir remaining milk into asparagus mixture. Cook, stirring occasionally, until thickened and bubbly, for about 10 minutes. Cook and stir for 2 minutes.

Stir chopped roasted peppers and chicken into asparagus mixture.

# TANDOORI CORNISH HENS

*Serves 6*

*One of the most popular Indian dishes, tandoori chicken is spicy but not hot. We used Cornish hens because they are low in fat and festive, but the recipe works well with chicken parts or a whole chicken, too.*

Vegetable oil spray

3 Cornish hens (about 1 pound each), thawed if frozen

3 tablespoons fresh lime juice (1 to 2 limes)

1 teaspoon chili powder, or to taste

½ teaspoon salt (optional)

Freshly ground pepper to taste

MARINADE

1 cup plain nonfat or low-fat yogurt

1 small onion, coarsely chopped

3 cloves garlic or 1½ teaspoons bottled minced garlic

1-inch piece fresh gingerroot, peeled and coarsely chopped

1 teaspoon cumin seeds or ground cumin

1 teaspoon sugar

½ teaspoon ground turmeric

½ teaspoon chili powder, or to taste

1 lime, cut into wedges

Fresh cilantro or parsley sprigs

**NUTRIENT ANALYSIS**

| | |
|---|---|
| Calories | 183 |
| Protein | 29 g |
| Carbohydrate | 1 g |
| Total Fat | 6 g |
| Saturated Fat | 2 g |
| Polyunsaturated Fat | 2 g |
| Monounsaturated Fat | 2 g |
| Cholesterol | 83 mg |
| Sodium | 84 mg |

Using vegetable oil spray, spray a broiler pan with rack or a shallow roasting pan and a wire rack. Set aside.

Remove giblets from hens and discard. Rinse hens and pat dry with paper towels. Make several slits in the skin, then split each hen in half along the breastbone.

In a small bowl, mix lime juice, chili powder, salt, and pepper. Rub mixture all over hens and set aside for about 15 minutes.

Meanwhile, in a blender or food processor, puree all marinade ingredients.

Place hens in a large bowl and add marinade. Mix well to coat all the pieces. Cover and refrigerate for at least 8 hours, turning occasionally.

Preheat oven to 400° F.

Place hens, skin side up, on prepared rack in broiler. Spoon marinade over the pieces. Bake, basting frequently with marinade, for 45 to 60 minutes, or until hens are thoroughly cooked and very tender. Test for doneness by pricking the skin of the thigh; the juice should run clear.

Remove skin before serving. Garnish hens with lime and cilantro.

# ROAST CORNISH HENS

*Serves 6*

*Add a dash of color to the serving platter with a variety of steamed vegetables. Nonfat chicken gravy packaged in a glass jar or made from a mix is a really easy accompaniment, too.*

3 Cornish hens (about 1 pound each), thawed if frozen

1 tablespoon whole peppercorns, coarsely crushed

3 tablespoons chopped fresh tarragon or 1 tablespoon dried, crumbled

1 medium pear, any kind, cut into thirds

1 cup fresh parsley sprigs

½ to ¾ cup low-sodium chicken broth (see page 55 or use commercial variety)

Water

¼ cup low-sodium chicken broth, if needed (see page 55 or use commercial variety)

Preheat oven to 425° F.

Remove giblets from hens and discard. Rinse hens and pat dry with paper towels. Gently loosen skin from meat on breast and legs by breaking the membrane that holds the skin to the meat and sliding your fingers between the two to loosen the skin.

Spread pepper and tarragon under the skin and in the cavity. Stuff each cavity with a piece of pear and about one third of the parsley.

Place the hens on a rack, breast side up, in a 3-inch-deep roaster pan. Soak 3 pieces of cheesecloth, each large enough to cover the top and sides of a hen, in ½ to ¾ cup of chicken broth. Cover hens with the cloth to keep the meat from drying out. Put water in the pan to a depth of 1 to 1½ inches to provide moisture.

Place hens in oven, reduce heat immediately to 325° F, and bake for 45 to 60 minutes. Baste occasionally with remaining broth if needed. Test for doneness by pricking the skin of the thigh; the juice should run clear.

Cut each hen in half and remove skin.

# TURKEY TETRAZZINI

*Serves 8*

*This is a great way to use turkey leftovers. Classic tetrazzini is made with spaghetti, but we used rotini because the sauce adheres to it so well.*

12 ounces dried rotini or other dried pasta

Vegetable oil spray

1 medium onion, diced

½ green bell pepper, diced

2 cloves garlic, minced, or 1 teaspoon bottled minced garlic

8 ounces fresh mushrooms, sliced

12 ounces cooked skinless turkey breast, cubed (about 2 cups)

10¾-ounce can low-fat, low-sodium cream of chicken soup

½ cup fat-free evaporated milk

2 tablespoons dry sherry, dry white wine, or nonalcoholic white wine (optional)

2 tablespoons grated or shredded Parmesan cheese

2 ounces diced pimientos, drained

⅛ teaspoon pepper

¼ cup plain dry bread crumbs

Cook pasta according to package directions, omitting salt and oil. Drain and set aside.

While pasta is cooking, preheat oven to 350° F.

Spray a deep skillet with vegetable oil spray. Sauté onion, bell pepper, and garlic over medium heat for 2 to 3 minutes, or until soft.

Add mushrooms and cook for 2 minutes, or until soft.

Add pasta to skillet. Stir in remaining ingredients except bread crumbs.

Spray a 3-quart casserole dish with vegetable oil spray. Pour pasta mixture into prepared casserole dish. Sprinkle top with bread crumbs.

Bake, covered, for 35 to 40 minutes.

**COOK'S TIP ON FRESH MUSHROOMS:**

Bulk-purchased mushrooms are best stored in a paper sack on your refrigerator shelf rather than in the vegetable crisper. You can refrigerate prepackaged mushrooms in their original container. Once opened, refrigerate them in a paper sack. Because mushrooms absorb water, clean them by wiping them gently with a damp towel or rinsing them briefly under cold water.

**NUTRIENT ANALYSIS**

Calories 308
Protein 22 g
Carbohydrate 44 g
Total Fat 4 g
Saturated Fat 1 g
Polyunsaturated Fat 1 g
Monounsaturated Fat 1 g
Cholesterol 35 mg
Sodium 252 mg

# TURKEY AND VEGETABLE CALZONE

*Serves 4*

**COOK'S TIP:**

To make the calzones when you don't have leftovers, cut about 5½ ounces of boneless, skinless turkey breast into bite-size pieces. About 5 to 7 minutes before the mushroom mixture is ready, stir in the raw turkey. Cook until the turkey is no longer pink in the center. Continue as directed above.

*Here's a fresh twist on the after-the-holidays turkey sandwich. For an exotic touch, use chanterelles, shiitake mushrooms, or oyster mushrooms.*

Vegetable oil spray

8 ounces fresh mushrooms, sliced

1 cup chopped onions or shallots (about 2 medium onions or 8 medium shallots)

½ cup chopped green, red, or yellow bell pepper

1 teaspoon dried oregano, crumbled

1 clove garlic, minced, or ½ teaspoon bottled minced garlic

½ teaspoon fennel seed, crushed using a mortar and pestle

¼ teaspoon crushed red pepper flakes

4 ounces cooked skinless turkey breast, finely chopped (about 1 cup)

Flour

10-ounce package refrigerated pizza dough

⅔ cup shredded part-skim mozzarella cheese (2½ to 3 ounces)

1 tablespoon fat-free milk

**NUTRIENT ANALYSIS**

Calories 314
Protein 20 g
Carbohydrate 42 g
Total Fat 7 g
Saturated Fat 3 g
Polyunsaturated Fat 1 g
Monounsaturated Fat 2 g
Cholesterol 32 mg
Sodium 452 mg

Spray a large skillet with vegetable oil spray. Add mushrooms, onion, bell pepper, oregano, garlic, fennel seed, and crushed red pepper. Cook over medium heat, stirring occasionally, for 15 to 20 minutes, or until mushrooms are tender and most of the liquid has evaporated.

Stir chopped turkey into mushroom mixture. Set aside.

Preheat oven to 375° F.

Lightly flour a flat surface and unroll pizza dough onto it. With a rolling pin, roll pizza dough into a

13-inch circle. (Hint: Fold in corners of dough before rolling.) Transfer to a baking sheet or pizza pan.

Spoon turkey mixture on half of the dough circle to within 1 inch of the edge. Sprinkle cheese over turkey mixture. Moisten edges of dough with water. Fold dough in half over filling. Seal edge by pressing with the tines of a fork. Prick top. Brush top with milk.

Bake, uncovered, for 30 to 35 minutes, or until crust is light brown and filling is heated through. Let stand 5 minutes. Cut into wedges to serve.

# MEATS

Braised Eye of Round Roast
with Brown Gravy

Peppery Beef with
Blue Cheese Sauce

Marinated Steak

Beef Stroganoff

Sloppy Joes

Meat Loaf
with Roasted Vegetables

Swedish Meat Loaf with
Dill Sauce

Shepherd's Pie

Bulgur and Ground Beef Casserole

Ground Beef Ragout

Mexican Beef and Corn Bread Pie

Chili

Vegetable-Beef Burgers

Lamb and Red Beans

Spicy Baked Pork Chops

Pork with Savory Sauce

Pork and Tofu Stir-fry

Pork with Corn-Cilantro Pesto

# BRAISED EYE OF ROUND ROAST WITH BROWN GRAVY

*Serves 8*

*This lean cut of meat is stuffed with whole cloves of garlic, rubbed with herbs, and braised to tender perfection. Pour the rich gravy, made from the braising liquid, over the beef and mashed potatoes or rice.*

2 pounds eye of round roast, all visible fat removed

4 cloves garlic, peeled

1 teaspoon dried thyme, crumbled

¼ teaspoon pepper

¼ teaspoon dried oregano, crumbled

Vegetable oil spray

1 medium onion, finely chopped

1 celery stalk, finely chopped

1 cup low-sodium beef broth (see page 56 or use commercial variety)

1 cup water

1 bay leaf

¼ teaspoon salt

½ cup water

¼ cup all-purpose flour

With a small, sharp knife, make 4 small cuts, evenly spaced and about 1½ inches deep, in the roast. Push the cloves of garlic into these cuts with your fingers (garlic should not be visible on the surface).

In a small bowl, combine thyme, pepper, and oregano. Sprinkle mixture evenly over the meat and lightly rub mixture into the surface with your fingers.

Heat a Dutch oven over medium-high heat. Lightly spray all surface areas of the roast with vegetable oil spray. When the Dutch oven is heated, spray it lightly with vegetable oil spray. Brown the entire roast (including the sides), about 3 minutes per surface area.

Add the onion and celery to the pot and cook for 2 to 3 minutes, stirring the vegetables occasionally.

Stir in the broth, water, bay leaf, and salt. Bring liquid to a boil over high heat. Reduce heat to low and cook, covered, for 2 to 2½ hours, or until meat is tender. Remove roast from pan and keep warm.

Bring braising liquid to a boil over high heat. Pour ½ cup water into a small bowl. Stir in flour. Add the flour mixture to the liquid and cook, stirring occasionally, until mixture is thickened, about 2 to 3 minutes.

Slice beef across the grain with a sharp knife and serve with the gravy.

# PEPPERY BEEF WITH BLUE CHEESE SAUCE

*Serves 4*

*Blue cheese has a strong flavor, so a little goes a long way. That means you get a rich, creamy sauce for only a few extra calories and a little extra total fat and saturated fat.*

12 ounces flank steak, all visible fat removed

2 teaspoons coarsely cracked pepper

Vegetable oil spray

SAUCE

1 teaspoon light margarine

1 clove garlic, minced, or ½ teaspoon bottled minced garlic

1 tablespoon all-purpose flour

⅔ cup fat-free milk

2 tablespoons crumbled blue cheese (about ½ ounce)

2 tablespoons finely chopped green onion (1 to 2)

1 tablespoon dry white wine or nonalcoholic white wine (optional)

Make 6 shallow crisscross slashes on the meat (3 in each direction). Rub meat with about half the pepper. Make 6 slashes on other side of meat. Rub with remaining pepper.

Lightly spray the unheated rack of a broiler pan with vegetable oil spray. Broil meat 3 to 5 inches from the heat for 5 minutes. Turn and broil 3 to 5 minutes, or until desired doneness.

Meanwhile, for sauce, melt margarine in a small saucepan over medium heat. Add garlic; cook for 1 minute.

Stir in flour, then stir in milk all at once (a whisk works well). Cook and stir until thickened and bubbly, about 5 minutes; cook and stir 1 minute more. Remove from heat. Stir in remaining sauce ingredients.

To serve, thinly slice meat diagonally across the grain. Serve with sauce.

NUTRIENT ANALYSIS

Calories 177
Protein 21 g
Carbohydrate 5 g
Total Fat 8 g
Saturated Fat 3 g
Polyunsaturated Fat 0 g
Monounsaturated Fat 3 g
Cholesterol 52 mg
Sodium 136 mg

# MARINATED STEAK

*Serves 6*

*This marinade is a favorite among steak lovers.*

1 to 1½ pounds flank steak, 1 inch thick, all visible fat removed

MARINADE

½ cup dry red wine, nonalcoholic red wine, or low-sodium beef broth (see page 56 or use commercial variety)

3 tablespoons minced fresh parsley

3 tablespoons tarragon vinegar or wine vinegar

1 teaspoon acceptable vegetable oil

1 tablespoon chopped fresh oregano or 1 teaspoon dried, crumbled

1 tablespoon chopped fresh tarragon or 1 teaspoon dried, crumbled

3 cloves garlic, crushed, or 1½ teaspoons bottled minced garlic

1 bay leaf

½ teaspoon freshly ground pepper

Vegetable oil spray

Freshly ground pepper to taste

Place steak in an airtight plastic bag or in a baking dish. In a small nonmetallic bowl, combine marinade ingredients. Pour over steak and turn to coat. Cover and refrigerate for at least 8 hours, turning occasionally.

Preheat broiler. Spray broiler pan with vegetable oil spray. Set aside.

Remove steak from marinade, pat dry, and sprinkle with pepper. Place meat on prepared broiler pan.

Broil 4 to 6 inches from heat until desired doneness, 4 to 7 minutes on each side for medium-well done, or 3 to 5 minutes on each side for medium-rare. Slice diagonally across the grain into thin slices.

## COOK'S TIP ON BEEF CUTS:

Steak on a cholesterol-lowering diet? Sure. Just select the cut of meat carefully and trim all visible fat. Besides flank steak, wise beef choices include tenderloin, sirloin, and round steak.

## NUTRIENT ANALYSIS

| | |
|---|---|
| Calories | 147 |
| Protein | 20 g |
| Carbohydrate | 0 g |
| Total Fat | 7 g |
| Saturated Fat | 3 g |
| Polyunsaturated Fat | 0 g |
| Monounsaturated Fat | 3 g |
| Cholesterol | 54 mg |
| Sodium | 48 mg |

# BEEF STROGANOFF

*Serves 10*

*Long, slow cooking tenderizes the meat and gives the stroganoff a chance to develop its full flavor. You'll love what yogurt cheese does for this recipe. Just be sure to plan ahead—the yogurt needs to drain for a long time.*

**NUTRIENT ANALYSIS**

*(With beef; includes yogurt cheese)*

| | |
|---|---|
| Calories | 320 |
| Protein | 28 g |
| Carbohydrate | 40 g |
| Total Fat | 5 g |
| Saturated Fat | 1 g |
| Polyunsaturated Fat | 1 g |
| Monounsaturated Fat | 1 g |
| Cholesterol | 51 mg |
| Sodium | 155 mg |

**NUTRIENT ANALYSIS**

*(With venison; includes yogurt cheese)*

| | |
|---|---|
| Calories | 319 |
| Protein | 30 g |
| Carbohydrate | 40 g |
| Total Fat | 4 g |
| Saturated Fat | 1 g |
| Polyunsaturated Fat | 1 g |
| Monounsaturated Fat | 1 g |
| Cholesterol | 76 mg |
| Sodium | 155 mg |

**NUTRIENT ANALYSIS**

*(For ½ cup yogurt cheese)*

| | |
|---|---|
| Calories | 137 |
| Protein | 14 g |
| Carbohydrate | 19 g |
| Total Fat | 0 g |
| Saturated Fat | 0 g |
| Polyunsaturated Fat | 0 g |
| Monounsaturated Fat | 0 g |
| Cholesterol | 4 mg |
| Sodium | 187 mg |

Vegetable oil spray

1 teaspoon acceptable vegetable oil

2 pounds boneless beef round steak or venison, all visible fat removed, cut into bite-size pieces

1 large onion, cut into ¼-inch-thick slices

1¾ cups low-sodium beef broth (see page 56 or use commercial variety)

¼ cup dry sherry

½ cup all-purpose flour

½ teaspoon freshly ground pepper

1 cup Yogurt Cheese (recipe follows)

2 tablespoons no-salt-added ketchup

1 tablespoon Worcestershire sauce

¼ teaspoon salt

12-ounce package macaroni

1 pound fresh mushrooms, thickly sliced

In a large nonstick skillet or Dutch oven sprayed with vegetable oil spray, heat oil over medium-high heat. Brown meat on all sides. Remove meat and set it aside.

Add onion and sauté, stirring frequently, for about 5 minutes.

Return meat to skillet and add broth, sherry, flour, and pepper. Stir well. Simmer, partially covered, stirring occasionally, for 1½ hours, or until meat is tender.

Meanwhile, put yogurt cheese, ketchup, Worcestershire sauce, and salt in a medium bowl. Whisk together to mix well and set aside.

Cook macaroni according to package directions, omitting salt and oil; drain.

In a nonstick skillet over medium heat, sauté mushrooms, stirring occasionally, until tender, about 10 to 15
minutes. Add mushrooms to cooked meat.

Add yogurt cheese mixture. Stir and heat for about 5
minutes.

Serve over macaroni.

### YOGURT CHEESE (ABOUT 2 CUPS)

**1 quart plain nonfat or low-fat yogurt without gelatin**

Place a double-thick layer of fine-mesh cotton cheesecloth or paper coffee filters inside a rustproof colander.
Place the colander in a bowl, leaving enough space for
about 2 cups of whey (watery liquid) to drain out of the
colander. Pour the yogurt into the prepared colander
and refrigerate for 8 hours. This will yield about 2 cups
of firm yogurt and 2 cups of drained whey.

**COOK'S TIP ON
YOGURT CHEESE:**

Use yogurt cheese almost
anywhere a recipe calls for
plain yogurt or sour cream.
Try the whey as a substitute
for fat-free milk, such as in
Potato Bread, page 252,
or Honey-Nut Bread,
page 254.

# SLOPPY JOES

*Serves 6*

*You can eat healthfully and still enjoy some old favorites. Here's a pared-down version of Sloppy Joes with perked-up flavor.*

### SAUCE

8-ounce can no-salt-added tomato sauce

½ cup low-sodium ketchup

1½ tablespoons Worcestershire sauce

1 teaspoon prepared mustard

1 teaspoon molasses

1 clove garlic, finely minced, or ½ teaspoon bottled minced garlic

½ teaspoon dry mustard

¼ teaspoon freshly grated orange rind

Pinch of ground cloves

1 pound lean ground beef (90 percent lean)

½ small onion, finely chopped

6 whole-wheat hamburger buns, toasted if desired

Hot pepper sauce to taste

In a small saucepan, combine sauce ingredients. Simmer, stirring occasionally, while preparing meat.

Heat a heavy nonstick skillet, at least 10 inches in diameter, over medium-high heat. Add beef and sauté, stirring occasionally, for 4 to 5 minutes, or until meat is no longer pink. Pour beef into a strainer or colander. Rinse under hot water.

Add onion to skillet and sauté, stirring frequently, for about 5 minutes, or until translucent.

Add beef and sauce to onion in skillet. Heat for 3 minutes, stirring occasionally.

Add hot pepper sauce, then spoon about ½ cup mixture over each bun. Serve immediately.

**NUTRIENT ANALYSIS**

Calories 249

Protein 23 g

Carbohydrate 30 g

Total Fat 5 g

Saturated Fat 1 g

Polyunsaturated Fat 1 g

Monounsaturated Fat 2 g

Cholesterol 47 mg

Sodium 324 mg

# MEAT LOAF WITH ROASTED VEGETABLES

*Serves 4*

*Using half beef and half chicken cuts the total fat and the saturated fat in this one-dish meal.*

¼ cup plain dry bread crumbs

¼ cup fat-free milk

Egg substitute equivalent to 1 egg, or 1 egg

½ pound lean ground beef (90 percent lean)

½ pound ground skinless chicken breast

¼ cup finely chopped green onions (2 to 3)

¼ cup finely chopped celery

½ teaspoon dried oregano, crumbled

¼ teaspoon ground sage

¼ teaspoon salt

⅛ teaspoon pepper

4 medium white potatoes, cut into 1-inch chunks

4 medium carrots, cut into ½-inch slices

1 medium onion, cut into 8 wedges

Vegetable oil spray

2 tablespoons barbecue sauce

Preheat oven to 350° F.

In a medium bowl, combine bread crumbs, milk, and egg substitute. Add beef, chicken, green onions, celery, oregano, sage, salt, and pepper. Mix well.

In a shallow baking dish or pan, pat meat mixture into a 7 × 3 × 2-inch loaf. Arrange vegetables around loaf. Spray vegetables with vegetable oil spray.

Bake, uncovered, for 1 hour, stirring vegetables once. When meat is almost done and vegetables are almost tender, warm sauce.

Pat meat loaf and vegetables with a paper towel to remove any grease. Transfer meat loaf and vegetables to a serving plate. Spoon barbecue sauce over meat loaf.

**NUTRIENT ANALYSIS**

Calories 296

Protein 30 g

Carbohydrate 29 g

Total Fat 6 g

Saturated Fat 2 g

Polyunsaturated Fat 1 g

Monounsaturated Fat 2 g

Cholesterol 64 mg

Sodium 387 mg

# SWEDISH MEAT LOAF
# WITH DILL SAUCE

*Serves 6*

*If you like Swedish meatballs, you'll love this moist and fla-vorful meat loaf.*

Vegetable oil spray

¾ cup rye bread crumbs (about 4 slices)

⅓ cup low-fat buttermilk

1 teaspoon acceptable vegetable oil

½ medium onion, finely minced

2 cloves garlic, finely minced, or 1 teaspoon bottled minced garlic

White of 1 large egg, lightly beaten

⅛ teaspoon freshly ground pepper

¼ teaspoon ground nutmeg

¼ teaspoon ground ginger

⅛ teaspoon ground allspice

1 tablespoon chopped fresh dill weed or 1 teaspoon dried

½ pound lean ground beef (90 percent lean)

¾ pound ground skinless chicken breast

### SAUCE

1 tablespoon light margarine

2 tablespoons all-purpose flour

1 cup low-sodium beef broth (see page 56 or use commercial variety)

¾ cup fat-free evaporated milk

3 tablespoons dry sherry or low-sodium beef broth

3 tablespoons chopped fresh dill weed or 1 tablespoon dried

¼ teaspoon ground nutmeg

¼ teaspoon ground allspice

¼ teaspoon ground ginger

⅛ teaspoon freshly ground pepper

Preheat oven to 425° F. Spray a 9 × 5-inch ovenproof loaf pan with vegetable oil spray. Set aside.

Mix bread crumbs and buttermilk in a large bowl and let soak 5 minutes.

Meanwhile, heat oil in a large nonstick skillet over medium heat. Add onion and sauté, stirring frequently, about 4 minutes.

Add garlic and continue to sauté, stirring constantly, 1 minute, or until onion is soft. Pour into bread crumb mixture.

Add egg white, pepper, nutmeg, ginger, allspice, and dill weed to bread crumbs. Use your hands to mix lightly.

Add ground beef and chicken. Mix well.

Lightly pat mixture into prepared loaf pan. Place in oven and reduce temperature to 350° F. Bake for 30 minutes.

While meat loaf is cooking, make the sauce. In a medium saucepan, melt margarine over medium heat.

Remove pan from heat and blend in flour.

Return pan to heat and gradually add broth, milk, and sherry. Cook, stirring constantly with a wire whisk, about 6 to 8 minutes, or until mixture thickens.

Remove pan from heat and blend in remaining ingredients.

Remove meat loaf from oven and pour off fat. Pour sauce over meat loaf, cover with foil, and return to oven. Bake for 15 minutes, or until done.

# SHEPHERD'S PIE

*Serves 6*

**COOK'S TIP ON GROUND BEEF:**

Wash that fat right out of your ground beef by browning the beef, then running it under hot water. Ninety-three percent lean ground beef that isn't rinsed has more fat than 90 percent lean—and even 85 percent lean—ground beef that is rinsed!

*Assemble this easy entrée ahead of time and bake it just before serving.*

Water

2 pounds russet potatoes, peeled and quartered

1 pound lean ground beef (90 percent lean)

1 large onion, finely chopped

3 medium carrots, chopped

1 large bell pepper, chopped

½ cup fresh or frozen no-salt-added green peas (about 8 ounces fresh unshelled or 5 ounces frozen)

1 medium tomato, chopped

¾ cup low-sodium beef broth (see page 56 or use commercial variety)

¼ cup chopped fresh parsley

2 tablespoons Worcestershire sauce

Freshly ground pepper to taste

⅓ cup fat-free milk

Freshly ground pepper to taste

2 tablespoons cold water

1 tablespoon cornstarch

**NUTRIENT ANALYSIS**

| | |
|---|---|
| Calories | 294 |
| Protein | 21 g |
| Carbohydrate | 40 g |
| Total Fat | 6 g |
| Saturated Fat | 2 g |
| Polyunsaturated Fat | 0 g |
| Monounsaturated Fat | 2 g |
| Cholesterol | 43 mg |
| Sodium | 115 mg |

Pour enough water into a large saucepan to cover potatoes. Bring water to a boil over high heat. Add potatoes and boil until tender, about 30 minutes. Drain. Return potatoes to saucepan.

Meanwhile, heat a heavy nonstick skillet, at least 10 inches in diameter, over medium-high heat. Add ground beef and sauté, stirring occasionally, 4 to 5 minutes, or until meat is no longer pink. Pour beef into a strainer or colander and rinse under hot water.

Return meat to skillet. Add onion and cook over medium-high heat until it's translucent, 4 to 5 minutes.

Add carrots, bell pepper, peas, tomato, broth, parsley, Worcestershire sauce, and pepper. Simmer, uncovered, for 15 minutes.

Add milk and pepper to potatoes and mash until smooth. Keep mixture warm.

Preheat oven to 350° F.

Pour 2 tablespoons water into a small bowl. Stir in cornstarch. Stir into meat mixture.

Spoon meat mixture into an ungreased 10 × 10 × 2-inch or 9 × 11 × 2-inch baking dish. Spread mashed potatoes over the surface, using a fork for texture.

Bake for 30 to 35 minutes, or until lightly browned.

# BULGUR AND GROUND BEEF CASSEROLE

*Serves 6*

*Bulgur, or cracked wheat, is available in most supermarkets and health food stores. It has a delicious, nutty flavor and is an excellent substitute for rice.*

1 cup bulgur (5 to 6 ounces)

1½ cups cold water

1 pound lean ground beef (90 percent lean)

2 medium onions, chopped

½ cup finely chopped fresh cilantro or parsley

1 tablespoon chopped fresh dill weed or 1 teaspoon dried

¼ teaspoon salt

Freshly ground pepper to taste

4 medium tomatoes, chopped

½ cup canned low-sodium vegetable juice

2 tablespoons fresh lemon juice

2 tomatoes, cut into wedges (optional)

1 lemon, thinly sliced (optional)

In a medium bowl, soak bulgur in cold water for 15 to 30 minutes, or until soft. Set aside.

Meanwhile, heat a heavy nonstick skillet, at least 10 inches in diameter, over medium-high heat. Add beef and sauté, stirring occasionally, for 4 to 5 minutes, or until meat is no longer pink. Pour beef into a strainer or colander. Rinse under hot water. Return beef to skillet.

Preheat oven to 350° F.

Add onions to skillet and cook until onions are translucent, 3 to 4 minutes.

Drain bulgur and add to meat mixture with cilantro, dill weed, salt, pepper, chopped tomatoes, vegetable juice, and lemon juice. Stir gently.

**NUTRIENT ANALYSIS**

Calories 221

Protein 22 g

Carbohydrate 27 g

Total Fat 3 g

Saturated Fat 1 g

Polyunsaturated Fat 0 g

Monounsaturated Fat 1 g

Cholesterol 47 mg

Sodium 153 mg

Place mixture in a 10 × 10 × 2-inch or 9 × 11 × 2-inch baking dish or ovenproof casserole dish.

Bake, uncovered, for 15 to 20 minutes, or until heated thoroughly. Garnish with tomato wedges and lemon slices.

# GROUND BEEF RAGOUT

*Serves 6*

**COOK'S TIP:**

Sometimes a small change makes a big difference. Substitute 1 cup of pearl onions (about 4 ounces) for the chopped onion in this recipe and see what we mean. Add the pearl onions with the wine, water, and other ingredients just after rinsing the cooked beef.

*The ingredients for this hearty dish sound a lot like those for chili, but the finished product is quite different. For economy in cost but not in taste, stretch the original recipe to serve 10 without increasing the amount of meat. Prepare about 2 ounces of dried spaghetti or yolk-free noodles per person to make a bed for the ragout.*

1½ pounds lean ground beef (90 percent lean)

1 large onion, chopped

2 large tomatoes, chopped

8-ounce can no-salt-added tomato sauce

¾ cup dry red wine, nonalcoholic red wine, or water

½ cup water

1 red chili pepper, seeded and chopped (optional)*

1 tablespoon fresh oregano or 1 teaspoon dried, crumbled

3 cloves garlic, minced, or 1½ teaspoons bottled minced garlic

1 teaspoon chili powder, or to taste

1 teaspoon ground cumin

½ teaspoon salt (optional)

Freshly ground pepper to taste

15-ounce can low-sodium kidney beans, drained

15-ounce can Great Northern, black, or lima beans, rinsed and drained

¼ cup chopped fresh parsley

**NUTRIENT ANALYSIS**

Calories 339
Protein 36 g
Carbohydrate 33 g
Total Fat 7 g
Saturated Fat 2 g
Polyunsaturated Fat 1 g
Monounsaturated Fat 3 g
Cholesterol 68 mg
Sodium 84 mg

Heat a 3-quart sauté pan or Dutch oven over medium-high heat. Add ground beef and sauté, stirring occasionally, for 4 to 5 minutes, or until meat is no longer pink. Pour beef into a strainer or colander. Rinse under hot water.

Return beef to the pan, add onion, and sauté for 4 to 5 minutes, or until onion is translucent.

Stir in remaining ingredients except beans. Bring mixture to a boil. Reduce heat and simmer, partially covered, for about 45 minutes, stirring occasionally.

Add beans and simmer for 10 to 15 minutes, or until beans are thoroughly heated. Sprinkle with parsley before serving.

* Hot chili peppers contain oils that can burn your skin, lips, and eyes. Wear rubber gloves or wash your hands thoroughly with warm, soapy water immediately after handling peppers.

# MEXICAN BEEF AND CORN BREAD PIE

*Serves 6*

*A blend of the Old South and South of the Border makes this a real winner. For a hearty family meal, serve with your favorite green salad and Gazpacho Salad Dressing (see page 84).*

### MEAT MIXTURE

1 pound lean ground beef (90 percent lean)

1 large onion, chopped

2 large tomatoes, chopped

1 large green bell pepper, chopped

10-ounce package frozen no-salt-added whole kernel corn (about 2 cups)

1 cup low-sodium chicken or beef broth (see pages 55 and 56 or use commercial variety)

1 tablespoon Worcestershire sauce

1 teaspoon ground cumin

1 teaspoon chili powder, or to taste

½ teaspoon salt (optional)

### CORN BREAD MIXTURE

1½ cups yellow cornmeal

¼ cup all-purpose flour

2 teaspoons baking powder

1 teaspoon sugar (optional)

¼ teaspoon salt (optional)

Whites of 3 large eggs, lightly beaten

½ cup fat-free milk

1 tablespoon acceptable vegetable oil

Preheat oven to 400° F.

Heat a heavy nonstick skillet, at least 10 inches in diameter, over medium-high heat. Add ground beef and sauté, stirring occasionally, for 4 to 5 minutes, or until meat is no longer pink. Pour beef into a strainer or colander. Rinse under hot water.

Return beef to the skillet and add onion. Cook until onion is translucent, about 3 minutes.

Add remaining meat mixture ingredients. Simmer, uncovered, for 20 to 25 minutes.

In a medium bowl, mix together cornmeal, flour, baking powder, sugar, and salt.

In a small bowl, combine egg whites, milk, and oil. Add to dry mixture. Mix lightly.

Place meat mixture in a $10 \times 10 \times 2$-inch baking dish. Spoon corn bread mixture over meat and spread lightly to cover surface.

Bake, uncovered, for 30 to 40 minutes, or until corn bread is golden-brown.

# CHILI

**COOK'S TIP:**

For that four-alarm taste, add 1 or 2 jalapeño peppers.

*Every cook has a favorite chili recipe. This one is destined to be yours! Like many other soups and stews, it tastes best when made the day before, allowing the flavors to mingle.*

Vegetable oil spray

1 pound lean ground beef (90 percent lean)

Vegetable oil spray

2 large onions, chopped

2 8-ounce cans no-salt-added tomato sauce

1½ cups water

2 to 4 cloves garlic, minced, or 1 to 2 teaspoons bottled minced garlic

2 15-ounce cans low-sodium pinto beans, drained

3 tablespoons chili powder

1 tablespoon chopped fresh oregano or 1 teaspoon dried, crumbled

1 teaspoon ground cumin

½ teaspoon salt (optional)

⅛ teaspoon cayenne, or to taste

Freshly ground pepper to taste

¼ cup cold water

2 tablespoons cornstarch

**NUTRIENT ANALYSIS**

Calories 301
Protein 28 g
Carbohydrate 40 g
Total Fat 4 g
Saturated Fat 1 g
Polyunsaturated Fat 1 g
Monounsaturated Fat 1 g
Cholesterol 47 mg
Sodium 101 mg

Heat a large, heavy saucepan or Dutch oven over medium-high heat. Spray with vegetable oil spray. Add ground beef and sauté, stirring occasionally, for 4 to 5 minutes, or until meat is no longer pink. Pour ground beef into a strainer or colander. Rinse under hot water. Set aside.

Spray the same pan with vegetable oil spray again and heat over medium-high heat. Add onions and sauté for 2 to 3 minutes, or until translucent.

Add beef, tomato sauce, 1½ cups water, and garlic. Simmer, partially covered, for 20 minutes.

Stir in beans, chili powder, oregano, cumin, salt, cayenne, and pepper. Simmer, partially covered, for 30 to 40 minutes.

Pour cold water into a small bowl. Stir in cornstarch. Stir into chili mixture. Cook for 3 to 4 minutes, or until desired consistency.

# VEGETABLE-BEEF BURGERS

*Serves 6*

*If you thought your hamburger days were over, think again. This recipe is low in fat and will be high on your list of favorites. For variety, replace the usual burger toppings with Salsa (see page 242) or a nonfat or low-fat salad dressing, such as honey mustard or Thousand Island.*

MEAT MIXTURE

1 pound lean ground beef (90 percent lean)

1 small tomato, finely chopped

1 medium onion, finely chopped

1 small green bell pepper, finely chopped

½ teaspoon freshly ground pepper, or to taste

1 teaspoon Worcestershire sauce

Vegetable oil spray

6 whole-wheat hamburger buns

1 large tomato, sliced

6 lettuce leaves

Mustard (optional)

Low-sodium ketchup (optional)

Fat-free, cholesterol-free mayonnaise (optional)

Combine ground beef, tomato, onion, bell pepper, pepper, and Worcestershire sauce. Mix well. Divide mixture into 6 portions and shape each into a patty about ½ inch thick.

Spray a heavy, nonstick skillet with vegetable oil spray and heat over medium-high heat. Handling patties very carefully to prevent breaking, place in skillet. Cook for 5 to 7 minutes on each side, or until desired doneness.

Place cooked patties on paper towels and blot to absorb fat. Serve patties on buns with tomato, lettuce, and mustard, ketchup, or mayonnaise.

**NUTRIENT ANALYSIS**

Calories 228

Protein 23 g

Carbohydrate 25 g

Total Fat 5 g

Saturated Fat 1 g

Polyunsaturated Fat 1 g

Monounsaturated Fat 2 g

Cholesterol 47 mg

Sodium 275 mg

# LAMB AND RED BEANS

*Serves 8*

*You'll feel as if you've arrived at an exotic spot in the Middle East when you try this dish.*

Vegetable oil spray

2 pounds lean lamb, all visible fat removed, cut into bite-size pieces

2 medium onions, chopped

3 cloves garlic, minced, or 1½ teaspoons bottled minced garlic

2 15-ounce cans low-sodium kidney beans, drained

6 medium tomatoes, chopped

¾ cup low-sodium chicken broth (see page 55 or use commercial variety)

¼ cup finely chopped fresh parsley

1 tablespoon fresh lemon juice

1 tablespoon finely chopped fresh mint or 1 teaspoon dried, crumbled

1 teaspoon turmeric

1 teaspoon freshly ground pepper, or to taste

½ cup plain nonfat or low-fat yogurt, lightly beaten with a fork

2 tablespoons fresh parsley, chopped

Preheat oven to 350° F.

In a Dutch oven sprayed with vegetable oil spray, brown lamb on all sides over medium-high heat, about 5 to 7 minutes.

Add onions and garlic and sauté until onions are soft.

Add beans, tomatoes, broth, ¼ cup parsley, lemon juice, mint, turmeric, and pepper. Bring to a boil over high heat, cover, and transfer to oven.

Bake for 1 to 1½ hours, or until lamb is tender.

Remove from oven. Stir in yogurt and sprinkle with 2 tablespoons parsley.

**COOK'S TIP:**

Make a double batch and freeze some for later. Omit the yogurt and parsley from the portion you freeze. When you need a quick meal, thaw the casserole, then reheat it in a pre-heated 350° F oven until thoroughly heated, about 30 to 35 minutes. Add yogurt and parsley just before serving.

**NUTRIENT ANALYSIS**

Calories 300
Protein 31 g
Carbohydrate 26 g
Total Fat 8 g
Saturated Fat 3 g
Polyunsaturated Fat 1 g
Monounsaturated Fat 3 g
Cholesterol 72 mg
Sodium 86 mg

# SPICY BAKED PORK CHOPS

*Serves 4*

*Fixing dinner will be as easy as 1-2-3! All you need to do to simplify preparation is set up an assembly line. Place the bowl with the milk mixture at the left, the plate of crumb mixture in the center, and the baking dish at the right.*

Vegetable oil spray

1 pound boneless pork loin chops, all visible fat removed

Egg substitute equivalent to 1 egg, or 1 egg

2 tablespoons fat-free milk

1/3 cup cornflake crumbs

2 tablespoons cornmeal

1/2 teaspoon dried marjoram, crumbled

1/8 teaspoon ground pepper

1/8 teaspoon dry mustard

1/8 teaspoon ground ginger

1/8 teaspoon cayenne

Preheat oven to 375° F. Using vegetable oil spray, spray a shallow baking pan large enough to hold pork chops in a single layer. Set aside.

Cut pork chops into 4 portions, if necessary. Set aside.

In a small, shallow bowl such as a soup bowl, combine egg substitute and milk.

In a shallow dish such as a pie pan, combine crumbs, cornmeal, marjoram, pepper, mustard, ginger, and cayenne. Using tongs, dip pork chops in milk mixture, letting excess liquid drip off. Coat both sides of pork chops with crumb mixture. Arrange pork chops in prepared pan.

Bake, uncovered, for 15 minutes. Turn chops with a spatula and bake for 10 minutes, or until chops are tender and slightly pink in center.

**NUTRIENT ANALYSIS**

Calories 234

Protein 27 g

Carbohydrate 11 g

Total Fat 9 g

Saturated Fat 3 g

Polyunsaturated Fat 1 g

Monounsaturated Fat 4 g

Cholesterol 70 mg

Sodium 142 mg

# PORK WITH SAVORY SAUCE

*Serves 4*

*The raspberry or balsamic vinegar gives this dish a dash of elegance.*

### SAUCE

¾ cup low-sodium chicken broth (see page 55 or use commercial variety)

¼ cup raspberry or balsamic vinegar (see Herbed or Fruit Vinegar, page 86, or use commercial variety)

2 tablespoons port

1 teaspoon olive oil

½ teaspoon coarsely ground pepper

½ teaspoon dried oregano, crumbled

1 clove garlic, minced, or ½ teaspoon bottled minced garlic

2 tablespoons cold water

1 teaspoon cornstarch

Vegetable oil spray

1 pound pork tenderloin, all visible fat removed, cut into ¼-inch medallions

In a small saucepan, combine broth, vinegar, wine, oil, pepper, oregano, and garlic. Cook, uncovered, over medium-high heat for about 20 minutes, or until liquid is reduced to ½ cup.

Pour water into a cup or small bowl. Add cornstarch and stir to dissolve.

Add cornstarch mixture to the sauce, stirring to mix well. Heat over medium heat, stirring until mixture thickens, about 1 minute. Cover, remove from heat, and set aside.

Spray a large nonstick skillet with vegetable oil spray and heat over medium-high heat. Add pork and sauté 3 to 4 minutes on each side, or until pork is no longer pink. Serve with sauce.

## NUTRIENT ANALYSIS

Calories 186
Protein 23 g
Carbohydrate 3 g
Total Fat 9 g
Saturated Fat 2 g
Polyunsaturated Fat 1 g
Monounsaturated Fat 5 g
Cholesterol 63 mg
Sodium 56 mg

# PORK AND TOFU STIR-FRY

*Serves 6*

**COOK'S TIP ON TOFU:**

Tofu is extremely versatile and you can use it creatively in many ways—in salads, dips, sandwiches, casseroles, burgers, and even desserts. Check the expiration date on tofu in aseptic containers or packaged in water in individual containers. Store tofu in a bowl of cold water in the refrigerator, changing water daily. (Tofu in aseptic packaging does not need to be refrigerated until opened.) Tofu keeps up to 1 week in the refrigerator and up to 2 months in the freezer (texture will be softer when thawed than before freezing).

*This recipe may look complicated because of the number of ingredients, but it isn't. If you marinate the pork and slice the vegetables in advance, you can put your meal together quickly. Once you taste the flavor of the sauce and marinade, you'll want to make this recipe often. For variety, substitute poultry or seafood for the pork, and switch vegetables to take advantage of seasonal specials at the supermarket.*

1 pound lean, boneless pork, all visible fat removed

### MARINADE

2 tablespoons minced fresh gingerroot or 1 teaspoon ground ginger

1 tablespoon low-sodium chicken broth (see page 55 or use commercial variety)

1 tablespoon dry sherry (optional)

1 tablespoon low-sodium soy sauce

2 cloves garlic, minced, or 1 teaspoon bottled minced garlic

### SAUCE

½ cup water

1 tablespoon Worcestershire sauce

1 tablespoon honey

1 tablespoon cornstarch

2 teaspoons low-sodium soy sauce

8 ounces reduced-fat firm tofu

1 teaspoon acceptable vegetable oil

### VEGETABLES

20 fresh snow peas, trimmed

1 cup thinly sliced red cabbage (3 to 4 ounces)

1 small green bell pepper, cut into 1-inch strips

1 small red or yellow bell pepper, cut into 1-inch strips

1 small onion, cut into wedges

6 green onions (green and white parts), sliced diagonally

2 celery stalks, sliced diagonally

1 teaspoon acceptable vegetable oil

10 to 12 cherry tomatoes, halved

Slice pork into 1-inch strips.

In a large bowl, combine all marinade ingredients. Add sliced pork and stir to coat. Set aside.

In a small bowl, combine all sauce ingredients. Stir to blend. Set aside.

Pour liquid from tofu. Drain. Place tofu on a double layer of paper towels. Pat dry. Cut into ½-inch cubes.

In a large nonstick skillet or wok, heat 1 teaspoon of the oil over high heat. Add vegetables and stir-fry for 2 minutes. Remove vegetables from pan. Set aside.

Using the same skillet, heat 1 teaspoon of oil and stir-fry tofu for 1 to 2 minutes, or until light golden-brown. Remove and set aside with vegetables.

Add pork and marinade. Stir-fry until meat loses its pink color.

Stir in tomatoes and reserved sauce. Cook until sauce starts to bubble and thicken.

Add reserved vegetables and heat thoroughly, 1 to 2 minutes.

# PORK WITH CORN-CILANTRO PESTO

*Serves 4*

The delicious pesto inside the pork pinwheels is the Southwest's rendition of an Italian favorite. The recipe makes more pesto than you need for the pork, so try some with pasta or spaghetti squash strands, or stir a dollop into vegetable soup for a fresh flavor boost.

Vegetable oil spray

¼ cup Corn-Cilantro Pesto (recipe follows)

1 pound pork tenderloin, all visible fat removed

1 cup Tomato Sauce (recipe follows)

### CORN-CILANTRO PESTO (ABOUT ¾ CUP)

1 cup firmly packed cilantro leaves

¼ cup firmly packed parsley leaves

¼ cup grated or shredded Parmesan or Romano cheese (about 1 ounce)

⅓ cup canned no-salt-added whole kernel corn, drained (about 3 ounces)

2 tablespoons chopped pecans, preferably dry-roasted

1 tablespoon chopped shallot

1 tablespoon fresh lime juice

2 cloves garlic, quartered

¼ teaspoon salt

4 teaspoons olive oil

Fresh lime juice or water (optional)

### TOMATO SAUCE (ABOUT 1 CUP)

Vegetable oil spray

½ cup chopped onion (about 1 medium)

1 clove garlic, minced, or 2 teaspoons bottled minced garlic

8-ounce can no-salt-added tomato sauce

¼ teaspoon sugar

**COOK'S TIP:**

Tenderloin usually comes packaged in 2 pieces. Wrap the unused piece and refrigerate or freeze for another recipe.

Refrigerate leftover pesto in a small airtight container for up to 1 week or freeze for up to 1 month.

**NUTRIENT ANALYSIS**

Calories 211
Protein 28 g
Carbohydrate 8 g
Total Fat 7 g
Saturated Fat 2 g
Polyunsaturated Fat 1 g
Monounsaturated Fat 4 g
Cholesterol 73 mg
Sodium 295 mg

¼ teaspoon salt

⅛ teaspoon pepper

Using vegetable oil spray, spray a broiler pan with rack or a wire rack and a shallow roasting pan.

Prepare pesto in a blender or food processor. Process cilantro, parsley, Parmesan, corn, pecans, shallot, 1 tablespoon lime juice, garlic, and salt until well combined, stopping and scraping sides occasionally.

With machine running, gradually add oil. Process until well combined. If the pesto is thicker than you like, add a teaspoon or so of lime juice.

Preheat oven to 425° F.

Butterfly the tenderloin by cutting it lengthwise almost in half. Lay out flat. Cover meat with plastic wrap. Use the flat side of a meat mallet to pound meat to a ¼-inch thickness.

Spread ¼ cup of pesto over cut surface of tenderloin. Roll up tenderloin from one of the short ends and tie in several places with string to secure. (Can be wrapped in plastic wrap at this point and stored in the refrigerator for 4 to 6 hours before cooking.)

Place tenderloin on prepared rack in broiler pan. Roast, uncovered, for 20 minutes, then turn tenderloin over and roast 10 to 20 minutes, or until a meat thermometer registers 160° F. Remove from oven and let stand 5 minutes.

Meanwhile, prepare Tomato Sauce. Spray a medium saucepan with vegetable oil spray. Add onion and garlic and cook over medium-low heat for about 5 minutes, or until tender.

Stir in remaining sauce ingredients. Bring to a boil over high heat. Reduce heat and simmer, uncovered, for 5 minutes, or until desired consistency.

Cut pork into medallions and serve with sauce.

# VEGETARIAN DISHES

Grilled Portobello Mushrooms
with Couscous and Greens

Pasta Primavera

Whole-Wheat Pasta
with Vegetarian Sauce

Penne and Cannellini Bean
Casserole with Sun-Dried
Tomatoes

Spinach-Stuffed Pizza

Soba Lo Mein with Bok Choy
and Sugar Snap Peas

Spicy Lentil Curry

Cranberry Bean and
Barley Stew with Sage

Quinoa in Vegetable Nests

Spinach and Black Bean
Enchiladas

Grilled Vegetable Quesadillas

Eggplant Parmigiana

Soybean Sauté

# GRILLED PORTOBELLO MUSHROOMS WITH COUSCOUS AND GREENS

*Serves 4*

*The grand size and meaty texture of the portobello mushroom make it a perfect base for fluffy couscous and vibrant greens. This is an eye-catching recipe that you can really sink your teeth into!*

4 whole portobello mushrooms

4 tablespoons balsamic vinegar

Vegetable oil spray

½ cup low-sodium vegetable broth (see page 57 or use commercial variety)

½ cup water

¼ teaspoon turmeric

⅔ cup couscous

¼ cup dried cranberries

½ teaspoon grated lemon rind

¼ teaspoon salt

1 teaspoon olive oil

2 cloves garlic

6 ounces fresh collard greens or kale or 8 ounces fresh spinach, chopped (about 4 cups)

2 tablespoons water

1 tablespoon light margarine

½ red bell pepper, finely chopped

In the top of each mushroom, cut 4 slits, each 2 to 3 inches long and about ½ inch deep. Remove stems. Place mushrooms, top side up, in a shallow casserole dish.

Sprinkle mushrooms with half the balsamic vinegar. Lightly spray top side of mushrooms with vegetable oil spray. Turn mushrooms over and sprinkle with remaining vinegar. Lightly spray bottom side with vegetable oil spray. Cover container with plastic wrap and set aside. (Will keep in refrigerator for up to 1 hour.)

Combine vegetable broth, water, and turmeric in a medium saucepan. Bring to a boil over high heat, 2 to 3 minutes.

Stir in the couscous, cranberries, lemon rind, and salt. Remove pan from heat and let stand, covered, for at least 5 minutes, or until time to serve.

Meanwhile, heat a medium saucepan over medium heat. Add oil and swirl to coat bottom of pan. When oil is hot, add garlic. Cook for 1 minute.

Add the collard greens and 2 tablespoons water. Cook, covered, for 2 to 3 minutes, or until greens are tender.

Add the margarine and stir until it melts, about 30 seconds. Remove pan from heat and cover to help retain heat.

Grill mushrooms over medium-hot coals (or medium-high heat if using gas, electric, propane, or stove-top grill) for 2 to 3 minutes on each side.

Place mushrooms stem side up on serving plates. Spoon couscous on top of each mushroom. Spoon greens on top of couscous. Sprinkle with bell pepper. Serve warm.

# PASTA PRIMAVERA

*Serves 4*

*You can make the sauce for this recipe as much as a day ahead and prepare the vegetables a few hours before meal-time. For full flavor, always use freshly grated Parmesan cheese.*

Water

3 cups broccoli florets, cut into bite-size pieces (about 6 ounces)

8 ounces fresh mushrooms, quartered

2 small zucchini, sliced into ¼-inch rounds

1 teaspoon olive oil

3 cloves garlic, minced, or 1½ teaspoons bottled minced garlic

1 pint cherry tomatoes, stemmed, cut in half

8 ounces dried no-yolk pasta

### SAUCE

¾ cup fat-free milk

⅔ cup nonfat or low-fat ricotta cheese

¼ cup grated or shredded Parmesan cheese (about 1 ounce)

2 tablespoons chopped fresh basil or 2 teaspoons dried, crumbled

2 teaspoons dry sherry (optional)

### TOPPING

2 tablespoons grated or shredded Parmesan cheese

Freshly ground pepper to taste

In a large saucepan, pour enough water to come slightly below bottom of steamer basket. Bring water to a boil. Place steamer in saucepan, being sure boiling water does not touch steamer. Layer broccoli, then mushrooms, then zucchini in steamer. Steam, tightly covered, for about 3 minutes, or until just tender-crisp. Set aside.

Heat a large nonstick skillet or nonstick wok over medium-high heat. Add oil and swirl to coat bottom of skillet. When oil is hot, add garlic. Sauté for 1 minute, stirring frequently.

Add tomatoes and sauté for 2 minutes, stirring frequently, until tomatoes are slightly cooked but not wilted. Set aside.

Cook pasta according to package directions, omitting salt and oil. Drain well.

In a blender or food processor, combine sauce ingredients. Process until smooth.

Pour sauce into a small saucepan and heat over low heat, stirring occasionally, until warm, 2 to 3 minutes.

In a large serving dish, stir pasta, vegetables, and sauce to coat well. Top with 2 tablespoons Parmesan and pepper.

# WHOLE-WHEAT PASTA WITH VEGETARIAN SAUCE

*Serves 6*

*Whole-wheat pasta gives this dish a wonderful, nutty flavor. You can make the sauce in advance and reheat it at serving time for extra flavor.*

### SAUCE

Vegetable oil spray

1 teaspoon olive oil

6 green onions (green and white parts), chopped

1 large red or white onion, chopped

4 cloves garlic, minced, or 2 teaspoons bottled minced garlic

16-ounce can low-sodium kidney beans or vegetarian beans

16-ounce can no-salt-added tomatoes

8 ounces fresh mushrooms, sliced

2 medium red, green, or yellow bell peppers, or any combination, chopped

2 celery stalks with leaves, chopped

1 cup water

½ cup dry red wine or nonalcoholic red wine (optional)

¼ cup minced fresh parsley

1 tablespoon chopped fresh oregano or 1 teaspoon dried, crumbled

1 tablespoon chopped fresh basil or ½ teaspoon dried, crumbled

1 bay leaf

Freshly ground pepper to taste

12 ounces dried whole-wheat pasta

4 ounces shredded nonfat or part-skim mozzarella cheese (about 1 cup)

### NUTRIENT ANALYSIS

Calories 336
Protein 21 g
Carbohydrate 62 g
Total Fat 2 g
Saturated Fat 0 g
Polyunsaturated Fat 1 g
Monounsaturated Fat 1 g
Cholesterol 0 mg
Sodium 164 mg

For sauce, spray a large saucepan or Dutch oven with vegetable oil spray. Heat over medium-high heat. Add oil and swirl to coat bottom of pan. When oil is heated, add onions and garlic. Sauté until onions are soft, 2 to 3 minutes.

Add remaining sauce ingredients and bring to a boil over high heat. Reduce heat and simmer, covered, for about 1 hour, stirring frequently. Remove bay leaf.

Meanwhile, cook pasta according to package directions, omitting salt and oil. Drain.

Serve sauce over hot pasta. Sprinkle with mozzarella.

# PENNE AND CANNELLINI BEAN CASSEROLE WITH SUN-DRIED TOMATOES

*Serves 8*

*Penne pasta (tube-shaped pasta cut diagonally) and vegetables team up with creamy cannellini beans (white kidney beans) for a winning casserole combination that could grace your table tonight!*

8 ounces dried penne pasta

8 sun-dried tomatoes (not packed in oil) (about 1 ounce)

Vegetable oil spray

1 tablespoon low-sodium vegetable broth (see page 57 or use commercial variety)

2 shallots, finely chopped

4 ounces asparagus, sliced diagonally into ½-inch pieces (about 1 cup)

½ red bell pepper, diced

1 teaspoon dried oregano, crumbled

⅛ teaspoon pepper

15-ounce can cannellini beans, drained and rinsed

½ cup low-sodium vegetable broth (see page 57 or use commercial variety)

¼ cup fat-free milk

4 ounces shredded part-skim mozzarella cheese (about 1 cup)

1 tablespoon light margarine, cut into small pieces

Cook pasta according to package directions, omitting salt and oil. Remove pasta with a large slotted spoon and set aside in a medium bowl.

Add tomatoes to the pasta cooking water, turn off heat, and let tomatoes soak for 15 to 20 minutes.

About halfway through soaking time, preheat oven to 350° F. Spray a 2½-quart shallow casserole dish with vegetable oil spray. Set aside.

Heat a nonstick skillet over medium heat. Add 1 tablespoon vegetable broth and shallots and cook for 1 minute.

Stir in asparagus, bell pepper, oregano, and pepper. Cook, stirring occasionally, for 1 to 2 minutes, or until vegetables are tender-crisp. Turn off heat.

Remove tomatoes from soaking liquid, squeeze out excess liquid, and dice tomatoes. Add them to the vegetables in skillet and stir to combine.

Layer half the cannellini beans, half the pasta, and half the vegetables in prepared casserole dish. Repeat the layers.

Pour the ½ cup vegetable broth and milk over all. Sprinkle evenly with cheese. Arrange margarine pieces over all.

Lightly cover casserole dish with foil. Bake for 20 minutes; uncover and bake for 5 minutes.

# SPINACH-STUFFED PIZZA

*Serves 6*

*The fresh spinach gives this pizza a delightful taste. Don't expect leftovers!*

## DOUGH

¾ cup very warm water (105° to 115° F)

1 teaspoon sugar

1 package rapid-rise yeast (¼ ounce)

1½ cups whole-wheat flour

¾ cup all-purpose flour

All-purpose flour

Vegetable oil spray

## FILLING

6 ounces fresh spinach (about 3 cups)

1½ cups shredded nonfat or part-skim mozzarella cheese (about 6 ounces)

⅓ cup grated or shredded Parmesan cheese (about 1 ounce)

## TOPPING

1 teaspoon olive oil

4 ounces fresh mushrooms, thinly sliced

1 cup no-salt-added meatless spaghetti sauce

To make the dough, combine water and sugar.

Add yeast and stir to dissolve. Let sit about 5 minutes. The yeast will bubble and develop a frothy head.

In a large bowl, mix the whole-wheat flour and ¾ cup all-purpose flour. Make a well in the center. While stirring, slowly add the yeast mixture.

Knead the dough for 6 to 8 minutes, or until a ball of smooth but elastic dough forms. If dough is sticky, gradually add a little more all-purpose flour while kneading. Lightly dust the ball of dough with all-purpose flour, put back into the bowl, and cover bowl loosely with a tea towel. Set in a warm, draft-free place and allow to rise until doubled in bulk, about 30 minutes.

Meanwhile, to prepare the filling, thoroughly rinse, stem, dry, and chop the spinach. Place in a large bowl.

Stir cheeses into spinach and set aside.

Preheat oven to 475° F.

Punch dough, then divide it into two balls. Keep one in the bowl, covered loosely with a tea towel, and place the other on a lightly floured surface. Using a lightly floured rolling pin, roll the ball into an 11-inch circle.

Spray the bottom and sides of a 9-inch glass pie pan with vegetable oil spray. Place the rolled dough in the pan so that it covers the bottom and sides. With a fork, prick the dough at about 1-inch intervals on the bottom.

Bake crust for 4 minutes, remove to a rack, and let cool.

Spread filling over the crust.

Roll the second dough ball into an 11-inch circle, place over the filling, and tuck edges of the dough around the bottom crust layer. Compress the filling by applying light pressure on the dough with the palms of your hands. Cut a 1-inch slit in the center of the top crust.

To make the topping, heat a small nonstick skillet over medium-high heat. Add oil and heat. Add mushrooms and sauté, stirring occasionally, for 3 to 4 minutes, or until soft.

Evenly spread the mushrooms over the crust and top with spaghetti sauce.

Place on middle rack of oven, reduce temperature to 450° F, and bake for 15 minutes. Reduce temperature to 400° F and bake for 5 to 10 minutes, or until edges are deep golden-brown.

# SOBA LO MEIN WITH BOK CHOY AND SUGAR SNAP PEAS

*Serves 4*

*The secret to success is to not overcook the noodles.*

**COOK'S TIP ON BOK CHOY:**

Both the crunchy white stems and the leafy green part of bok choy are edible. Cook the stems or eat them raw like celery. Cook the delicate leafy green parts as you would spinach. Both stems and greens are good stir-fried or added to soups (the greens cook quickly, so add them near the end of cooking time). Tofu, bok choy, and broth are a great combination in either soup or a stir-fry.

8 cups water

SAUCE

¼ cup low-sodium vegetable broth (see page 57 or use commercial variety)

2 tablespoons hoisin sauce

1 tablespoon reduced-sodium soy sauce

1 teaspoon sugar (optional)

4 ounces soba noodles

1 teaspoon acceptable vegetable oil

2 cloves garlic, minced, or 1 teaspoon bottled minced garlic

2 carrots, thinly sliced

4 ounces sugar snap peas, ends trimmed (about 1 cup)

2 stalks bok choy, stems and leaves thinly sliced

½ medium onion, thinly sliced

In a large saucepan, bring water to a boil over high heat.

While water heats, mix sauce ingredients in a small bowl. Set aside.

Add noodles to boiling water, reduce heat to medium-high, and cook, stirring occasionally, for 2 to 3 minutes, or until tender. Drain; set noodles aside.

Heat a wok or large skillet over medium-high heat. Add oil and garlic and cook for 15 seconds.

Add carrot and peas and stir-fry for 1 minute.

Add bok choy and onion and stir-fry for 1 to 2 minutes, or until vegetables are tender-crisp.

Add the sauce and noodles and stir-fry for 1 minute, or until mixture is warmed through.

**NUTRIENT ANALYSIS**

| | |
|---|---|
| Calories | 194 |
| Protein | 8 g |
| Carbohydrate | 38 g |
| Total Fat | 2 g |
| Saturated Fat | 0 g |
| Polyunsaturated Fat | 1 g |
| Monounsaturated Fat | 0 g |
| Cholesterol | 0 mg |
| Sodium | 202 mg |

# SPICY LENTIL CURRY

*Serves 6*

*Try this curry over rice with a dollop of nonfat or low-fat yogurt. One delicious way to use leftovers is in pita pockets.*

1½ cups dried lentils, rinsed and drained (about 8 ounces)

6 cups water

1 teaspoon cumin seeds or ground cumin

1 teaspoon acceptable vegetable oil

1 large onion, chopped

1 medium tomato, chopped

1 red hot chili pepper (optional)*

1 tablespoon grated fresh gingerroot or 1 teaspoon powdered ginger

1 clove garlic, minced, or ½ teaspoon bottled minced garlic

½ teaspoon ground turmeric

½ teaspoon salt

2 tablespoons chopped fresh cilantro or parsley

In a heavy saucepan, bring lentils and water to a boil over medium-high heat. Reduce heat and simmer, partially covered, occasionally skimming off the foam and stirring, for 45 to 50 minutes, or until lentils are tender.

Meanwhile, heat a nonstick skillet over medium-high heat. Sauté cumin seeds for about 1 minute, being careful not to burn them. Add oil and onion and cook until onion is light brown, 4 to 5 minutes.

Add tomato and hot pepper and continue to cook, stirring frequently, until tomato is reduced to a pulp, about 5 minutes. Remove hot pepper.

When lentils are tender, stir in all ingredients except cilantro. Cook for 10 to 15 minutes. Garnish with cilantro.

* Hot chili peppers contain oils that can burn your skin, lips, and eyes. Wear rubber gloves or wash your hands thoroughly with warm, soapy water immediately after handling peppers.

| NUTRIENT ANALYSIS | |
| --- | --- |
| Calories | 186 |
| Protein | 13 g |
| Carbohydrate | 32 g |
| Total Fat | 2 g |
| Saturated Fat | 0 g |
| Polyunsaturated Fat | 1 g |
| Monounsaturated Fat | 0 g |
| Cholesterol | 0 mg |
| Sodium | 185 mg |

# CRANBERRY BEAN AND BARLEY STEW WITH SAGE

*Serves 8*

**COOK'S TIP ON CRANBERRY BEANS:**

Dried cranberry beans, also known as shell beans and Romano beans, are creamy or pinkish beige and streaked with crimson. You can substitute them when a recipe calls for kidney beans.

*The sweet potato imparts a subtly different taste to this stew while sneaking in vitamin A and vitamin C.*

1 cup dried cranberry beans (6 ounces)

Water

6 cups cold water

½ cup pearl barley

2 cups low-sodium vegetable broth (see page 57 or use commercial variety)

1 medium sweet potato, peeled and diced

2 celery stalks, diced

2 parsnips, peeled and cut into ½-inch slices

1 medium onion, diced

½ teaspoon salt

⅛ teaspoon pepper

1 tablespoon chopped fresh sage leaves (about 10 leaves), or 1 teaspoon dried

Sort through beans, removing any shriveled beans or stones. Place beans in a large bowl and fill with cold water to cover beans by 2 inches. Let soak, covered, for 4 to 8 hours. Drain and rinse beans, discarding soaking liquid. (You may simmer beans for 5 minutes in enough water to cover them by 2 inches, then remove them from heat and let stand, covered, for 1 hour. Drain and rinse beans and continue with the recipe.)

In a large pot, combine beans and 6 cups cold water. Bring to a boil over high heat. Reduce heat and simmer, partially covered, stirring occasionally, for 1½ hours.

**NUTRIENT ANALYSIS**

Calories 169
Protein 7 g
Carbohydrate 36 g
Total Fat 1 g
Saturated Fat 0 g
Polyunsaturated Fat 0 g
Monounsaturated Fat 0 g
Cholesterol 0 mg
Sodium 223 mg

Add barley and cook, partially covered, stirring occasionally, for 1 hour.

Add the remaining ingredients except fresh sage (dried sage goes in at this point) and cook, partially covered, stirring occasionally, for 30 minutes. Add fresh sage and cook for 5 minutes.

# QUINOA IN VEGETABLE NESTS

*Serves 4*

**COOK'S TIP:**

You can prepare this recipe up to 4 days in advance, keeping vegetable-sprout mixture and quinoa mixture separate. Warm both mixtures, combine as described and garnish with green onions.

**COOK'S TIP ON ALFALFA SPROUTS:**

Looking for some easy ways to use leftover sprouts? Add them to salads or sandwiches, use them as a delicate garnish for creamy or broth-type vegetable soups, or make a bed for grilled vegetables. Use them quickly, though—alfalfa sprouts stay fresh for only about 2 days.

*Quinoa (keen'-wah) cooks quickly and is very nutritious— although a grain, it's a complete protein. Rinsing before cooking is important to remove the coating, which can impart a bitter flavor. If you don't find quinoa at your supermarket, try health food stores.*

¾ cup quinoa

1½ cups water

2 carrots, cut into very thin strips

½ yellow bell pepper, cut into very thin strips

1 cup thinly sliced red cabbage (3 to 4 ounces)

1 cup bean sprouts (about 2 ounces)

1 cup alfalfa sprouts (about 2 ounces)

2 teaspoons lime juice

2 teaspoons rice vinegar

2 teaspoons reduced-sodium soy sauce

1 clove garlic, minced, or ½ teaspoon bottled minced garlic

⅛ teaspoon pepper

2 green onions (green and white parts), cut into very thin strips

Rinse quinoa in a fine strainer under cold running water for 1 to 2 minutes. Shake off excess water.

Toast quinoa in a dry saucepan for about 5 minutes over medium heat, stirring occasionally.

Add 1½ cups water to quinoa and bring to a boil over high heat. Reduce heat to low and cook, covered, for 15 minutes.

Remove from heat and let stand, covered, for 5 minutes. Refrigerate, covered, for at least 30 minutes.

Meanwhile, in a medium bowl, combine carrots, bell pepper, cabbage, bean sprouts, and alfalfa sprouts. Set aside.

**NUTRIENT ANALYSIS**

Calories 171
Protein 8 g
Carbohydrate 31 g
Total Fat 3 g
Saturated Fat 0 g
Polyunsaturated Fat 2 g
Monounsaturated Fat 1 g
Cholesterol 0 mg
Sodium 128 mg

In a large bowl, combine lime juice, rice vinegar, soy sauce, garlic, pepper, and cooled quinoa.

For each serving, place one fourth of the vegetable mixture in a shallow bowl. Make an indentation in the middle of the vegetables and place one fourth of the quinoa mixture in the "nest." Garnish with green onions.

# SPINACH AND BLACK BEAN ENCHILADAS

*Serves 6*

**COOK'S TIP:**

This dish freezes so well that you might want to make a batch to keep on hand for unexpected guests or evenings when you just don't want to cook. After rolling the enchiladas, place them in a container and cover tightly with foil or put them in an airtight plastic freezer bag. Increase baking time to 35 to 40 minutes.

You can substitute a 10-ounce package of no-salt-added frozen spinach for the fresh spinach. Cook according to package directions, omitting salt and oil, then continue with the recipe.

**NUTRIENT ANALYSIS**

| | |
|---|---|
| Calories | 201 |
| Protein | 17 g |
| Carbohydrate | 34 g |
| Total Fat | 1 g |
| Saturated Fat | 0 g |
| Polyunsaturated Fat | 1 g |
| Monounsaturated Fat | 0 g |
| Cholesterol | 3 mg |
| Sodium | 374 mg |

*Dress up these hearty enchiladas with a side of seasoned rice or corn on the cob and sliced watermelon or other seasonal fruit.*

Several quarts of water

8 cups fresh spinach leaves, stemmed (1 pound)

Vegetable oil spray, if needed

15-ounce can black beans, drained and rinsed

½ cup low-sodium salsa (see page 242 or use commercial variety)

¼ teaspoon ground cumin

¼ teaspoon chili powder

6 6-inch corn tortillas or nonfat or low-fat flour tortillas*

½ cup nonfat or low-fat sour cream

1½ to 2 teaspoons fresh lime juice

4 ounces shredded nonfat or low-fat Monterey Jack cheese (about 1 cup)

2 Italian plum tomatoes, diced

2 green onions (green and white parts), thinly sliced

In a large pot, bring water to a boil over high heat.

While water heats, thoroughly rinse spinach. Add spinach to boiling water and cook for 1 minute. Remove with a slotted spoon and drain well in a colander. Press out as much liquid as possible with the back of a large spoon. (Discard water or save for vegetable stock.)

Preheat oven to 350° F. If using a casserole dish, spray it with vegetable oil spray and set aside.

In a medium bowl, combine spinach, black beans, salsa, cumin, and chili powder.

Spoon one sixth of the mixture down the middle of one tortilla. Roll the tortilla around the filling (jelly-roll style). Place tortilla seam side down in a shallow non-stick baking pan or prepared casserole dish. Repeat process with remaining tortillas.

Bake enchiladas, uncovered, for 15 minutes.

Meanwhile, combine sour cream and lime juice. Remove enchiladas from oven and spread sour cream mixture evenly over enchiladas. Top with cheese, tomatoes, and green onions and bake for 5 minutes.

* Nonfat and low-fat flour tortillas can be high in sodium. When shopping, select the one with the lowest sodium value or substitute corn tortillas.

# GRILLED VEGETABLE QUESADILLAS

*Serves 4*

*Quesadillas are the answer to the modern-day last-minute appetizer or lunch. Tortillas enclose various fillings, such as meat, vegetables, or cheese, then are lightly heated. Our version includes grilled vegetables—a great way to add healthful variety to your meals.*

Vegetable oil spray

1 ear of corn, shucked and desilked

1 red bell pepper, cut in half, seeds and ribs removed

1 medium yellow squash, ends trimmed, cut in half lengthwise

½ small onion

4 ounces shredded low-fat Monterey Jack cheese (about 1 cup)

1 Italian plum tomato, diced

2 teaspoons lime juice

¼ teaspoon chili powder

⅛ teaspoon pepper

Vegetable oil spray

4 6-inch corn tortillas

½ cup low-sodium salsa (see page 242 or use commercial variety)

½ cup nonfat or low-fat sour cream

Using vegetable oil spray, lightly spray all surface areas of corn, bell pepper, squash, and onion.

Over medium-hot coals (or medium-high heat if using gas, electric, propane, or stove-top grill), grill corn on all sides until done, about 2 minutes per side; bell pepper, squash, and onion should take 1 to 2 minutes. Place vegetables on a cutting board; let cool for about 10 minutes.

Dice bell pepper, squash, and onion and place in a medium bowl.

Using a sharp knife, slice corn kernels off cob. Stir corn, cheese, tomato, lime juice, chili powder, and pepper into vegetable mixture. Set aside.

Preheat a nonstick griddle or cast-iron skillet over medium heat. Using vegetable oil spray, lightly spray one side of a tortilla. Place tortilla, sprayed side down, on the griddle. Spread a heaping ⅓ cup of the vegetable-cheese mixture on half of the tortilla. Fold the other half of the tortilla over the filling. Cook for 1 to 2 minutes on each side, or until tortilla is golden-brown and cheese is melted. Remove and place on a cutting board. Repeat with remaining tortillas and filling.

To serve, cut quesadillas in half and place on a serving platter. Top each quesadilla with 1 tablespoon each of salsa and sour cream.

# EGGPLANT PARMIGIANA

*Serves 6*

*Broiling the eggplant instead of frying it is the key to reducing the fat in this recipe. To complete the meal, add a garden salad and Whole-Wheat French Bread (see page 250).*

### SAUCE

2 8-ounce cans no-salt-added tomato sauce

14-ounce can artichoke hearts, drained

6-ounce can no-salt-added tomato paste

1 tablespoon salt-free Italian herb seasoning

2 cloves garlic, finely minced, or 1 teaspoon bottled minced garlic

1 teaspoon olive oil

¼ teaspoon fennel seeds, crushed (optional)

⅛ teaspoon freshly ground pepper

Dash hot pepper sauce


1 eggplant, sliced into ⅜-inch-thick rounds (about 1 pound)

10 ounces firm reduced-fat tofu, drained

White of 1 large egg

1 cup shredded nonfat or part-skim mozzarella cheese (about 4 ounces)

1 tablespoon all-purpose flour

⅓ cup grated or shredded Parmesan cheese (about 1 ounce)

⅓ cup crumbs from French or sourdough bread

**NUTRIENT ANALYSIS**

Calories 157
Protein 15 g
Carbohydrate 23 g
Total Fat 2 g
Saturated Fat 0 g
Polyunsaturated Fat 1 g
Monounsaturated Fat 1 g
Cholesterol 0 mg
Sodium 345 mg

In a blender or food processor, blend sauce ingredients for about 30 seconds, or until no lumps remain. Set aside.

Preheat broiler.

Place eggplant slices on baking sheet; do not overlap. Broil 4 inches from heat, 3 to 4 minutes per side, being careful not to burn the eggplant. Remove eggplant from broiler; let eggplant cool.

Preheat oven to 350° F.

Pour liquid from tofu. Drain. Place tofu on a double layer of paper towels. Pat dry.

In a blender or food processor, process tofu and egg white until smooth. Set aside.

Mix mozzarella with flour to keep cheese from clumping.

In an 8 × 11½ × 2-inch ovenproof glass casserole dish, layer ingredients: one third of the sauce, one half of the eggplant slices, one third of the sauce, all the mozzarella, tofu-egg mixture, remaining eggplant slices, remaining sauce, Parmesan, and bread crumbs.

Bake, uncovered, for 35 minutes. Let sit for 5 minutes before serving.

# SOYBEAN SAUTÉ

*Serves 8*

**COOK'S TIP ON FRESH SOYBEANS:**
Fresh soybeans are sometimes available in Asian markets and specialty stores in late summer and early fall. Rinse fresh soybeans in cold water, combine them with vegetable broth or water, and bring to a boil over high heat. Reduce heat to medium-low and cook for 3 to 5 minutes. Drain.

*High in nutrition and mild in flavor, soybeans can be enhanced with aromatic vegetables and assertive spices. Serve this colorful dish warm or chilled. If you are pressed for time, substitute low-sodium canned pinto beans, Great Northern beans, or kidney beans.*

¾ cup dried soybeans (about 5 ounces)

Water

4 cups low-sodium vegetable broth (see page 57 or use commercial variety) or cold water

¼ medium head red cabbage (about 6 ounces)

2 medium yellow squash

1 red bell pepper

1 medium onion

4 cloves garlic

Vegetable oil spray

1 cup frozen no-salt-added whole kernel corn (5 to 6 ounces)

4-ounce can diced green chili peppers, drained

3 tablespoons fresh lemon juice

1 teaspoon coriander seeds, crushed in a mortar and pestle, or 1 teaspoon ground coriander

½ teaspoon salt

⅛ teaspoon black pepper

Sort through soybeans, removing any stones or shriveled beans. Place soybeans in a large bowl and fill with cold water to cover the soybeans by 4 inches. Cover and refrigerate for at least 8 hours. Drain; set beans aside.

Place beans in a large saucepan and add vegetable broth. Bring mixture to a boil over high heat. Reduce heat to low and cook, partially covered, for 2½ to 3 hours, or until soybeans are tender. Drain; set beans aside.

While beans are cooking, core and thinly slice red cabbage, dice squash, core and dice bell pepper, dice onion, and mince garlic (don't combine). Set aside.

Lightly spray a medium sauté pan with vegetable oil spray. Sauté the garlic over medium-low heat for 30 seconds.

Add the squash, bell pepper, onion, and corn. Cook, stirring occasionally, for 2 to 3 minutes, or until vegetables are tender-crisp.

Add soybeans and remaining ingredients except cabbage and cook for 1 to 2 minutes, or until mixture is warmed through.

Spoon mixture into serving bowls and garnish each with cabbage.

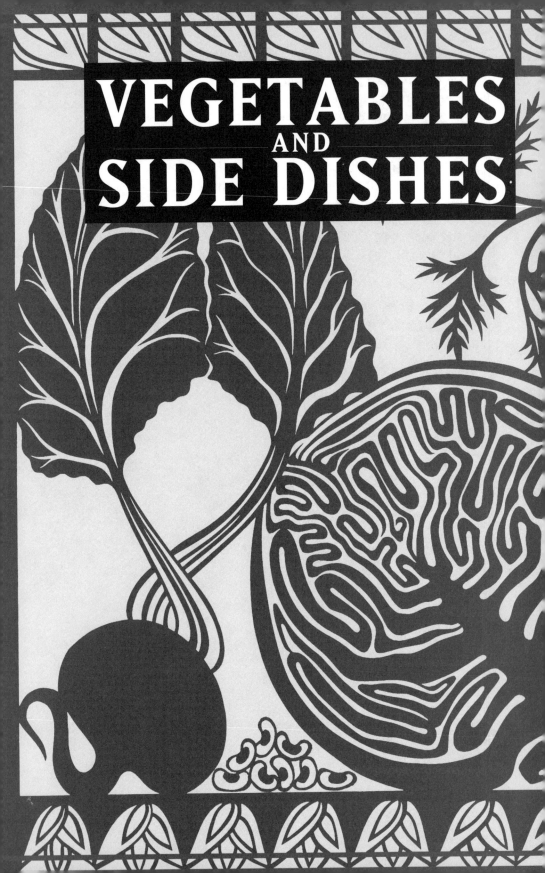

# VEGETABLES
## AND
# SIDE DISHES

Boston Baked Beans
with Chipotle Peppers

Green Beans Almondine

Refried Beans

Beets in Orange Sauce

Stir-Fried Broccoli

Braised Brussels Sprouts with
Pimiento and Water Chestnuts

Honey Carrots

Sautéed Carrots

Corn Bread Dressing

Sautéed Greens

Pan-Fried Pasta Pancake
with Vegetables

Southern-Style Black-Eyed Peas

Baked Potatoes with
Vegetable Topping

Twice-Baked Potatoes and Herbs

Herbed Baby Potatoes

Home-Fried Potatoes

Scalloped Potatoes

Steamed Red Potatoes with
Garlic Sauce

Red and Green Pilaf

Golden Rice

Spinach-Cheese Strudel

Praline Butternut Squash

Oven-Fried Green Tomatoes
with Poppy Seeds

Sautéed Cherry Tomatoes

Sautéed Zucchini

Ratatouille

Vegetable Stir-Fry

# BOSTON BAKED BEANS WITH CHIPOTLE PEPPERS

*Serves 10*

**COOK'S TIP ON CHIPOTLE PEPPERS:**

Look for chipotle peppers—dried, smoked jalapeño peppers—in your supermarket produce section or in Hispanic markets.

*Chipotle chili peppers make a great substitute for high-fat bacon or salt pork in this classic bean recipe.*

2 chipotle chili peppers, rinsed*

1 pound dried navy beans or Great Northern beans (about 2½ cups), rinsed and picked over for stones and shriveled beans

8 cups cold water

8 cups water

1 cup chopped onion (about 2 medium)

¼ cup firmly packed dark brown sugar

¼ cup molasses

¼ cup reduced-calorie maple-flavored syrup

2 tablespoons Worcestershire sauce

1 teaspoon dry mustard

½ teaspoon salt

¼ teaspoon pepper

Using a sharp knife, slit open chili peppers and remove seeds and stems. Place peppers in a Dutch oven.

Add beans and cold water to chili peppers. Bring to a boil over high heat. Reduce heat and simmer, uncovered, for 2 minutes. Remove from heat. Cover and let stand for 1 hour. (Or skip boiling the water and soak beans and chili peppers overnight in covered Dutch oven.) Drain and rinse beans and chili peppers, discarding liquid. Finely chop chili peppers.

Return beans and chili peppers to same pot. Add 8 cups fresh water and onion. Bring to a boil over high heat. Reduce heat and simmer, covered, stirring occasionally, for about 1¼ hours, or until tender. Drain bean mixture, reserving liquid.

Preheat oven to 300° F.

**NUTRIENT ANALYSIS**

Calories 214
Protein 9 g
Carbohydrate 44 g
Total Fat 1 g
Saturated Fat 0 g
Polyunsaturated Fat 0 g
Monounsaturated Fat 0 g
Cholesterol 0 mg
Sodium 151 mg

In same pot, combine drained bean mixture and remaining ingredients except bean liquid.

Stir in ½ cup of the reserved bean liquid.

Transfer to a 2-quart casserole dish. Bake, uncovered, for 1 hour. Stir beans. Bake, stirring occasionally, for 30 to 60 minutes, or until desired consistency. If mixture becomes dry, stir in additional reserved bean liquid.

* Hot chili peppers contain oils that can burn your skin, lips, and eyes. Wear rubber gloves or wash your hands thoroughly with warm, soapy water immediately after handling peppers.

# GREEN BEANS ALMONDINE

*Serves 6*

**COOK'S TIP ON FRESH GREEN BEANS:**

When green beans are in season, buy extra to freeze. Trim and slice beans. Blanch them in boiling water to cover by 1 inch for 1 minute. Remove them from the hot water and run them under cold water. Cool beans, then freeze them for up to 6 months. Thaw and use in this recipe as directed.

*Fresh green beans get a quick sauté, preserving their color and texture. Oregano adds flavor and almonds add crunch, making this an ideal side dish for roast turkey or grilled chicken or fish.*

1 pound fresh green beans (about 3 cups)

1 teaspoon light margarine

¼ cup low-sodium vegetable or chicken broth (see pages 57 and 55 or use commercial variety)

1 tablespoon chopped fresh oregano or 1 teaspoon dried, crumbled

Freshly ground pepper to taste

1 cup frozen pearl onions (about 4 ounces)

2 tablespoons sliced almonds

¼ cup seasoned bread crumbs

Trim green beans and slice into 2-inch sections.

In a large nonstick skillet, heat margarine over medium-high heat. Add green beans and sauté for 1 to 2 minutes, stirring constantly so beans cook evenly.

Add broth, oregano, and pepper; sauté for 20 to 30 seconds.

Add onions. Cook, covered, over medium-low heat for 6 to 8 minutes, or until beans are tender-crisp.

Meanwhile, in a small nonstick pan over medium heat, dry-roast almonds, stirring occasionally, for 2 to 3 minutes. Sprinkle bread crumbs and almonds over cooked beans.

**NUTRIENT ANALYSIS**

Calories 66

Protein 2 g

Carbohydrate 10 g

Total Fat 1 g

Saturated Fat 0 g

Polyunsaturated Fat 1 g

Monounsaturated Fat 1 g

Cholesterol 0 mg

Sodium 64 mg

# REFRIED BEANS

*Serves 5*

*Canned nonfat refried beans tend to be high in sodium. Make this simple version instead—it's low in fat, saturated fat, and sodium and has no cholesterol, but the seasonings make it high in taste.*

1 teaspoon acceptable vegetable oil

2 tablespoons finely chopped onion

2 cloves garlic, minced, or 1 teaspoon bottled minced garlic

2 15-ounce cans no-salt-added pinto beans

1 tablespoon low-sodium ketchup

2 tablespoons canned diced green chili peppers

In a large nonstick skillet, heat oil over medium heat. Add onion and sauté for about 5 minutes, or until soft.

Add garlic and sauté for 2 to 3 minutes. Set aside.

Drain beans well, reserving ½ cup liquid. Put beans in a shallow bowl and mash with a potato masher or fork. Add ketchup and reserved liquid and mash again.

Add bean mixture and chili peppers to the sautéed garlic and onion. Mix well.

Heat beans thoroughly over medium heat, stirring constantly.

**COOK'S TIP ON CANNED CHILI PEPPERS:**

Canned green chili peppers are a perfect flavor booster. They are mildly spicy, adding just enough zip to make a difference in your finished dish. Add them to soups, dips, spreads, yeast breads, and marinades.

**NUTRIENT ANALYSIS**

| | |
|---|---|
| Calories | 174 |
| Protein | 10 g |
| Carbohydrate | 31 g |
| Total Fat | 2 g |
| Saturated Fat | 0 g |
| Polyunsaturated Fat | 1 g |
| Monounsaturated Fat | 0 g |
| Cholesterol | 0 mg |
| Sodium | 43 mg |

# BEETS IN ORANGE SAUCE

*Serves 6*

*Fresh orange sauce adds zest and flair to brightly colored beets.*

2 pounds fresh beets

2 quarts water

Sᴀᴜᴄᴇ

1 tablespoon sugar

1 tablespoon cornstarch

¼ teaspoon salt (optional)

2 teaspoons grated orange rind, or to taste

⅔ cup fresh orange juice (2 to 3 medium oranges)

1 teaspoon light margarine

1 orange, peeled and divided into sections (optional)

Cut off all but about 1 to 2 inches of stems from beets. In a large saucepan, bring water to a boil over high heat. Add beets and reduce heat. Simmer, covered, for 40 to 50 minutes, or until tender. Drain beets. Let them cool slightly, then slip off the skins. Slice beets into wedges.

Meanwhile, to prepare sauce, combine sugar, cornstarch, and salt in a small saucepan.

Slowly add orange rind and orange juice, stirring until smooth. Cook over medium heat, stirring constantly, until thickened, 5 to 8 minutes.

Add margarine and stir until melted.

Pour sauce over warm beets and garnish with orange sections.

---

**COOK'S TIP ON BEETS:**

Leaving some stem on beets prevents the color from "bleeding." Rinse raw beets *gently* to keep from piercing the skin. After cooking fresh beets, cool them, then hold them under running water while slipping off the skins.

**COOK'S TIP:**

You can substitute 2 16- or 17-ounce cans of beets for the fresh beets. Heat them in a medium saucepan over medium heat until warmed through. Drain. Sauce and garnish as described in recipe.

---

**NUTRIENT ANALYSIS**

Calories 93
Protein 3 g
Carbohydrate 21 g
Total Fat 1 g
Saturated Fat 0 g
Polyunsaturated Fat 0 g
Monounsaturated Fat 0 g
Cholesterol 0 mg
Sodium 120 mg

# STIR-FRIED BROCCOLI

*Serves 6*

*This recipe features only the florets of the broccoli. Save the stems for use in soups, stir-fries, or side dishes.*

1½ pounds fresh broccoli

Vegetable oil spray

4 green onions (green and white parts), cut into 1-inch
    strips

1 tablespoon light margarine

1 teaspoon salt-free lemon-herb seasoning

Trim broccoli and break florets into bite-size pieces.

Spray a nonstick skillet with vegetable oil spray. Over medium-high heat, stir-fry broccoli and green onions for 2 to 3 minutes. Broccoli should be tender-crisp.

Add margarine, sprinkle with seasoning, and stir to coat evenly.

# BRAISED BRUSSELS SPROUTS WITH PIMIENTO AND WATER CHESTNUTS

*Serves 4*

*Try this quick and colorful side dish for an elegant touch with lean roast beef or pork.*

### COOK'S TIP ON BRUSSELS SPROUTS:

When sprouts have simmered for 1 to 2 minutes, remove the lid for 15 to 20 seconds, replace lid, and continue cooking as usual. This allows discharge of the sulfurous compounds that can give the sprouts a bitter flavor.

8 ounces fresh brussels sprouts (about 2 cups)

1 cup low-sodium chicken broth (see page 55 or use commercial variety)

2 ounces diced pimientos, drained (about ¼ cup)

¼ teaspoon salt

⅛ teaspoon pepper

2 tablespoons sliced water chestnuts

1 teaspoon light margarine

1 teaspoon all-purpose flour

1 tablespoon water

2 tablespoons sliced almonds, preferably dry-roasted

Remove any yellow outer leaves from brussels sprouts. With a small knife, trim a small amount from the bottom of the stem. Slice a shallow *X* into the stem (this will help the brussels sprouts cook evenly). Rinse sprouts in cool water.

In a medium saucepan over high heat, bring chicken broth, pimientos, salt, and pepper to a boil. Add the sprouts and cook, covered, on medium-low heat for 6 to 7 minutes, or until tender.

Remove sprouts, reserving liquid in the pan; keep sprouts warm. Reduce the liquid to ½ cup by cooking over high heat for about 5 minutes (without stirring).

Add the water chestnuts and margarine and cook over medium heat for 1 minute, stirring occasionally.

### NUTRIENT ANALYSIS

Calories 58
Protein 3 g
Carbohydrate 7 g
Total Fat 2 g
Saturated Fat 0 g
Polyunsaturated Fat 1 g
Monounsaturated Fat 1 g
Cholesterol 0 mg
Sodium 183 mg

Place the flour in a cup or small bowl and stir in 1 tablespoon water.

Add to the chicken broth mixture and cook, stirring occasionally, over medium heat for 1 to 2 minutes, or until sauce is thick. Pour over brussels sprouts and sprinkle with sliced almonds.

# HONEY CARROTS

*Serves 6*

*Carrots prepared this way will be a favorite—even among the young ones in your family.*

1½ pounds fresh or no-salt-added frozen baby carrots
½ cup water
1 tablespoon light margarine
2 tablespoons honey
½ tablespoon light brown sugar
2 to 3 tablespoons minced fresh parsley

Rinse and trim fresh carrots.

In a medium saucepan, bring water to a boil over high heat. Add carrots, reduce heat, and simmer, covered, for about 10 minutes, or until tender-crisp. (If using frozen carrots, follow package directions, omitting margarine and salt.) Drain.

In a large nonstick skillet, melt margarine over medium heat.

Add honey, sugar, and carrots. Reduce heat to medium-low and cook, stirring frequently, until carrots are well glazed, 1 to 2 minutes.

Sprinkle with parsley before serving.

**NUTRIENT ANALYSIS**

Calories 90
Protein 1 g
Carbohydrate 18 g
Total Fat 2 g
Saturated Fat 1 g
Polyunsaturated Fat 1 g
Monounsaturated Fat 1 g
Cholesterol 0 mg
Sodium 93 mg

# SAUTÉED CARROTS

*Serves 6*

*Tired of plain carrots? Try these for a distinctive change.*
*The apple and lemon juices make the difference.*

1 pound carrots, peeled and grated (about 4 cups)

2 tablespoons frozen unsweetened apple juice
　　concentrate, thawed

1 tablespoon fresh lemon juice

1 teaspoon light margarine

1 teaspoon poppy seeds

In a nonstick skillet, combine carrots, apple juice, and lemon juice. Place over medium-high heat and sauté, stirring constantly, for about 3 minutes.

Add margarine and stir to coat evenly.

Sprinkle with poppy seeds.

**NUTRIENT ANALYSIS**

Calories 47
Protein 1 g
Carbohydrate 10 g
Total Fat 1 g
Saturated Fat 0 g
Polyunsaturated Fat 0 g
Monounsaturated Fat 0 g
Cholesterol 0 mg
Sodium 55 mg

# CORN BREAD DRESSING

*Serves 10*

**COOK'S TIP ON DEFATTING BROTH:**

To defat homemade or canned broth, refrigerate it to allow the fat to harden. (Leave commercially prepared broth in the unopened can.) Remove and discard the fat before using the broth.

*When it comes to dressing, everyone seems to have a traditional family recipe. Here's a winner with real southern flavor.*

¼ cup water

1½ cups chopped celery (about 4 stalks)

1 cup chopped onion (about 2 medium)

3 cups corn bread crumbs (about half the Southern-Style Corn Bread recipe, see page 257)

4 slices stale or toasted whole-grain bread, cut into cubes

¼ cup chopped fresh parsley

1 teaspoon rubbed sage

1 teaspoon poultry seasoning

1½ cups low-sodium chicken broth (see page 55 or use commercial variety)

Whites of 2 large eggs, lightly beaten

Vegetable oil spray

1 tablespoon light margarine

Preheat oven to 350° F.

In a small saucepan over high heat, bring water to a boil. Add celery and onion and cook for 2 to 3 minutes, or until soft.

In a medium bowl, stir in corn bread crumbs, bread cubes, parsley, sage, and poultry seasoning, mixing well.

Add broth and egg whites and mix again.

Pour the celery, onion, and cooking liquid into the bowl and mix well.

Spray a 2-quart casserole dish with vegetable oil spray. Pour mixture into prepared dish and dot with margarine.

Bake, uncovered, for 30 minutes.

# SAUTÉED GREENS

*Serves 6*

*Cabbage and rice vinegar enhance the flavor of the collard greens in this simple dish.*

3 quarts water

1 bunch collard greens, kale, mustard greens, or spinach, stemmed and finely chopped (12 to 16 ounces)

⅓ medium head cabbage, coarsely shredded (2½ to 3 cups)

Nonfat olive oil spray

1 teaspoon olive oil

1 medium onion, cut into quarters and sliced

1 clove garlic, minced, or ½ teaspoon bottled minced garlic

1 to 2 teaspoons rice vinegar or white wine vinegar

In a large saucepan over high heat, bring water to a boil. Add collard greens, return to a boil, and cook for 3 to 4 minutes, or until greens are tender-crisp.

With a slotted spoon, remove greens, leaving the water in the pan. Place greens in a colander, rinse, let drain, and set aside.

Return water to a boil, add cabbage, and cook for 1 minute. Pour into the colander and let drain. Set aside.

Heat a large skillet over medium-low heat. Spray with olive oil spray. Add oil and swirl to coat bottom of skillet. When oil is hot, add onion and garlic. Sauté for 3 to 4 minutes, or until onion is tender-crisp.

Add greens and cabbage and sauté, stirring occasionally, for 2 to 3 minutes. Stir in vinegar.

**NUTRIENT ANALYSIS**

Calories 43
Protein 2 g
Carbohydrate 8 g
Total Fat 1 g
Saturated Fat 0 g
Polyunsaturated Fat 0 g
Monounsaturated Fat 1 g
Cholesterol 0 mg
Sodium 15 mg

# PAN-FRIED PASTA PANCAKE WITH VEGETABLES

*Serves 4*

*Try this for a tasty alternative to plain pasta. It's fun to make and reheats well.*

8 ounces dried pasta, such as linguine, vermicelli, or spaghetti (2 to 2½ cups)

1 medium carrot, shredded

2 green onions, thinly sliced

½ cup snow peas, cut into ½-inch pieces (about 2 ounces)

1 teaspoon fragrant toasted sesame oil

1 teaspoon acceptable vegetable oil

Egg substitute equivalent to 4 eggs

⅛ teaspoon black pepper

Cook pasta according to package directions, omitting oil and salt. Drain, place in large bowl, and refrigerate for at least 10 minutes.

Add carrot, green onions, snow peas, and sesame oil to pasta.

Heat a 10-inch nonstick omelet pan over medium heat. Add oil and heat for 30 seconds. Carefully spread the pasta mixture evenly in the pan; cook for 1 minute without stirring.

Combine the egg substitute and black pepper in a small bowl. Pour over the pasta, tilting the pan to distribute the egg evenly (do not stir).

Cook, covered, over low heat for 10 to 12 minutes, or until eggs are thoroughly cooked. If you wish to brown the other side, invert the pancake onto a plate, then slide it back into the pan to cook for 1 to 2 minutes.

**NUTRIENT ANALYSIS**

Calories 290
Protein 14 g
Carbohydrate 50 g
Total Fat 3 g
Saturated Fat 0 g
Polyunsaturated Fat 2 g
Monounsaturated Fat 1 g
Cholesterol 0 mg
Sodium 133 mg

# SOUTHERN-STYLE BLACK-EYED PEAS

*Serves 12 as a side dish*
*Serves 4 as an entrée*

*Black-eyed peas are rich in protein and contain a soluble fiber that may help lower blood cholesterol slightly. Seasoning the peas with lean ham instead of the traditional salt pork reduces the fat content.*

1 pound dried black-eyed peas

5 to 7 cups water

4 ounces smoke-flavored lean, low-sodium ham, all visible fat removed, diced

½ medium onion, diced

1 medium carrot, thinly sliced

1 serrano pepper, seeded and thinly sliced (optional)*

### SLOW COOKER DIRECTIONS

Place peas in a colander and rinse under cold running water. Using 5 cups of water, place all ingredients in slow cooker. Cook on low setting for 8 to 10 hours, or until peas are tender.

### STOVE-TOP DIRECTIONS

Rinse peas under cold running water. Using 7 cups of water, place all ingredients in a large saucepan or Dutch oven. Bring to a boil over high heat. Skim off any foam. Reduce heat to medium-low and simmer, covered, for 2 hours, or until peas are tender.

* Hot chili peppers contain oils that can burn your skin, lips, and eyes. Wear rubber gloves or wash your hands thoroughly with warm, soapy water immediately after handling peppers.

**NUTRIENT ANALYSIS**
*(For side dish)*

| | |
|---|---|
| Calories | 136 |
| Protein | 10 g |
| Carbohydrate | 23 g |
| Total Fat | 1 g |
| Saturated Fat | 0 g |
| Polyunsaturated Fat | 0 g |
| Monounsaturated Fat | 0 g |
| Cholesterol | 5 mg |
| Sodium | 87 mg |

# BAKED POTATOES WITH VEGETABLE TOPPING

*Serves 6*

**COOK'S TIP ON BAKING POTATOES:**

For light, fluffy potatoes with crisp skins, pierce the surface in a few places with a fork to help release steam. Wrap the potatoes in foil for a moist texture.

*If you enjoy a baked potato with salad, you'll love this recipe. It offers the best of both worlds: A twice-baked potato with a piping-hot, creamy filling is topped with crispy vegetables.*

6 medium baking potatoes

1 small onion, finely chopped

2 green onions (green and white parts), finely chopped

1 small carrot, shredded

¼ cup peeled, finely chopped cucumber

2 radishes, shredded

2 tablespoons cider vinegar

1 tablespoon chopped fresh basil or 1 teaspoon dried, crumbled

½ cup plain nonfat or low-fat yogurt

¼ cup grated Parmesan cheese (about 1 ounce)

¼ cup fat-free milk

1 teaspoon light margarine

Freshly ground pepper to taste

Preheat oven to 425° F.

Scrub potatoes with a brush. Pat dry. Prick in several places. Bake on a baking sheet for 40 to 60 minutes, or until tender. Lower heat to 350° F.

Meanwhile, combine onion, green onions, carrot, cucumber, radishes, vinegar, and basil. Mix well; set aside.

Cut a 1-inch slice from the top of each potato. Using a spoon, carefully scoop out the pulp from each potato, leaving a thin shell.

With an electric mixer on low speed or a potato masher, beat or mash potato pulp with yogurt, Parmesan, milk, margarine, and pepper until smooth.

**NUTRIENT ANALYSIS**

Calories 178
Protein 6 g
Carbohydrate 36 g
Total Fat 2 g
Saturated Fat 1 g
Polyunsaturated Fat 0 g
Monounsaturated Fat 0 g
Cholesterol 3 mg
Sodium 105 mg

Stuff potato mixture into shells. Place on baking sheet and bake for 25 to 30 minutes. Serve hot, topped with vegetable mixture.

## MICROWAVE DIRECTIONS

On a microwave-safe plate, arrange prepared potatoes in spoke fashion. Cook, uncovered, on 100 percent power (high) for 18 to 22 minutes, or until tender, rearranging and turning potatoes over once. Remove potatoes from microwave and wrap in foil. Let stand for 5 to 10 minutes. Continue as directed in recipe (bake stuffed potatoes in conventional oven for best results).

# TWICE-BAKED POTATOES AND HERBS

*Serves 4*

*Idaho license plates read "Famous Potatoes" and for good reason. That state produces about one third of the U.S. potato crop. Most Idaho potatoes are russets, your best choice for this dish.*

4 medium baking potatoes

⅓ cup nonfat or low-fat sour cream or nonfat or low-fat plain yogurt

2 tablespoons chopped fresh herbs (basil, chives, thyme, marjoram, oregano, parsley, etc.), any combination

2 tablespoons grated or shredded Parmesan cheese (about ½ ounce)

Fat-free milk (optional)

¼ cup shredded nonfat or part-skim mozzarella cheese (about ½ ounce)

Preheat oven to 425° F.

Scrub potatoes with a brush. Pat dry. Prick in several places. Bake on a baking sheet for 40 to 60 minutes, or until tender.

Cut a 1-inch slice from the top of each potato. Discard skin from slice and place pulp in a bowl. Using a spoon, carefully scoop the pulp from each potato, leaving a thin shell. Add pulp to the bowl.

With an electric mixer on low speed or a potato masher, beat or mash potato pulp. Add sour cream, herbs, and Parmesan. Beat or mash until smooth. If necessary, stir in 1 to 2 tablespoons milk to make desired consistency.

Stuff potato mixture into shells. Sprinkle 1 tablespoon mozzarella on each potato. Place in a shallow baking dish and bake for 15 to 20 minutes, or until lightly browned.

**NUTRIENT ANALYSIS**

Calories 172
Protein 8 g
Carbohydrate 33 g
Total Fat 1 g
Saturated Fat 1 g
Polyunsaturated Fat 0 g
Monounsaturated Fat 0 g
Cholesterol 3 mg
Sodium 133 mg

On a microwave-safe plate, arrange prepared potatoes in spoke fashion. Cook, uncovered, on 100 percent power (high) for 11 to 15 minutes, or until tender, rearranging and turning potatoes over once. Remove potatoes from microwave and wrap in foil. Let stand for 5 to 10 minutes. Continue as directed in recipe (bake stuffed potatoes in conventional oven for best results).

# HERBED BABY POTATOES

*Take simple kitchen staples, add to red potatoes, and you have a tasty side dish that goes well with almost any main course.*

1½ pounds unpeeled small red potatoes, quartered

2 tablespoons light margarine, melted

Vegetable oil spray, preferably olive oil flavored

2 tablespoons minced fresh parsley

1 tablespoon chopped fresh oregano or 1 teaspoon dried, crumbled

½ teaspoon paprika

½ teaspoon garlic powder

Freshly ground pepper to taste

2 tablespoons minced fresh parsley (optional)

Preheat oven to 350° F.

In a 2-quart casserole dish, toss potatoes in margarine to coat each piece. Spray potatoes lightly with cooking spray.

Stir in remaining ingredients except optional parsley.

Bake for 30 to 40 minutes, or until lightly browned. Sprinkle with remaining parsley.

**NUTRIENT ANALYSIS**

Calories 119
Protein 2 g
Carbohydrate 24 g
Total Fat 2 g
Saturated Fat 0 g
Polyunsaturated Fat 1 g
Monounsaturated Fat 1 g
Cholesterol 0 mg
Sodium 54 mg

# HOME-FRIED POTATOES

*Serves 6*

*These potatoes are delicious with Chicken with Mustard and Herbs or Crispy Oven-Fried Chicken (see pages 126 and 137).*

1 tablespoon acceptable vegetable oil

1½ pounds small red potatoes, unpeeled, cooked and quartered

2 medium shallots, chopped

1 teaspoon paprika

½ teaspoon dried rosemary, crushed

½ teaspoon dry mustard

¼ teaspoon salt (optional)

Freshly ground black pepper to taste

In a large, heavy nonstick skillet, heat oil over medium-high heat. Sauté potatoes on one side for 3 to 4 minutes.

Turn potatoes, add shallots, and sauté for 3 to 4 minutes.

Stir in remaining ingredients. Cook for 1 to 2 minutes, or until potatoes are tender.

**NUTRIENT ANALYSIS**

Calories 122
Protein 2 g
Carbohydrate 24 g
Total Fat 2 g
Saturated Fat 0 g
Polyunsaturated Fat 1 g
Monounsaturated Fat 1 g
Cholesterol 0 mg
Sodium 8 mg

# SCALLOPED POTATOES

*Serves 6*

*The nonfat and low-fat dairy products available today make it a snap to prepare low-fat scalloped potatoes. Your heart—and your taste buds—will love you for it.*

Vegetable oil spray

1¾ cups fat-free milk

1 cup nonfat or low-fat sour cream

3 tablespoons light margarine, softened

1 tablespoon cornstarch

⅛ teaspoon freshly ground pepper

4 medium potatoes (about 1½ pounds), unpeeled and cut into ⅛- to ¼-inch-thick slices

½ medium onion, diced

Paprika to taste

Preheat oven to 350° F. Spray an 8 × 11½ × 2-inch baking pan with vegetable oil spray.

In a medium bowl, whisk together milk, sour cream, margarine, cornstarch, and pepper.

Line pan with one third of the potatoes. Pour one third of the sour cream mixture over the potatoes. Sprinkle with half the onion. Repeat the layers. Top with remaining potatoes, then with remaining sour cream mixture.

Cover with aluminum foil and bake for 1 hour. Uncover and bake for 20 minutes. Sprinkle with paprika. Let stand 5 minutes before serving.

**NUTRIENT ANALYSIS**

Calories 175
Protein 7 g
Carbohydrate 30 g
Total Fat 3 g
Saturated Fat 1 g
Polyunsaturated Fat 1 g
Monounsaturated Fat 1 g
Cholesterol 3 mg
Sodium 153 mg

# STEAMED RED POTATOES
# WITH GARLIC SAUCE

*Serves 4*

*The steamed garlic used in this sauce has a surprisingly mild flavor. The dish is easy to fix and offers a nice change of pace.*

Water

4 large or 8 small red potatoes (about 1¼ pounds), unpeeled

2 heads garlic

2 teaspoons fat-free milk

1 teaspoon acceptable vegetable oil

1 teaspoon light margarine

2 teaspoons chopped fresh parsley

Freshly ground pepper to taste

Place a steamer basket in a medium saucepan and add water to a depth of 1 to 2 inches. Be sure the water does not reach the bottom of the basket. Cover saucepan and bring water to a boil over medium-high heat.

Meanwhile, cut large potatoes in half. Place potatoes in steamer basket in boiling water.

Separate cloves of garlic, but do not peel the paper-thin skins. Scatter cloves around potatoes. Cover and steam for about 20 minutes, or until a fork can be easily inserted into potatoes.

Remove garlic from pan. Remove skins by pressing cloves in a garlic press, peeling skins off with your fingers, or pushing the garlic pulp out of the cloves. Discard skins and mash garlic pulp with milk, oil, and margarine. Warm sauce slightly over low heat, if desired.

Remove potatoes from pan and cut them in half. Serve with a dollop of garlic sauce, parsley, and pepper.

**NUTRIENT ANALYSIS**

Calories 237
Protein 6 g
Carbohydrate 51 g
Total Fat 2 g
Saturated Fat 0 g
Polyunsaturated Fat 1 g
Monounsaturated Fat 0 g
Cholesterol 0 mg
Sodium 31 mg

# RED AND GREEN PILAF

*Serves 4*

*This pretty rice dish is speckled with sliced okra or green peas and bits of red and green bell pepper, then seasoned with a touch of cayenne.*

Vegetable oil spray

½ cup chopped onion

⅓ cup chopped green bell pepper

⅓ cup chopped red bell pepper

½ cup brown rice

2 cloves garlic, minced, or 1 teaspoon bottled minced garlic

1½ cups low-sodium chicken broth (see page 55 or use commercial variety)

¼ teaspoon salt

⅛ teaspoon cayenne

1 cup sliced fresh or frozen okra, thawed, or ⅔ cup no-salt-added green peas (6 to 8 ounces fresh or 8 to 10 ounces frozen okra or 3 to 4 ounces peas)

1 medium Italian plum tomato, seeded and chopped

Spray a medium saucepan with vegetable oil spray. Add onion and bell peppers and cook over medium-high heat for 5 minutes, stirring occasionally.

Stir in rice and garlic and cook for 1 minute.

Add broth, salt, and cayenne. Bring to a boil over high heat. Reduce heat and simmer, covered, for 30 minutes.

Stir in okra. Cook, covered, for 5 to 10 minutes, or until rice is tender and liquid is absorbed.

Stir in tomato. Let stand for 5 minutes before serving.

**NUTRIENT ANALYSIS**

Calories 119
Protein 4 g
Carbohydrate 24 g
Total Fat 1 g
Saturated Fat 0 g
Polyunsaturated Fat 0 g
Monounsaturated Fat 0 g
Cholesterol 0 mg
Sodium 173 mg

# GOLDEN RICE

*Serves 6*

*This dish is known as "pilau" in Indian cuisine and as "pilaf" in Middle Eastern and Greek cuisine. Basmati is an aromatic, long-grain rice from India and Pakistan.*

1 cup basmati or other long-grain rice (6 to 8 ounces)

1 cup low-sodium chicken broth (see page 55 or use commercial variety)

1 cup water

1 cinnamon stick

1 bay leaf

¼ teaspoon salt (optional)

¼ teaspoon ground turmeric or saffron

2 tablespoons slivered almonds, dry-roasted

Rinse rice in several changes of water before cooking.

In a 2-quart saucepan over medium-high heat, bring broth and water to a boil.

Stir in rice, cinnamon stick, bay leaf, and salt. Reduce heat and simmer, covered, for 20 minutes.

Add turmeric and stir lightly with a fork. Continue to cook, covered, over low heat for 10 minutes, or until rice is tender and liquid is absorbed.

Remove cinnamon stick and bay leaf. Sprinkle with almonds just before serving.

## NUTRIENT ANALYSIS

Calories 144

Protein 4 g

Carbohydrate 27 g

Total Fat 2 g

Saturated Fat 0 g

Polyunsaturated Fat 0 g

Monounsaturated Fat 1 g

Cholesterol 0 mg

Sodium 11 mg

# SPINACH-CHEESE STRUDEL

*Serves 6*

*Spinach, caraway, and honey may seem to be an unlikely combination, but they're delicious together.*

8 ounces fresh spinach

1 teaspoon light margarine

6 green onions (green and white parts), chopped

Whites of 2 eggs

2 tablespoons water

8 sheets phyllo dough

1½ ounces low-fat feta cheese, soaked in cold water and drained

½ teaspoon caraway seeds

¼ teaspoon freshly ground black pepper, or to taste

1 tablespoon honey

Preheat oven to 350° F.

Thoroughly rinse spinach; drain. Remove stems from spinach, then tear leaves into bite-size pieces. Place in a medium bowl and set aside.

In a nonstick skillet, heat margarine over medium-high heat. Add green onions and sauté until soft, about 1 to 2 minutes.

Pour cooked onions over spinach and mix while still hot enough to wilt spinach.

In a small bowl, combine egg whites and water, beating lightly with a fork or a small whisk.

Keeping unused dough covered with a damp tea towel to prevent drying, lightly brush 4 sheets of phyllo with egg white mixture. Stack all phyllo sheets, alternating brushed and unbrushed sheets.

Spread spinach-onion mixture over the phyllo, leaving a 1-inch border on all sides.

Crumble the feta cheese. Sprinkle cheese, caraway seeds, and pepper over spinach mixture. Drizzle with honey.

Starting with a long side, roll phyllo, jelly-roll style, and place seam side down on a nonstick baking sheet, making sure that the ends of the roll are tucked under.

Brush the top lightly with remaining egg white mixture. At 1½-inch intervals, cut through the pastry to the spinach to provide vents for steam to escape. Bake for 20 to 30 minutes, or until a light golden-brown. Slice, using vent lines as guides.

**COOK'S TIP:**

This recipe freezes well. Prepare as above but omit the final brushing and the baking. Freeze overnight on a baking sheet, then wrap well in freezer paper or foil. To prevent the pastry from getting soggy, do not defrost before baking. Place on a baking sheet, brush with egg white wash, and bake at 350° F for 35 to 45 minutes, or until light golden-brown.

**COOK'S TIP ON PHYLLO:**

Phyllo is a paper-thin dough, available frozen in most large supermarkets and specialty groceries. Thaw phyllo in the refrigerator. Unopened, the thawed dough will keep for a month if refrigerated. Refreezing can make the dough crumbly.

# PRALINE BUTTERNUT SQUASH

*Serves 8*

*Sweet, maple-flavored fruit tops pureed butternut squash. Perfect for fall entertaining, especially when the holidays roll around!*

2- to 2½-pound butternut squash

1 cup water

15¼-ounce can pineapple chunks, packed in juice, drained

½ cup dried fruit (apricots, peaches, apples, or any combination), diced

2 tablespoons chopped pecans, dry-roasted

2 tablespoons maple syrup

1 tablespoon brown sugar

1 teaspoon grated lemon rind

Preheat oven to 350° F.

Cut squash in half. Scoop out the seeds with a spoon. Lay squash, cut side down, in a shallow baking dish. Add 1 cup water to dish.

Bake for 45 to 50 minutes, or until squash is tender. Remove from oven and cool for at least 15 minutes.

Remove flesh from rind with a spoon. Place flesh in a food processor and process for 1 minute, or until mixture is smooth. (You may use a potato masher if you wish.) Spoon squash into an ungreased 1-quart casserole dish.

In a medium bowl, combine remaining ingredients. Spoon mixture over squash.

Bake, uncovered, for 30 minutes, or until mixture is warmed through.

**NUTRIENT ANALYSIS**

Calories 112
Protein 1 g
Carbohydrate 26 g
Total Fat 1 g
Saturated Fat 0 g
Polyunsaturated Fat 0 g
Monounsaturated Fat 1 g
Cholesterol 0 mg
Sodium 7 mg

# OVEN-FRIED GREEN TOMATOES WITH POPPY SEEDS

*Serves 6*

*A typical end-of-summer tradition in the South is to pick the last of the garden tomatoes while they are still green, slice them, coat them with cornmeal, and fry them to eat as a side dish. This dish captures that same tradition and flavor, minus the fat.*

1 pound green tomatoes or firm red tomatoes (about 3 medium)

Egg substitute equivalent to 1 egg, or 1 egg

2 tablespoons fat-free milk

½ cup cornmeal

¼ cup all-purpose flour

1 teaspoon poppy seeds

¼ teaspoon salt

⅛ teaspoon pepper

Vegetable oil spray

Preheat oven to 450° F.

Cut tomatoes into ¼-inch-thick slices.

In a small bowl, combine egg substitute and milk.

In a pie pan or shallow baking dish, combine cornmeal, flour, poppy seeds, salt, and pepper.

Spray a baking sheet with vegetable oil spray. Line up, in order, tomato slices, egg mixture, cornmeal mixture, and baking sheet.

Using tongs, dip tomato slices in egg mixture, letting excess drip off. Lightly coat both sides of tomatoes with cornmeal mixture. Arrange tomatoes in a single layer on baking sheet.

Bake, uncovered, for 10 minutes. Turn and bake for 5 minutes, or until golden-brown.

**NUTRIENT ANALYSIS**

Calories 86
Protein 3 g
Carbohydrate 17 g
Total Fat 1 g
Saturated Fat 0 g
Polyunsaturated Fat 0 g
Monounsaturated Fat 0 g
Cholesterol 0 mg
Sodium 120 mg

# SAUTÉED CHERRY TOMATOES

*Serves 5*

*Don't put all the cherry tomatoes in your salad—save some for this creative side dish. It adds color and variety to any meal.*

1 pint cherry tomatoes, stemmed

2 teaspoons olive oil

1 clove garlic, finely minced, or ½ teaspoon bottled minced garlic

3 tablespoons finely chopped fresh parsley

½ shredded wheat biscuit, crushed

⅛ teaspoon freshly ground pepper, or to taste

Cut tomatoes in half.

Heat a medium nonstick skillet over medium-high heat. Add oil and swirl to coat bottom of skillet. When oil is hot, add garlic. Sauté for 30 seconds.

Add tomatoes and parsley and sauté, stirring constantly, for 20 to 30 seconds, or until tomato skins just begin to wilt.

Add biscuit crumbs and pepper. Stir well.

**NUTRIENT ANALYSIS**

Calories 43

Protein 1 g

Carbohydrate 6 g

Total Fat 2 g

Saturated Fat 0 g

Polyunsaturated Fat 0 g

Monounsaturated Fat 1 g

Cholesterol 0 mg

Sodium 8 mg

# SAUTÉED ZUCCHINI

*Serves 6*

*Add a touch of Italy to your menu. The herbs and spices blend for a unique-tasting side dish.*

1 teaspoon acceptable vegetable oil

2 pounds zucchini, sliced ½ inch thick

½ cup whole-wheat bread crumbs, toasted

¼ cup finely chopped fresh parsley

2 tablespoons minced almonds, dry-roasted

1 tablespoon grated Parmesan cheese

1 tablespoon chopped fresh oregano or 1 teaspoon dried, crumbled

1 clove garlic, minced, or ½ teaspoon bottled minced garlic (optional)

Freshly ground pepper to taste

In a large nonstick skillet, heat oil over medium-high heat. Swirl oil. Add zucchini and sauté for 5 to 8 minutes, or until just tender and lightly browned.

Combine remaining ingredients in a medium bowl and add to zucchini. Remove from heat and mix gently.

## NUTRIENT ANALYSIS

| | |
|---|---|
| Calories | 84 |
| Protein | 3 g |
| Carbohydrate | 12 g |
| Total Fat | 3 g |
| Saturated Fat | 1 g |
| Polyunsaturated Fat | 1 g |
| Monounsaturated Fat | 2 g |
| Cholesterol | 1 mg |
| Sodium | 96 mg |

# RATATOUILLE

*Serves 6*

*Excellent with chicken or fish, this French stew is also wonderful served hot on a baked potato or cold with crusty bread.*

1 large eggplant, cut into 1-inch cubes
4 medium zucchini, sliced ½ inch thick
1 teaspoon salt
1 teaspoon olive oil
2 medium onions, sliced
2 medium red, green, or yellow bell peppers, or any combination, chopped
2 large tomatoes, chopped
1 tablespoon chopped fresh thyme or 1 teaspoon dried, crumbled
1 tablespoon chopped fresh oregano or 1 teaspoon dried, crumbled
1 tablespoon chopped fresh basil or 1 teaspoon dried, crumbled
2 cloves garlic, minced, or 1 teaspoon bottled minced garlic
Freshly ground pepper to taste

Unless eggplant is very young, remove peel.

Place eggplant and zucchini in a colander, sprinkle with salt, and toss lightly. Allow to drain for at least 30 minutes. Rinse and pat dry with paper towels.

Heat a large, heavy nonstick skillet over medium-high heat. Add oil and swirl to coat bottom of skillet. When oil is hot, add onions. Sauté until translucent, 2 to 3 minutes.

Stir in eggplant, zucchini, and remaining ingredients. Reduce heat and simmer, covered, stirring occasionally to prevent sticking, for 30 to 45 minutes, or until vegetables are thoroughly cooked. Uncover and cook for 5 minutes to reduce liquid.

Ratatouille is best made a day ahead to allow flavors to blend. Serve warm or cold.

**NUTRIENT ANALYSIS**

Calories 93
Protein 3 g
Carbohydrate 20 g
Total Fat 1 g
Saturated Fat 0 g
Polyunsaturated Fat 0 g
Monounsaturated Fat 1 g
Cholesterol 0 mg
Sodium 370 mg

# VEGETABLE STIR-FRY

*Serves 6*

*The secret here is to prepare all the vegetables ahead of time so you can work quickly. Stir-fry them just before serving so they'll be crisp and crunchy. You can be creative with the combinations to showcase your family's favorite vegetables.*

¼ cup low-sodium chicken broth (see page 55 or use commercial variety)

1½ tablespoons low-sodium soy sauce

1 tablespoon acceptable vegetable oil

Vegetable oil spray

2 cups shredded red cabbage (6 to 8 ounces)

2 medium bell peppers, any color or combination, cut into 1-inch strips

4 ounces fresh mushrooms, thinly sliced

1 large carrot, cut into very thin strips

1 cup fresh snow peas, stems and strings removed (about 4 ounces)

4 green onions (green and white parts), cut into 1-inch strips

1 teaspoon grated fresh gingerroot or ¼ teaspoon ground ginger

1 tablespoon sesame seeds, toasted (optional)

Combine broth, soy sauce, and oil.

Spray a nonstick wok or skillet with vegetable oil spray and place over high heat. Add soy sauce mixture. Stir-fry remaining ingredients except sesame seeds, stirring constantly, for 2 minutes. Remove from heat. Vegetables should be tender-crisp.

Sprinkle with sesame seeds and serve immediately.

| NUTRIENT ANALYSIS | |
|---|---|
| Calories | 60 |
| Protein | 2 g |
| Carbohydrate | 8 g |
| Total Fat | 3 g |
| Saturated Fat | 0 g |
| Polyunsaturated Fat | 1 g |
| Monounsaturated Fat | 1 g |
| Cholesterol | 0 mg |
| Sodium | 169 mg |

# SAUCES

# CUCUMBER RAITA

*Serves 7, ¼ cup per serving*

*Raita (rī′-ta) is an Indian yogurt sauce. It makes a cool and refreshing accompaniment to any spicy dish.*

8 ounces plain nonfat or low-fat yogurt
1 small cucumber, peeled, seeded, and finely diced
¼ cup finely diced green bell pepper
2 tablespoons finely chopped fresh parsley or cilantro
¼ teaspoon cumin seeds or ground cumin
Freshly ground black pepper to taste

In a medium bowl, whisk yogurt until smooth.

Add remaining ingredients except black pepper. Stir well.

Cover and refrigerate until ready to serve. Sprinkle with pepper before serving.

**NUTRIENT ANALYSIS**

| | |
|---|---|
| Calories | 23 |
| Protein | 2 g |
| Carbohydrate | 3 g |
| Total Fat | 0 g |
| Saturated Fat | 0 g |
| Polyunsaturated Fat | 0 g |
| Monounsaturated Fat | 0 g |
| Cholesterol | 1 mg |
| Sodium | 26 mg |

SAUCES

# TOMATO-MINT RAITA

*Serves 7, ¼ cup per serving*

*This sauce makes delicious use of two of summer's trademark items, tomatoes and mint. Like its cousin, Cucumber Raita, this dish complements the fiery flavors of much Indian food.*

8 ounces plain nonfat or low-fat yogurt

2 medium tomatoes, finely chopped

4 green onions (green and white parts), finely chopped

1 red chili pepper, seeded and finely chopped (optional)*

¼ cup finely chopped fresh mint

¼ teaspoon cumin seeds or ground cumin

¼ teaspoon salt (optional)

Paprika to taste

Fresh mint sprigs

In a medium bowl, whisk yogurt until smooth.

Add tomatoes, green onions, chili pepper, chopped mint, cumin seeds, and salt. Stir well.

Cover and refrigerate until ready to serve. Sprinkle with paprika and garnish with mint before serving.

* Hot chili peppers contain oils that can burn your skin, lips, and eyes. Wear rubber gloves or wash your hands thoroughly with warm, soapy water immediately after handling peppers.

| NUTRIENT ANALYSIS | |
| --- | --- |
| Calories | 28 |
| Protein | 2 g |
| Carbohydrate | 5 g |
| Total Fat | 0 g |
| Saturated Fat | 0 g |
| Polyunsaturated Fat | 0 g |
| Monounsaturated Fat | 0 g |
| Cholesterol | 1 mg |
| Sodium | 29 mg |

# SALSA

*Serves 5, ¼ cup per serving*

*This spicy Mexican sauce is excellent as a topping or a dip. It can also be used to perk up dishes from scrambled eggs to grilled chicken. Make it several hours in advance to allow its flavors to blend.*

6 small ripe tomatoes, chopped

⅓ cup fresh lime juice (3 to 4 medium limes)

2 tablespoons finely chopped red onion

2 tablespoons finely chopped fresh cilantro or parsley

1 to 2 jalapeño peppers, seeded and minced, or to taste*

2 teaspoons red wine vinegar

⅛ teaspoon salt (optional)

Freshly ground pepper to taste

For a smooth sauce, thoroughly process all ingredients in a blender or food processor. If you prefer a chunky sauce, simply combine the ingredients.

Cover and refrigerate until needed.

* Hot chili peppers contain oils that can burn your skin, lips, and eyes. Wear rubber gloves or wash your hands thoroughly with warm, soapy water immediately after handling peppers.

## NUTRIENT ANALYSIS

Calories 34

Protein 1 g

Carbohydrate 8 g

Total Fat 0 g

Saturated Fat 0 g

Polyunsaturated Fat 0 g

Monounsaturated Fat 0 g

Cholesterol 0 mg

Sodium 15 mg

# CREAMY DESSERT TOPPING

*Serves 8, 2 tablespoons per serving*

*Reminiscent of cheesecake, this topping is luscious when drizzled over fruit, spread on muffins, or poured on a slice of angel food cake.*

½ cup plain nonfat or low-fat yogurt
½ cup nonfat or low-fat cottage cheese
2 tablespoons honey
½ to ¾ teaspoon vanilla extract (optional)

In a blender or food processor, process all ingredients until light and creamy.

Cover and refrigerate. Serve chilled.

# BERRY SAUCE

*Serves 6, 1/4 cup per serving*

*This topping is as easy to make as it is colorful and flavorful. It's great on fruit salads, nonfat or low-fat yogurt, sorbet, French toast, waffles, or even nonfat or low-fat cottage cheese.*

**16-ounce bag frozen unsweetened strawberries, raspberries, or other berries**

**1 teaspoon cornstarch**

Defrost berries and puree in a blender or food processor.

Place berry puree and cornstarch in a medium saucepan. Bring to a boil over medium-high heat, stirring frequently. Cook, continuing to stir frequently, until mixture thickens.

Cover and refrigerate. Serve chilled.

**NUTRIENT ANALYSIS**

Calories 24
Protein 0 g
Carbohydrate 6 g
Total Fat 0 g
Saturated Fat 0 g
Polyunsaturated Fat 0 g
Monounsaturated Fat 0 g
Cholesterol 0 mg
Sodium 1 mg

# APPLE-RAISIN SAUCE

*Serves 6, ½ cup per serving*

*Instead of apple strudel à la mode, try this delicious fruit sauce over nonfat or low-fat ice cream or frozen yogurt. You'll get the same taste combination but a lot less fat.*

3 medium apples

2 cups unsweetened apple juice

¼ cup raisins or dried cranberries

1 teaspoon ground cinnamon

2 tablespoons cold water

1 tablespoon cornstarch

Peel apples, if desired. Core and chop coarsely.

In a large saucepan, combine apples, juice, raisins, and cinnamon. Bring to a boil over medium-high heat. Reduce heat and simmer for 15 minutes, or until apples are tender.

Meanwhile, pour water into a cup or small bowl. Add cornstarch and stir until dissolved.

Add cornstarch mixture to apple mixture and cook, stirring constantly, for 1 to 2 minutes, or until thick and smooth. Serve warm.

## NUTRIENT ANALYSIS

Calories 114

Protein 1 g

Carbohydrate 29 g

Total Fat 1 g

Saturated Fat 0 g

Polyunsaturated Fat 0 g

Monounsaturated Fat 0 g

Cholesterol 0 mg

Sodium 5 mg

# BREADS
## AND
# BREAKFAST
# DISHES

Savory Dill Bread

Whole-Wheat French Bread

Potato Bread

Honey-Nut Bread

Zucchini Bread

Speckled Spoon Bread

Southern-Style Corn Bread

Buttermilk Biscuits

Oat Bran Muffins

Oatmeal-Fruit Muffins

Cardamom-Lemon Muffins

Gingerbread Pancakes
with Apple-Berry Topping

Breakfast Tortilla Wrap

Spanish-Style Scrambled Eggs

Seasoned Bread Crumbs

# SAVORY DILL BREAD

*Serves 16, 1 slice per serving*

*The aroma that fills the air when this bread is baking will entice you to devour your slice warm from the oven (or bread machine) before you even think of spreading margarine—and fat—on top.*

**NUTRIENT ANALYSIS**

| | |
|---|---|
| Calories | 114 |
| Protein | 3 g |
| Carbohydrate | 21 g |
| Total Fat | 2 g |
| Saturated Fat | 0 g |
| Polyunsaturated Fat | 1 g |
| Monounsaturated Fat | 1 g |
| Cholesterol | 0 mg |
| Sodium | 93 mg |

**NUTRIENT ANALYSIS**

*(For 1-lb bread machine)*

| | |
|---|---|
| Calories | 69 |
| Protein | 2 g |
| Carbohydrate | 12 g |
| Total Fat | 1 g |
| Saturated Fat | 0 g |
| Polyunsaturated Fat | 0 g |
| Monounsaturated Fat | 0 g |
| Cholesterol | 0 mg |
| Sodium | 51 mg |

**NUTRIENT ANALYSIS**

*(For 1½- to 2-lb bread machine)*

| | |
|---|---|
| Calories | 67 |
| Protein | 2 g |
| Carbohydrate | 12 g |
| Total Fat | 1 g |
| Saturated Fat | 0 g |
| Polyunsaturated Fat | 0 g |
| Monounsaturated Fat | 0 g |
| Cholesterol | 0 mg |
| Sodium | 62 mg |

Vegetable oil spray

1¼ cups warm water (105° F)

1 tablespoon active dry yeast (1 envelope)

2 cups all-purpose flour

2 tablespoons acceptable margarine

1 teaspoon dried dill weed

1 teaspoon onion powder

½ teaspoon garlic powder

½ teaspoon dried oregano, crumbled

½ teaspoon salt

1½ cups all-purpose flour

Vegetable oil spray

Spray a baking sheet with vegetable oil spray. Set aside.

Pour water into a medium bowl; dissolve yeast in the water. Let stand 5 minutes.

Meanwhile, in a large bowl, combine 2 cups flour, margarine, dill weed, onion powder, garlic powder, oregano, and salt.

Add yeast mixture to flour mixture, stirring with a sturdy spoon for about 30 seconds.

Stir in small amounts of remaining flour until dough starts to pull away from the sides of the bowl.

Turn dough onto a floured surface. Knead in enough remaining flour for dough to become smooth and elastic, about 7 to 8 minutes. (You may or may not knead in all the flour.) Shape into a ball.

With paper towels, wipe out the flour mixture bowl, then spray it with vegetable oil spray. Place dough in bowl, turning to coat all sides. Cover the bowl with a tea towel and set in a warm, draft-free place for dough to rise for 1 hour, or until doubled in bulk.

Punch dough down and shape it into a round loaf. Place on the prepared baking sheet. Flatten loaf slightly with your hands. Using a serrated knife, cut an X into the top of the loaf. Cover loaf with a tea towel. Allow dough to rise for 30 minutes, or until doubled in bulk. Near the end of the rising cycle, preheat oven to 375° F.

Remove tea towel and bake loaf on the middle oven rack for 35 to 40 minutes, or until loaf sounds hollow when tapped. Remove from oven and cool on a wire rack for 15 minutes before cutting. (The longest wait!)

## BREAD MACHINE INSTRUCTIONS

| *1-Pound Bread Machine (16 slices)* | *1½- to 2-Pound Bread Machine (24 slices)* |
|---|---|
| ¾ cup water (tap) | 1¼ cups water (tap) |
| 2 cups all-purpose flour | 3 cups all-purpose flour |
| 1½ tablespoons acceptable margarine | 2 tablespoons acceptable margarine |
| ¾ teaspoon dried dill weed | 1 teaspoon dried dill weed |
| ¾ teaspoon onion powder | 1 teaspoon onion powder |
| ¼ teaspoon garlic powder | ½ teaspoon garlic powder |
| ¼ teaspoon dried oregano | ½ teaspoon dried oregano |
| ¼ teaspoon salt | ½ teaspoon salt |
| 2 teaspoons active dry yeast | 1 tablespoon active dry yeast (1 envelope) |

Follow manufacturer's instructions for the regular baking cycle or the dough cycle. If you use the latter, shape the loaf by hand when the dough is ready and bake in the oven as directed in the main recipe.

# WHOLE-WHEAT FRENCH BREAD

*Serves 24, 2 slices per serving*

*This dense bread has a wonderful texture. The recipe makes 4 loaves—they'll disappear quickly!*

Vegetable oil spray

2 cups very warm water (110° F to 115° F)

2 tablespoons honey

1½ teaspoons active dry yeast (½ envelope)

1 teaspoon salt

4 cups whole-wheat flour

3 cups all-purpose flour

White of 1 large egg, lightly beaten

1 teaspoon sesame seeds (optional)

Spray 2 large baking sheets and 1 large bowl with vegetable oil spray. Set aside.

In a second large bowl, mix water, honey, yeast, and salt.

In a third large bowl, combine whole-wheat and all-purpose flours; mix well.

Add 2 cups of combined flours to the yeast mixture and stir well. Gradually stir in 3 more cups of flour.

Turn dough onto a floured surface. Knead in enough of remaining 2 cups of flour to make a soft, but not sticky, dough. Knead dough for 8 to 10 minutes, or until smooth and elastic.

Shape dough into a ball and place in prepared bowl, turning to coat all sides. Cover the bowl with a clean tea towel and set in a warm, draft-free place to rise for about 1½ hours, or until doubled in bulk.

Turn dough onto a lightly floured surface, punch down, and knead out the large air bubbles. Divide dough into four equal pieces. Shape each piece into a skinny loaf, about 12 inches long. Place on prepared baking sheets and cover with a clean tea towel. Allow to rise again in a warm, draft-free place for 45 minutes, or until doubled in bulk. Near the end of the rising cycle, preheat oven to 350° F.

Brush each loaf with egg white.

Bake for 40 to 50 minutes, or until loaves are golden-brown and sound hollow when tapped. About 5 minutes before end of baking cycle, reglaze loaves with egg white and sprinkle with sesame seeds.

# POTATO BREAD

*Serves 24, 2 slices per serving*

*The next time you make mashed potatoes, plan ahead and make extra—leftovers work perfectly here. This recipe makes 4 loaves, so you'll have some to freeze.*

**COOK'S TIP ON BAKING BREAD:**
A familiar phrase describing the doneness of bread is "Sounds hollow when tapped." Using an instant-read thermometer helps take the guesswork out of this method. Insert the thermometer in the bread when your timer goes off (this type of thermometer is not meant to remain in the food while the food bakes). If the temperature is 190° F, your bread should be done.

Vegetable oil spray

4 cups whole-wheat flour

4 cups all-purpose flour

2 tablespoons active dry yeast (2 envelopes)

2 tablespoons honey

2½ teaspoons salt

1½ cups mashed potatoes

1½ cups fat-free milk

½ cup water

¼ cup acceptable margarine

Whites of 4 large eggs

GLAZE

¼ cup fat-free milk

Spray 2 large baking sheets and 1 large bowl with vegetable oil spray. Set aside.

In another large bowl, combine whole-wheat and all-purpose flours.

In a third large bowl, mix yeast, honey, salt, and 1½ cups of combined flours.

In a 2-quart saucepan, combine mashed potatoes, 1½ cups milk, water, and margarine. Heat over medium-high heat, stirring frequently, until very warm, 120° F to 130° F. The margarine does not need to melt completely.

With an electric mixer on low speed, beat potato mixture into yeast mixture.

Add egg whites. Increase mixer speed to medium and beat for 2 minutes, scraping bowl occasionally.

Stir in 1 cup of combined flours; beat 2 minutes. Gradually stir in 3 more cups of flour.

**NUTRIENT ANALYSIS**

Calories 192

Protein 7 g

Carbohydrate 35 g

Total Fat 3 g

Saturated Fat 1 g

Polyunsaturated Fat 1 g

Monounsaturated Fat 1 g

Cholesterol 0 mg

Sodium 283 mg

Turn the dough onto a well-floured surface. Knead in enough of the remaining 2½ cups of flour to make a soft, but not sticky, dough. Knead the dough for about 10 minutes, or until smooth and elastic. Shape into a ball and place in the prepared bowl, turning to coat all sides. Cover the bowl with a clean tea towel and set in a warm, draft-free place to rise for 1½ hours, or until doubled in bulk.

Turn dough onto a lightly floured surface, punch down, and knead out the large air bubbles. Divide dough into 4 equal pieces. Shape each piece into an oval, about 10 inches long. Using a serrated knife, cut 2 parallel slashes into top of each loaf.

Place 2 loaves on each prepared baking sheet and cover with clean tea towels. Allow to rise in a warm, draft-free place for 1 hour, or until doubled in bulk. Near the end of the rising cycle, preheat oven to 350° F.

Brush each loaf with 1 tablespoon milk.

Bake for 35 to 45 minutes, or until loaves are golden-brown and sound hollow when tapped. Serve warm or at room temperature.

# HONEY-NUT BREAD

*Serves 20, 1 slice per serving*

*Freeze single slices of this delicious bread for a lunch-box addition. When packed frozen, a slice will thaw in less than an hour.*

1 cup fat-free milk

1 cup honey

1¼ cups whole-wheat flour

1¼ cups all-purpose flour

1 tablespoon baking powder

½ teaspoon salt

¼ cup light margarine

Egg substitute equivalent to 1 egg, or 1 egg

Whites of 2 eggs, lightly beaten

¼ cup finely chopped walnuts, preferably dry-roasted (1 to 2 ounces)

Vegetable oil spray

Preheat oven to 325° F.

In a small saucepan over medium-high heat, heat milk and honey until very warm, 120° F to 130° F.

In a large bowl, combine whole-wheat and all-purpose flours, baking powder, and salt.

Add liquid mixture to dry mixture and stir until just moistened.

Add margarine, egg substitute, and egg whites and stir until blended. (Overmixing will produce a rubbery texture.)

Fold in nuts.

Lightly spray two 9 × 5 × 3-inch loaf pans with vegetable oil spray. Pour in bread mixture.

Bake for 50 to 60 minutes, or until a cake tester inserted into the center of the loaf comes out moist but not wet. Cool on a wire rack.

To store, wrap each loaf in foil to preserve moisture.

**NUTRIENT ANALYSIS**

Calories 143
Protein 3 g
Carbohydrate 27 g
Total Fat 3 g
Saturated Fat 1 g
Polyunsaturated Fat 1 g
Monounsaturated Fat 1 g
Cholesterol 0 mg
Sodium 159 mg

# ZUCCHINI BREAD

*Serves 16, 1 slice per serving*

*A perfect luncheon bread is hard to find, but this comes close—good nutrition and great taste rolled into one!*

Vegetable oil spray

1½ cups all-purpose flour

½ cup firmly packed light brown sugar

1½ teaspoons baking powder

½ teaspoon ground cinnamon

¼ teaspoon baking soda

⅛ teaspoon salt

1 cup shredded zucchini (about 4 ounces)

¼ cup raisins (optional)

1 tablespoon finely chopped walnuts, preferably dry-roasted

½ cup pineapple juice

Egg substitute equivalent to 1 egg, or 1 egg

1 tablespoon acceptable vegetable oil

1 tablespoon corn syrup

½ teaspoon vanilla extract

Preheat oven to 350° F. Spray a 9 × 5 × 3-inch loaf pan with vegetable oil spray. Set aside.

In a large bowl, combine flour, brown sugar, baking powder, cinnamon, baking soda, and salt.

Stir in zucchini, raisins, and nuts. Set aside.

In a smaller bowl, beat together remaining ingredients. Add liquid ingredients to flour mixture and stir until just moistened.

Pour batter into prepared pan and bake for 1 hour, or until a cake tester inserted into the center of the loaf comes out clean. Let cool in pan for 10 minutes, then turn out onto a wire rack and cool completely.

To store, wrap loaf in plastic wrap and refrigerate for up to 7 days.

**NUTRIENT ANALYSIS**

Calories 91
Protein 2 g
Carbohydrate 18 g
Total Fat 1 g
Saturated Fat 0 g
Polyunsaturated Fat 1 g
Monounsaturated Fat 0 g
Cholesterol 0 mg
Sodium 63 mg

# SPECKLED SPOON BREAD

*Serves 6*

**COOK'S TIP:**

Don't worry if you can't serve this as soon as it comes out of the oven. It will deflate slightly but still be light and fluffy.

*This soufflélike bread requires a spoon for serving. Pair it with lean roasted meat or poultry and a fresh green salad.*

1 cup water

½ cup cornmeal

½ cup canned or frozen no-salt-added whole kernel corn (about 4 ounces canned or 3 ounces frozen)

¼ cup chopped fresh parsley

2 tablespoons chopped pimiento

1 tablespoon light margarine

2 cloves garlic, minced, or 1 teaspoon bottled minced garlic

¾ cup fat-free milk

Egg substitute equivalent to 1 egg, or 1 egg

1 teaspoon baking powder

Whites of 3 eggs*

Vegetable oil spray

Preheat oven to 325° F.

In a medium saucepan, combine water and cornmeal. Bring to a boil over high heat; reduce heat to medium-low. Cook and stir for about 1 minute, or until very thick. Remove from heat.

Stir in corn, parsley, pimiento, margarine, and garlic, then stir in milk.

In a small bowl, stir together egg substitute and baking powder until well combined. Stir into cornmeal mixture.

Beat egg whites with an electric mixer until stiff peaks form. Fold beaten whites into cornmeal mixture.

Spray a 1½-quart casserole dish with vegetable oil spray. Spoon cornmeal mixture into casserole dish.

Bake, uncovered, for 50 to 60 minutes, or until a knife inserted near the center comes out clean.

* Even a single drop of egg yolk will prevent egg whites from rising, so separate eggs very carefully.

**NUTRIENT ANALYSIS**

Calories 88

Protein 5 g

Carbohydrate 14 g

Total Fat 1 g

Saturated Fat 0 g

Polyunsaturated Fat 0 g

Monounsaturated Fat 1 g

Cholesterol 1 mg

Sodium 165 mg

# SOUTHERN-STYLE CORN BREAD

*Serves 12*

*This corn bread has a crispy crust and a flavorful, moist center. For a simple yet satisfying meal, serve it with South-ern-Style Black-Eyed Peas and Sautéed Greens (see pages 219 and 217).*

1½ teaspoons acceptable vegetable oil

1½ cups yellow cornmeal, whole-grain if possible

1½ cups whole-wheat flour

⅓ cup nonfat dry milk

1 to 3 tablespoons sugar (optional)

1½ tablespoons baking powder

½ teaspoon salt

Whites of 3 large eggs

1½ cups fat-free milk

Pour oil into a 10½-inch cast-iron skillet or 9 × 11-inch ovenproof glass casserole dish. Swirl oil. Set aside.

Preheat oven to 450° F for cast iron or 425° F for glass.

In a large bowl, mix cornmeal, flour, dry milk, sugar, baking powder, and salt. Set aside.

In a small bowl, beat egg whites with a whisk until slightly frothy.

Add milk and whisk again.

Pour liquid ingredients into dry ingredients and mix, leaving some lumps. Do not overmix.

Place skillet in oven for 1 to 2 minutes to heat the oil. *Be careful not to let it burn!* Watch the time carefully.

Pour batter into hot skillet. Bake for about 20 min-utes. Immediately remove corn bread from pan by turn-ing onto a cutting board.

**NUTRIENT ANALYSIS**

Calories 141
Protein 6 g
Carbohydrate 27 g
Total Fat 1 g
Saturated Fat 0 g
Polyunsaturated Fat 1 g
Monounsaturated Fat 0 g
Cholesterol 1 mg
Sodium 281 mg

# BUTTERMILK BISCUITS

*Serves 8*

*A drizzle of honey instead of lots of margarine is perfect for these fluffy biscuits. The secret to success? Don't overmix the dough, or the biscuits will be tough.*

Vegetable oil spray

1 cup all-purpose flour

2 teaspoons baking powder

1 teaspoon sugar

⅛ teaspoon baking soda

⅛ teaspoon salt

1 tablespoon acceptable margarine

⅓ cup low-fat buttermilk

¼ cup nonfat or low-fat plain yogurt

Flour

Preheat oven to 425° F. Spray an 8-inch round cake pan lightly with vegetable oil spray. Set aside.

In a medium bowl, mix the flour, baking powder, sugar, baking soda, and salt.

With a pastry blender or fork, cut in the margarine until it is in small pieces throughout the flour.

Stir buttermilk and yogurt into the flour mixture with a fork until mixture is just moistened.

Turn dough out onto a lightly floured board. Sprinkle dough with a small amount of flour and shape into a disk. With your hands or a rolling pin, pat out the dough until it is about ½ inch thick. Cut out biscuits with a 2½-inch round cutter. Place biscuits in the prepared cake pan.

Bake for 10 to 12 minutes, or until biscuits are done through the middle (they will be golden-brown on the bottom). Remove from pan and place in a tea towel to keep warm.

**NUTRIENT ANALYSIS**

Calories 81
Protein 2 g
Carbohydrate 14 g
Total Fat 2 g
Saturated Fat 0 g
Polyunsaturated Fat 1 g
Monounsaturated Fat 1 g
Cholesterol 1 mg
Sodium 214 mg

# OAT BRAN MUFFINS

*Serves 18*

*You've heard about the healthfulness of oat bran—now taste how good it can be. The almond extract "stretches" the nutty flavor the pecans provide. Make an extra batch to freeze so you can enjoy these moist muffins at breakfast, lunch, or snack time.*

2½ cups oat bran, uncooked

¼ cup firmly packed light brown sugar

¼ cup currants (1 to 2 ounces)

⅛ cup chopped pecans or other nuts, preferably dry-roasted (about ½ ounce)

1 tablespoon baking powder

¼ teaspoon salt (optional)

Whites of 4 large eggs, lightly beaten

¾ cup fat-free milk

¼ cup honey

2 tablespoons acceptable vegetable oil

1 teaspoon almond extract

1 teaspoon vanilla extract

Vegetable oil spray

Preheat oven to 350° F.

In a large bowl, combine oat bran, sugar, currants, nuts, baking powder, and salt. Mix well.

In a small bowl, combine remaining ingredients except vegetable oil spray. Add to dry ingredients and stir until just moistened.

Spray a 12-chamber muffin tin and a 6-chamber muffin tin lightly with vegetable oil spray or use paper bake cups in the muffin tins. Spoon mixture evenly into muffin tins.

Bake for 20 to 25 minutes, or until light brown. Serve warm or at room temperature.

**NUTRIENT ANALYSIS**

Calories 92

Protein 4 g

Carbohydrate 18 g

Total Fat 3 g

Saturated Fat 0 g

Polyunsaturated Fat 1 g

Monounsaturated Fat 1 g

Cholesterol 0 mg

Sodium 87 mg

# OATMEAL-FRUIT MUFFINS

*Serves 12*

*Oats, wheat germ, milk, and fruit—so many healthful ingredients in such tasty muffins!*

Vegetable oil spray

1 cup all-purpose flour

¾ cup quick or regular rolled oats

⅓ cup toasted wheat germ

2 teaspoons baking powder

1 teaspoon ground cinnamon

½ teaspoon baking soda

⅛ teaspoon salt

¾ cup fat-free milk

½ cup firmly packed light brown sugar

Egg substitute equivalent to 1 egg, or 1 egg

¼ cup unsweetened applesauce

½ teaspoon vanilla

½ cup snipped dried figs or apricots (about 8 ounces figs or 3½ ounces apricots)

Preheat oven to 400° F. Line 12 muffin cups with paper bake cups or spray with vegetable oil spray. Set aside.

In a medium bowl, stir together flour, oats, wheat germ, baking powder, cinnamon, baking soda, and salt. Make a well in the center.

In another medium bowl, combine remaining ingredients except figs.

Add wet mixture to dry mixture. Stir until just moistened (batter should be lumpy).

Fold in figs.

Spoon batter into muffin cups, using about ¼ cup batter for each cup.

Bake for 10 to 12 minutes, or until a toothpick inserted near the center comes out clean. Cool on a wire rack for 5 minutes; remove muffins from bake cups. Serve warm or at room temperature.

**NUTRIENT ANALYSIS**

Calories 136
Protein 4 g
Carbohydrate 29 g
Total Fat 1 g
Saturated Fat 0 g
Polyunsaturated Fat 0 g
Monounsaturated Fat 0 g
Cholesterol 0 mg
Sodium 178 mg

# CARDAMOM-LEMON MUFFINS

*Serves 24*

Cardamom adds a distinctive flavor and enhances the
sweetness of these muffins. Instead of using a lot of fat for
moistness, this recipe calls on applesauce. Oat bran contains soluble fibers that may help lower blood cholesterol
slightly.

Vegetable oil spray

2½ cups oat bran, uncooked

2 cups all-purpose flour

2 teaspoons baking powder

1½ teaspoons baking soda

1 teaspoon ground cardamom

2 cups unsweetened applesauce

Whites of 4 large eggs

½ cup pineapple juice

½ cup honey

2 tablespoons acceptable vegetable oil

¼ teaspoon almond extract

Grated rind of 1 lemon

Preheat oven to 400° F.

Spray two 12-chamber muffin tins with vegetable oil
spray or use paper bake cups in the tins. Set aside.

In a medium bowl, combine oat bran, flour, baking
powder, baking soda, and cardamom. Mix well.

In a large bowl, combine remaining ingredients. Mix
well.

Add dry ingredients to wet ingredients. Stir until just
moistened (batter should be lumpy).

Fill prepared muffin cups almost full. Place in oven
and reduce heat to 375° F. Bake for 18 to 20 minutes, or
until golden-brown. Serve warm or at room temperature.

**NUTRIENT ANALYSIS**

| | |
|---|---|
| Calories | 108 |
| Protein | 3 g |
| Carbohydrate | 23 g |
| Total Fat | 2 g |
| Saturated Fat | 0 g |
| Polyunsaturated Fat | 1 g |
| Monounsaturated Fat | 1 g |
| Cholesterol | 0 mg |
| Sodium | 95 mg |

# GINGERBREAD PANCAKES WITH APPLE-BERRY TOPPING

*Serves 4*

*You don't need cold weather to enjoy these pancakes, and you don't need an excuse to eat them for dinner! Look for boysenberry syrup near the pancake syrup at the super-market.*

1 cup all-purpose flour

2 tablespoons sugar

2 teaspoons baking powder

½ teaspoon ground cinnamon

¼ teaspoon ground ginger

¼ teaspoon ground allspice

¾ cup fat-free milk

Egg substitute equivalent to 1 egg, or 1 egg

2 tablespoons molasses

1 tablespoon acceptable vegetable oil

8 ounces light apple pie filling

½ cup boysenberry, blueberry, or strawberry syrup

4 tablespoons dried cranberries (optional)

Preheat nonstick griddle over medium heat.

In a medium bowl, combine flour, sugar, baking powder, cinnamon, ginger, and allspice.

In a small bowl, combine milk, egg substitute, molasses, and vegetable oil.

Pour wet mixture into dry mixture and stir until just combined. (Do not overmix or pancakes will be tough.)

Test griddle by sprinkling a few drops of water on it. If water evaporates quickly, the griddle is ready. Pour about ¼ cup of the batter onto the griddle. Cook for 2 to 3 minutes, or until bubbles appear all over the surface. Flip over, and cook for 2 minutes, or until bottom is golden-brown. Repeat until all of the batter is used.

**NUTRIENT ANALYSIS**

Calories 394
Protein 6 g
Carbohydrate 87 g
Total Fat 4 g
Saturated Fat 1 g
Polyunsaturated Fat 2 g
Monounsaturated Fat 1 g
Cholesterol 1 mg
Sodium 342 mg

While pancakes are cooking, heat the apple pie filling in a small saucepan over low heat for 2 to 3 minutes, or until filling is warmed through. Set aside.

To serve, place 2 pancakes on a plate. Spoon about 2 tablespoons of syrup on pancakes. Spread ¼ cup apple pie filling on top and sprinkle with 1 tablespoon dried cranberries. Repeat with remaining pancakes.

# BREAKFAST TORTILLA WRAP

*Serves 4*

*This hearty breakfast sandwich combines fluffy scrambled eggs, Canadian bacon, hash browns, red bell pepper for color, and a bit of cheese for flair. Perfect for busy people on the go—wrap some up today!*

Vegetable oil spray

Egg substitute equivalent to 2 eggs, or 2 eggs

⅛ teaspoon black pepper

4 6-inch nonfat or low-fat flour tortillas* or corn tortillas

1 cup fat-free frozen shredded potatoes (about 3 ounces)

½ red bell pepper, diced

¼ cup chopped Canadian bacon (about 1 ounce)

¼ teaspoon salt

⅛ teaspoon black pepper

Vegetable oil spray

1 ounce nonfat or low-fat Cheddar cheese, shredded (about ¼ cup)

Preheat oven to 350° F.

Spray a small nonstick skillet with vegetable oil spray. Heat skillet over medium-low heat. Pour egg substitute into skillet and add ⅛ teaspoon black pepper. Cook, stirring occasionally, for 3 to 4 minutes, or until eggs are cooked through. Set aside.

Wrap tortillas in aluminum foil and warm in oven for 5 minutes.

Meanwhile, in a medium bowl, mix potatoes, bell pepper, Canadian bacon, salt, and remaining black pepper.

Spray a medium-size nonstick skillet with vegetable oil spray. Heat over medium-high heat.

Using a rubber scraper, spread potato mixture evenly over the bottom of the skillet. Cook for 6 to 7 minutes on one side, or until potatoes are a light golden-brown.

Turn potato mixture over with a spatula and cook for 5 to 6 minutes.

To assemble using flour tortillas, layer ingredients vertically down the middle of a tortilla as follows: one quarter of the scrambled eggs, one quarter of the potato mixture, and one quarter of the cheese. Fold the left third of the tortilla to the center. Roll the bottom edge all the way up to the top. Repeat with remaining tortillas.

To assemble using corn tortillas, layer ingredients horizontally across the middle of each tortilla as described above. Roll like a jelly roll, starting at the bottom. Secure each wrap with a toothpick, if desired.

Serve immediately, keep in an airtight container, or store individually in plastic wrap. To reheat, place 1 or 2 wraps on a microwave-safe plate. Microwave on 100 percent power (high) for 1 to 1½ minutes.

* Nonfat and low-fat flour tortillas can be high in sodium. When shopping, select the one with the lowest sodium value.

# SPANISH-STYLE SCRAMBLED EGGS

*Serves 3*

*Eggs with a peppy personality, this recipe is perfect for a jump start of flavor in the morning. Or wrap the warm mixture in a tortilla and enjoy it for breakfast, lunch, or dinner.*

1 teaspoon acceptable vegetable oil

1 small ripe tomato, finely chopped

1 green onion, finely chopped

Egg substitute equivalent to 6 eggs, or whites of 6 large eggs

1 tablespoon low-sodium salsa (see page 242 or use commercial variety) or picante sauce

Freshly ground pepper to taste

1 tablespoon minced fresh cilantro or parsley

Fresh cilantro or parsley sprigs (optional)

1 tomato, cut into wedges (optional)

In a large nonstick skillet, heat oil over medium-high heat. Add tomato and onion and sauté until onion is soft, 1 to 2 minutes. Reduce heat to low.

In a bowl, combine egg substitute, salsa, and pepper. Beat until frothy.

Add egg mixture to skillet. Cook over low heat, stirring occasionally, until almost set.

Add minced cilantro and stir until eggs are fully set. Garnish with cilantro sprigs and tomato.

**NUTRIENT ANALYSIS**

Calories 81

Protein 12 g

Carbohydrate 5 g

Total Fat 2 g

Saturated Fat 0 g

Polyunsaturated Fat 1 g

Monounsaturated Fat 0 g

Cholesterol 0 mg

Sodium 242 mg

# SEASONED BREAD CRUMBS

*Makes about 1 cup*

*These bread crumbs are a good staple to have on hand. They perk up steamed vegetables, add crunch to broiled fish, garnish soups or salads, and make a tasty topping for casseroles.*

4 slices whole-wheat bread

¼ cup grated or shredded Parmesan cheese (about 1 ounce)

1 tablespoon dried parsley flakes, crumbled

1 teaspoon dried onion flakes

½ teaspoon dried basil, crumbled

½ teaspoon dried oregano, crumbled

Preheat oven to 275° F.

Arrange bread slices in a single layer on a baking sheet.

Bake for 15 to 20 minutes, or until crisp and dry.

Break slices into pieces and place in a blender or food processor. Process until desired size. If you prefer, place bread pieces in a plastic bag and crush with a rolling pin.

Add remaining ingredients and stir to mix well. Store refrigerated in an airtight container.

## NUTRIENT ANALYSIS
*(For 1 tablespoon)*

| | |
|---|---|
| Calories | 24 |
| Protein | 1 g |
| Carbohydrate | 3 g |
| Total Fat | 1 g |
| Saturated Fat | 0 g |
| Polyunsaturated Fat | 0 g |
| Monounsaturated Fat | 0 g |
| Cholesterol | 1 mg |
| Sodium | 61 mg |

# BEVERAGES

Orange Juice Cooler
Orange-Strawberry Froth
Spiced Apple Cider
Chocolate Cappuccino

# ORANGE JUICE COOLER

*Serves 4*

*Here's a yummy drink to add fizz to your next brunch.*

¼ cup frozen orange juice concentrate
3 cups club soda
Crushed ice
4 fresh strawberries or 4 fresh mint sprigs (optional)

Put orange juice concentrate in a 2-quart pitcher. Add club soda and whisk or stir until concentrate has melted.

Place desired amount of crushed ice in each glass. Pour juice mixture into glasses.

Garnish each glass with a strawberry or a fresh mint sprig. Serve immediately.

**NUTRIENT ANALYSIS**

Calories 28
Protein 0 g
Carbohydrate 7 g
Total Fat 0 g
Saturated Fat 0 g
Polyunsaturated Fat 0 g
Monounsaturated Fat 0 g
Cholesterol 0 mg
Sodium 38 mg

# ORANGE-STRAWBERRY FROTH

*Serves 6*

*When you crave something sweet, try this drink. You'll think it's nectar from the gods!*

2 cups fresh orange juice (6 to 8 medium oranges)
1½ cups apricot nectar (12 ounces)
1 cup frozen unsweetened strawberries (5 to 6 ounces)

In a blender or food processor, process ingredients for about 20 seconds, or until smooth and frothy. Serve immediately.

# SPICED APPLE CIDER

*Serves 16*

**COOK'S TIP ON BOUQUET GARNI:**

For easy removal of the allspice and cloves from the juice mixture, make a bouquet garni. Tie the spices in cheesecloth or put them in a tea ball. When the cider is ready, you won't have to round up the spices, piece by piece. Most often made of parsley, thyme, and bay leaf, bouquets garnis are time-savers in soups and stews also.

*A warm fire. A cozy room. A comfy chair. This cold-weather favorite completes the scene.*

2 quarts unsweetened apple juice or apple cider

1 quart water

3 tea bags, regular or decaffeinated

½ orange with peel, thinly sliced

½ lemon with peel, thinly sliced

12 whole allspice

6 whole cloves

2 cinnamon sticks

Ground allspice to taste

1 orange with peel, thinly sliced (optional)

1 lemon with peel, thinly sliced (optional)

In a large saucepan over high heat, bring apple juice, water, tea bags, orange slices, lemon slices, whole allspice, cloves, and cinnamon sticks to a boil. Reduce heat and simmer for 3 minutes.

Remove tea bags, orange and lemon slices, allspice, and cloves. Simmer for 5 minutes. Add ground allspice.

Serve hot or chilled. Garnish with fresh slices of orange and lemon.

**NUTRIENT ANALYSIS**

Calories 61
Protein 0 g
Carbohydrate 15 g
Total Fat 0 g
Saturated Fat 0 g
Polyunsaturated Fat 0 g
Monounsaturated Fat 0 g
Cholesterol 0 mg
Sodium 6 mg

# CHOCOLATE CAPPUCCINO

*Serves 4*

*Cappuccino is a mixture of espresso, steamed milk, and the foam from the milk. Add chocolate syrup or cocoa powder and you have chocolate cappuccino, also known as mocha. Besides tasting terrific, this cappuccino is convenient—you don't need an espresso/cappuccino machine. A blender produces amazing results when frothing the milk. (See the Cook's Tip if you do own an espresso/cappuccino machine.)*

**COOK'S TIP:**

If you have an espresso/ cappuccino maker, brew coffee, steam, and froth milk according to manufacturer's directions. Add chocolate syrup, sugar, and whipped topping as directed in the recipe.

**2 cups fat-free milk**

**1⅓ cups strong brewed coffee (dark roast recommended)**

**¼ cup nonfat or low-fat chocolate syrup**

**4 teaspoons sugar**

**¼ cup nonfat or low-fat frozen whipped topping, thawed (optional)**

**¼ teaspoon unsweetened cocoa powder**

Heat the milk in a medium saucepan over medium heat until warm (do not boil), 2 to 3 minutes. No stirring is needed.

Place milk in a blender and blend on high speed for 1 minute. Set aside.

Measure ⅓ cup of hot coffee into a coffee mug or cappuccino cup. Spoon 1 tablespoon chocolate syrup and 1 teaspoon sugar into each mug. Stir.

Pour ½ cup of milk into each mug (do not stir). Top each serving with a dollop of whipped topping and a sprinkle of cocoa powder.

**NUTRIENT ANALYSIS**

Calories 80
Protein 4 g
Carbohydrate 16 g
Total Fat 0 g
Saturated Fat 0 g
Polyunsaturated Fat 0 g
Monounsaturated Fat 0 g
Cholesterol 2 mg
Sodium 73 mg

# DESSERTS

Chocolate Strawberry Shortcake

Chocolate Custard Cake
with Raspberries

Lemon Poppy Seed Cake

Peach-Raspberry Cobbler

Apple-Rhubarb Crisp

Pumpkin Pie

Meringue Shells

Gingersnap and
Graham Cracker Crust

Baklava

Sugar-Dusted Mocha Brownies

Cocoa-Almond Meringue Kisses

Gingerbread Bars

Mocha Cheesecake

Chocolate Soufflé with
Vanilla Sauce

Tapioca Pudding

Orange Fluff

Bananas Foster Plus

Cherries Jubilee

Melon with Sherbet

Strawberries Romanoff

Yogurt-Fruit Cup

Mango Brûlée with Pine Nuts

Very Berry Sorbet

Strawberry Margarita Ice

Baked Apples

# CHOCOLATE STRAWBERRY SHORTCAKE

*Serves 8*

*Yummy chocolate and sweet, succulent strawberries come together to treat your taste buds in this new twist on an old favorite.*

2 pounds fresh strawberries, sliced (5½ to 6 cups)
¼ cup sugar

### CAKE

1⅔ cups all-purpose flour
⅓ cup unsweetened cocoa powder
¼ cup sugar
1 tablespoon baking powder
⅓ cup acceptable margarine
⅔ cup fat-free milk
Egg substitute equivalent to 1 egg, or 1 egg
1 teaspoon vanilla
Vegetable oil spray

16-ounce container nonfat or low-fat vanilla yogurt

Preheat oven to 450° F.

In a large bowl, combine strawberries and ¼ cup sugar. Stir gently until well combined. Set aside.

For cake, in a medium bowl, combine flour, cocoa powder, ¼ cup sugar, and baking powder. Using a pastry blender, cut in margarine until mixture resembles coarse crumbs.

In a small bowl, combine milk, egg substitute, and vanilla. Add to dry ingredients and stir just to moisten.

Spray an 8-inch round baking pan with vegetable oil spray. Spread dough in pan, building up sides slightly.

Bake for 15 to 18 minutes, or until a toothpick inserted near the center comes out clean. Cool for 10 minutes on a wire rack. Remove cake from pan; place on a serving plate.

To serve, stir yogurt until smooth and creamy. Slice cake in half horizontally. Spoon half the strawberries onto bottom half of cake. Cover with top of cake. Spoon remaining strawberries and any juice on top of cake and dollop with yogurt. Serve warm or at room temperature. Cover any leftovers and refrigerate.

# CHOCOLATE CUSTARD CAKE WITH RASPBERRIES

*Serves 10*

**COOK'S TIP:**

This flanlike cake isn't a high riser—it doesn't contain any flour or leavening agent.

*You'll love the richness and creamy texture of this cake. Serve it warm or chilled with a double dose of raspberries.*

**Vegetable oil spray**

C A K E

14-ounce can nonfat sweetened condensed milk

Egg substitute equivalent to 5 eggs

½ cup fat-free milk

½ cup sugar

¼ cup unsweetened cocoa powder

¼ cup nonfat or low-fat chocolate syrup

1¼ cups seedless all-fruit raspberry preserves

10 ounces fresh or frozen raspberries, thawed

1 tablespoon powdered sugar (optional)

Preheat oven to 350° F. Spray an 8-inch nonstick round cake pan with vegetable oil spray. Cut a circle of parchment paper or wax paper to fit the bottom of the pan. Place paper in pan. If using wax paper, spray the top with vegetable oil spray.

In a large bowl, whisk together all cake ingredients. Pour into prepared pan.

Place the pan in the middle of a $12 \times 17 \times 1$-inch jelly-roll pan and fill jelly-roll pan half full with warm water, or place cake pan in a baking pan (the bottom of a broiler pan works well) and add warm water to a depth of 1 inch.

Bake for 40 to 45 minutes, or until a toothpick inserted in the center of cake comes out clean. Remove cake pan from water and let cool on a wire rack for 10 minutes. Carefully invert onto a plate (it is not neces-

**NUTRIENT ANALYSIS**

Calories 293

Protein 8 g

Carbohydrate 68 g

Total Fat 1 g

Saturated Fat 0 g

Polyunsaturated Fat 0 g

Monounsaturated Fat 0 g

Cholesterol 2 mg

Sodium 103 mg

sary to loosen sides first) and remove paper. Let cool for 15 minutes.

While cake is cooling, heat preserves in a small saucepan over low heat, stirring occasionally.

Top the cake with a thin coating of the preserves. Sprinkle with about half the raspberries. Cut the cake into 10 pie-shaped slices. Spoon remaining preserves on each dessert plate. Place each cake slice on preserves. Top with remaining raspberries, then dust lightly with powdered sugar.

For a more formal presentation, place raspberries in a ring around the top of the cake before cutting. Sprinkle any remaining berries on the dessert plates.

# LEMON POPPY SEED CAKE

*Serves 10*

**COOK'S TIP ON POPPY SEEDS AND SESAME SEEDS:**

Store poppy seeds and sesame seeds in the refrigerator. Otherwise, the oil in the seeds will turn rancid after a few months.

*Perfect with an afternoon cup of tea, this moist cake has a bold lemon flavor accented with the delicate crunch of poppy seeds.*

Vegetable oil spray

2 cups all-purpose flour

¾ cup sugar

1 tablespoon poppy seeds

2 teaspoons baking powder

¼ teaspoon baking soda

¼ teaspoon salt

¾ cup unsweetened applesauce (about 6 ounces)

1 teaspoon grated lemon rind

¼ cup fresh lemon juice (1 to 2 lemons)

2½ tablespoons acceptable vegetable oil

2 tablespoons corn syrup

1 teaspoon lemon extract

Whites of 4 eggs*

Preheat oven to 350° F. Lightly spray a 9-inch round cake pan with vegetable oil spray. Set aside.

In a medium bowl, combine flour, sugar, poppy seeds, baking powder, baking soda, and salt. Set aside.

In another medium bowl, combine applesauce, lemon peel, lemon juice, vegetable oil, corn syrup, and lemon extract. Pour the applesauce mixture into the flour mixture. Stir until just combined.

In a large bowl, beat the egg whites with an electric hand or stand mixer until they form stiff peaks.

Using a rubber scraper, fold the flour/applesauce mixture into the beaten egg whites. Pour mixture into the prepared cake pan and smooth top with a spatula.

Bake for 30 minutes, or until a toothpick inserted in the center comes out clean. Cool in pan for 10 minutes,

**NUTRIENT ANALYSIS**

Calories 207

Protein 4 g

Carbohydrate 40 g

Total Fat 3 g

Saturated Fat 0 g

Polyunsaturated Fat 2 g

Monounsaturated Fat 1 g

Cholesterol 0 mg

Sodium 217 mg

loosen sides of cake with a thin metal spatula, and invert cake onto a cooling rack. Cake can be served warm, at room temperature, or chilled.

* Even a single drop of egg yolk will prevent egg whites from rising, so separate eggs very carefully.

# PEACH-RASPBERRY COBBLER

*Serves 4*

*Cobblers get their name from the cobbled or bumpy appearance of the biscuitlike topping that bakes on a bubbly fruit filling. Serve this one warm on its own or with a scoop of nonfat or low-fat vanilla frozen yogurt or ice milk.*

### TOPPING

⅓ cup all-purpose flour

¼ cup whole-wheat flour

2 tablespoons light brown sugar

1 tablespoon wheat germ

1 teaspoon baking powder

2 tablespoons light margarine

### FILLING

⅓ cup sugar

1 tablespoon all-purpose flour

¼ teaspoon ground ginger

2 cups fresh or frozen unsweetened sliced peaches or nectarines (about 4 medium fresh or 16 ounces frozen)

2 cups fresh or frozen raspberries (10 to 12 ounces)

2 tablespoons water

Egg substitute equivalent to 1 egg, or 1 egg

2 tablespoons fat-free milk

Preheat oven to 400° F.

In a medium bowl, stir together all topping ingredients except margarine.

Using a pastry blender, cut in margarine until mixture resembles coarse crumbs. Make a well in the center. Set aside.

For filling, in a small bowl stir together sugar, 1 tablespoon all-purpose flour, and ginger.

In a large saucepan, combine peaches, raspberries, and water (it's not necessary to thaw frozen fruit). Bring to a boil over high heat. Reduce heat and simmer, covered, stirring often, for about 5 minutes, or until soft.

Stir in flour-ginger mixture. Cook and stir until thickened and bubbly. Reduce heat and keep filling hot.

In a small bowl, stir together egg substitute and milk. Add to topping mixture. Using a fork, stir just until moistened.

Transfer hot filling to an ungreased 1½-quart baking dish. Immediately spoon small mounds of topping onto hot filling.

Bake, uncovered, for 20 to 25 minutes, or until a wooden toothpick inserted into one of the biscuit mounds comes out clean. Serve warm.

# APPLE-RHUBARB CRISP

*Serves 6*

The apples give sweetness and the rhubarb contributes tartness to this fruit crisp. Since most baked fruit desserts taste best when eaten warm, let this dish cool for about 20 minutes after you remove it from the oven.

## FILLING

2 cups fresh or frozen unsweetened sliced rhubarb, thawed and drained (about 10 ounces fresh or 16 ounces frozen)

2 medium cooking apples, cored, peeled, and sliced (about 2 cups)

½ cup sugar

1 tablespoon cornstarch

## TOPPING

⅔ cup regular or quick-cooking rolled oats

½ cup all-purpose flour

¼ cup firmly packed light brown sugar

3½ tablespoons light margarine

In a large bowl, combine the filling ingredients. Stir to mix well. Let stand for 1 hour. Spoon into an ungreased 8 × 8 × 2-inch baking pan or 1-quart casserole dish.

Preheat oven to 375° F.

In a medium bowl, stir together the topping ingredients except margarine.

Using a pastry blender, cut in margarine until mixture resembles coarse crumbs. Sprinkle topping over rhubarb mixture.

Bake, uncovered, for 30 to 40 minutes, or until topping is light brown. Let cool for about 20 minutes before serving.

**COOK'S TIP ON COOKING APPLES:**

Apples that retain their shape and flavor are especially good for baking. Among the best are Rome Beauty, Baldwin, Winesap, Granny Smith, Jonathan, and Cortland.

**COOK'S TIP ON RHUBARB:**

When buying fresh rhubarb, look for crisp, brightly colored stalks. The leaves (which are inedible) should look fresh and be free of blemishes. To store rhubarb, wrap it tightly in plastic wrap or a plastic bag and refrigerate it for up to 3 days. Remove and discard the leaves just before using the stalks.

**NUTRIENT ANALYSIS**

| | |
|---|---|
| Calories | 236 |
| Protein | 3 g |
| Carbohydrate | 49 g |
| Total Fat | 4 g |
| Saturated Fat | 1 g |
| Polyunsaturated Fat | 1 g |
| Monounsaturated Fat | 2 g |
| Cholesterol | 0 mg |
| Sodium | 87 mg |

# PUMPKIN PIE

*Serves 8*

*Fat-free evaporated milk is rich in taste and texture. Use it in cooking in place of whole milk or cream, as we've done here.*

9-inch unbaked low-fat piecrust, such as Gingersnap and Graham Cracker Crust (see page 288)

### FILLING

16-ounce can pumpkin puree

1¼ cups fat-free evaporated milk

Whites of 3 large eggs

½ cup firmly packed dark brown sugar

1 teaspoon ground cinnamon

1 teaspoon ground ginger

¼ teaspoon ground nutmeg

Pinch of ground cloves

½ cup nonfat or low-fat frozen whipped topping, thawed (optional)

Preheat oven to 350° F.

Bake piecrust until lightly browned, about 10 minutes. Remove from oven and let cool to room temperature.

Preheat oven to 450° F.

In a large bowl, beat all filling ingredients until no lumps remain. Pour into piecrust. Bake for 10 minutes. Reduce heat to 325° F and bake for 50 minutes, or until a knife inserted into the center comes out clean. When serving, top each slice with a dollop of whipped topping.

**NUTRIENT ANALYSIS**

Calories 220
Protein 6 g
Carbohydrate 46 g
Total Fat 2 g
Saturated Fat 1 g
Polyunsaturated Fat 0 g
Monounsaturated Fat 1 g
Cholesterol 1 mg
Sodium 222 mg

# MERINGUE SHELLS

*Serves 10 as individual shells*
*Serves 8 as 9-inch pie shell*

*For an elegant dessert that's light and delicious, fill these shells with nonfat or low-fat vanilla ice cream or frozen yogurt drizzled with Berry Sauce (see page 244). Experiment with other fruits and nonfat or low-fat custards and frozen treats to come up with your own creations.*

Vegetable oil spray
Whites of 2 large eggs*
⅛ teaspoon cream of tartar
½ cup sugar
½ teaspoon white vinegar
½ teaspoon vanilla extract

## NUTRIENT ANALYSIS
*(For individual shell)*

| | |
|---|---|
| Calories | 42 |
| Protein | 1 g |
| Carbohydrate | 10 g |
| Total Fat | 0 g |
| Saturated Fat | 0 g |
| Polyunsaturated Fat | 0 g |
| Monounsaturated Fat | 0 g |
| Cholesterol | 0 mg |
| Sodium | 11 mg |

## NUTRIENT ANALYSIS
*(For ⅛ of large shell)*

| | |
|---|---|
| Calories | 53 |
| Protein | 1 g |
| Carbohydrate | 13 g |
| Total Fat | 0 g |
| Saturated Fat | 0 g |
| Polyunsaturated Fat | 0 g |
| Monounsaturated Fat | 0 g |
| Cholesterol | 0 mg |
| Sodium | 14 mg |

Preheat oven to 275° F. Line 2 large baking sheets with wax paper, then lightly spray with vegetable oil spray.

In a large bowl, beat egg whites and cream of tartar with an electric beater until stiff peaks form.

Add sugar 2 tablespoons at a time, beating well after each addition. To test whether sugar has dissolved completely, rub meringue mixture between fingers; if meringue is grainy, continue beating.

Add vinegar and vanilla; beat well to blend.

Drop mixture by heaping tablespoonfuls about 2 inches apart on prepared baking sheets. Spread each spoonful into a 2½-inch circle, pushing the mixture against the edges to resemble a nest. Bake for 45 minutes. Reduce heat to 250° F and bake for about 15 minutes, until each meringue is firm and crisp but not brown.

Remove shells from wax paper while warm. Allow shells to cool on a rack before filling. Empty shells can be stored in a plastic bag in an airtight container for up to 2 weeks.

For a 9-inch pie shell, lightly spray pie pan with vegetable oil spray. Prepare meringue as directed above. Spoon meringue into prepared pie pan, heaping the mixture higher along the sides so that it resembles a large nest. Bake at 275° F for 1 hour. Reduce heat to 250° F and bake for 30 minutes, or until meringue is firm and crisp but not brown. Let cool to room temperature before filling.

* Even a single drop of egg yolk will prevent egg whites from rising, so separate eggs very carefully.

# GINGERSNAP AND GRAHAM CRACKER CRUST

*Makes 1 9-inch piecrust*

*The flavorful pairing of gingersnaps and graham crackers makes this crust almost a dessert in itself! The corn syrup and apple juice bind the dough and make it easy to shape the piecrust.*

¾ cup crushed low-fat graham crackers (about 9 squares)

¾ cup crushed low-fat gingersnaps (about 18 cookies)

2 tablespoons corn syrup

2 tablespoons unsweetened apple juice

In a medium bowl, mix all ingredients with a spoon. Using your fingers, press mixture evenly in a 9-inch pie pan.

The crust is ready to fill and bake. If you need a pre-baked crust, bake it at 350° F for 10 minutes, then cool and fill.

**NUTRIENT ANALYSIS**

*(For ⅛ of piecrust)*

Calories 109
Protein 1 g
Carbohydrate 23 g
Total Fat 2 g
Saturated Fat 0 g
Polyunsaturated Fat 0 g
Monounsaturated Fat 1 g
Cholesterol 0 mg
Sodium 147 mg

# BAKLAVA

*Serves 12*

*This decadent Greek sweet usually is full of butter and therefore loaded with fat and saturated fat. Through the wonders of modern technology—in the form of butter-flavor vegetable oil spray—baklava is back on the menu!*

1 cup raisins (5 to 6 ounces)

⅓ cup finely chopped pecans or walnuts, dry-roasted (about 1 ounce)

8 sheets phyllo dough, thawed

Butter-flavor vegetable oil spray

½ cup honey

2 teaspoons ground cinnamon

1 tablespoon acceptable margarine, melted

Preheat oven to 350° F.

In a small bowl, mix raisins and nuts. Set aside.

Lightly spray every other sheet of phyllo with vegetable oil spray, stacking all the sheets.

Spread raisin-nut mixture over the phyllo, leaving a 1-inch border on all sides.

Drizzle with honey and sprinkle with cinnamon.

Starting on a long side, roll lengthwise, jelly-roll fashion, and place, seam side down, on a nonstick baking sheet, making sure the ends of the roll are tucked under.

Brush the top lightly with margarine. Cut through the pastry to the raisin-nut mixture, at 1½-inch intervals, to provide vents for steam to escape.

Bake for 20 to 30 minutes, or until light golden-brown. Slice, using vent lines as guides.

**COOK'S TIP:**

This dish freezes well. Prepare as above but omit brushing with margarine and baking. (Do cut the steam vents.) Freeze overnight on a baking sheet, then wrap well in freezer paper or foil. To prevent the pastry from getting soggy, do not defrost before baking. Place on a baking sheet, brush with margarine, and bake at 350° F for 35 to 45 minutes, or until golden.

**NUTRIENT ANALYSIS**

Calories 156
Protein 2 g
Carbohydrate 32 g
Total Fat 3 g
Saturated Fat 0 g
Polyunsaturated Fat 1 g
Monounsaturated Fat 2 g
Cholesterol 0 mg
Sodium 65 mg

# SUGAR-DUSTED MOCHA BROWNIES

*Serves 12*

**COOK'S TIP:**
For a decorative topping, place a doily on top of the brownies before sifting powdered sugar. Remove doily before cutting brownies.

*This light, yet fudgy version of a countrywide favorite features a touch of coffee and a pretty powdered-sugar top.*

½ cup all-purpose flour

½ cup unsweetened cocoa powder

½ teaspoon baking powder

4 tablespoons light margarine (¼ cup)

1 tablespoon instant coffee crystals

1 cup sugar

Egg substitute equivalent to 2 eggs, or 2 eggs

¼ cup prune baby food

2 teaspoons vanilla

Vegetable oil spray

2 tablespoons powdered sugar

Preheat oven to 350° F.

In a small bowl, combine flour, cocoa powder, and baking powder. Set aside.

In a medium saucepan over medium-low heat, melt margarine.

Add coffee crystals and stir until dissolved. Remove from heat and let cool slightly.

Using a wooden spoon, add sugar, egg substitute, prune baby food, and vanilla to coffee mixture. Stir until well combined.

Fold cocoa mixture into sugar mixture until well combined.

Spray an 8 × 8 × 2-inch cake pan with vegetable oil spray. Spoon batter into baking pan.

Bake, uncovered, for 18 to 20 minutes, or until a toothpick inserted near the center comes out almost clean (it should have a few fudgy crumbs on it).

Cool brownies in the pan on a wire rack. Sift powdered sugar over brownies.

**NUTRIENT ANALYSIS**

Calories 124
Protein 2 g
Carbohydrate 25 g
Total Fat 2 g
Saturated Fat 1 g
Polyunsaturated Fat 1 g
Monounsaturated Fat 1 g
Cholesterol 0 mg
Sodium 82 mg

# COCOA-ALMOND MERINGUE KISSES

*Serves 14*

*These meringues are crisp on the outside and chewy on the inside.*

Vegetable oil spray

Whites of 3 large eggs*

⅛ teaspoon cream of tartar

¾ cup sugar

3 tablespoons unsweetened cocoa powder

½ teaspoon vanilla extract

¼ cup sliced almonds (about 1 ounce)

Preheat oven to 325° F. Spray 2 large baking sheets with vegetable oil spray. Set aside.

In a large bowl, beat egg whites and cream of tartar until stiff peaks form.

Add sugar, 2 tablespoons at a time, beating well after each addition.

Add cocoa and vanilla. Beat well to blend.

Fold in almonds.

Drop mixture by tablespoonfuls onto prepared baking sheets.

Bake for 25 minutes, or until meringues are crisp on the outside. Remove from baking sheets immediately and allow to cool on a rack. Store in an airtight container.

* Even a single drop of egg yolk will prevent egg whites from rising, so separate eggs very carefully.

**NUTRIENT ANALYSIS**

Calories 62

Protein 1 g

Carbohydrate 12 g

Total Fat 1 g

Saturated Fat 0 g

Polyunsaturated Fat 0 g

Monounsaturated Fat 1 g

Cholesterol 0 mg

Sodium 12 mg

# GINGERBREAD BARS

*The wonderful, spicy aroma of these cookies baking will have the whole family lined up in the kitchen. The cookies are great any time, and they freeze well.*

Vegetable oil spray

6 tablespoons acceptable margarine, at room temperature

1 cup firmly packed dark brown sugar

Whites of 2 large eggs

¼ cup molasses

1¼ cups all-purpose flour

1 cup whole-wheat flour

¼ cup nonfat dry milk powder

¾ teaspoon baking powder

¾ teaspoon baking soda

¾ teaspoon ground ginger

½ teaspoon ground cinnamon

½ teaspoon ground nutmeg

⅛ teaspoon ground cloves

¼ cup finely chopped walnuts, preferably dry-roasted (about 1 ounce)

**NUTRIENT ANALYSIS**

Calories 195
Protein 3 g
Carbohydrate 33 g
Total Fat 6 g
Saturated Fat 1 g
Polyunsaturated Fat 2 g
Monounsaturated Fat 2 g
Cholesterol 0 mg
Sodium 137 mg

Preheat oven to 350° F. Spray a 12½ × 8-inch baking pan with vegetable oil spray.

In a large bowl, beat margarine at medium speed until creamy.

Add brown sugar and beat at high speed until light, 1 to 2 minutes.

Beat in egg whites.

Add molasses and beat until no lumps remain.

In a separate bowl, sift together remaining ingredients except nuts. Add sifted ingredients to margarine mixture and blend thoroughly.

Stir in nuts and mix well. The dough will be sticky.

Place the dough in center of prepared pan. Using a spatula or wet hands, spread dough evenly. Place pan on center rack of oven.

Bake for 25 minutes. Allow to cool for at least 5 minutes. Cut into 30 bars. Refrigerate in an airtight container for up to 1 week. Serve at room temperature.

# MOCHA CHEESECAKE

*Serves 10*

*With this recipe, you can indulge yourself! Yogurt cheese
and nonfat or low-fat ricotta cheese replace the high-fat
cream cheese found in most cheesecakes. Also, egg whites
and cocoa powder are used instead of whole eggs and chocolate. The result is a delectable cake that tastes sinful but
isn't. It freezes well if wrapped tightly before freezing.*

## CRUST

Vegetable oil spray

4 slices whole-wheat bread, toasted

¼ cup honey

Whites of 2 large eggs

3 tablespoons wheat germ

2 tablespoons unsweetened cocoa powder

1½ teaspoons vanilla extract

1½ teaspoons coffee liqueur

## FILLING

2 cups Yogurt Cheese (see page 155)

2 cups nonfat or low-fat ricotta cheese

⅔ cup sugar

Whites of 2 large eggs

2 tablespoons all-purpose flour

2 tablespoons unsweetened cocoa powder

1 tablespoon vanilla extract

1 tablespoon coffee liqueur

Grated rind of ½ orange

Fresh fruit, thinly sliced (optional)

Preheat oven to 300° F. Spray a 9-inch springform pan
with vegetable oil spray.

    Break bread into quarters and place in a food proces-
sor. Process into fine crumbs.

In a medium bowl, mix bread crumbs with remaining crust ingredients until coarse and moist. Using a fork, press mixture evenly on the bottom of the prepared pan.

Bake for 10 minutes, or until firm to the touch. Cool on wire rack.

In a food processor, process all filling ingredients until fully blended, scraping the sides of the bowl as needed. Pour batter over cooled crust.

Bake on middle rack of oven for 1 hour. Turn off heat and let cake remain in the oven for 15 minutes. Remove cake from oven and let cool. Cover and refrigerate for at least 3 hours, preferably overnight, before removing sides of pan.

Garnish with fresh fruit. Serve chilled or at room temperature.

# CHOCOLATE SOUFFLÉ WITH VANILLA SAUCE

*Serves 6*

**COOK'S TIP ON COCOA POWDER:**
Cocoas are different colors and have different acidities and different tastes. Dutch-process cocoa is less acid than other cocoas, so its taste is mellower. Combine various cocoas to experience different flavors.

*This wonderful soufflé uses cocoa instead of chocolate. You'll think this dessert tastes just like its high-fat counterpart.*

**Vegetable oil spray**

⅓ **cup fresh orange juice**

⅓ **cup sugar**

**Whites of 4 large eggs***

¼ **cup unsweetened cocoa powder (Dutch process preferred)**

**2 tablespoons orange liqueur**

¾ **cup vanilla ice milk, softened**

Preheat oven to 300° F. Lightly spray six 5-ounce custard cups with vegetable oil spray.

In a small saucepan over medium-high heat, cook orange juice and sugar until mixture has a syrupy consistency, about 3 to 4 minutes, stirring occasionally. Remove from heat and set aside.

In a large bowl, beat egg whites until stiff, but stop before dry peaks form.

Pour syrup over the egg whites and continue beating for 2 minutes.

Add cocoa and liqueur and beat only until well mixed. Pour into prepared custard cups.

Bake for 12 minutes, or until soufflés have puffed. Do not overbake or soufflés will become tough.

To serve, spoon 2 tablespoons softened ice milk into the center of each soufflé. Serve immediately.

* Even a single drop of egg yolk will prevent egg whites from rising, so separate eggs very carefully.

**NUTRIENT ANALYSIS**

Calories 105
Protein 4 g
Carbohydrate 20 g
Total Fat 1 g
Saturated Fat 1 g
Polyunsaturated Fat 0 g
Monounsaturated Fat 0 g
Cholesterol 2 mg
Sodium 52 mg

# TAPIOCA PUDDING

*Serves 4*

*When you need to soothe your taste buds after a spicy meal, try this rich tapioca pudding. A touch of nutmeg contributes to the inviting taste of this comfort food, and toasted slivered almonds add a flavorful crunch.*

2¾ cups fat-free milk

⅓ cup sugar

Whites of 2 large eggs, lightly beaten

3 tablespoons quick-cooking tapioca

¾ teaspoon vanilla extract

Pinch ground nutmeg

¼ cup slivered almonds, dry-roasted (about 1 ounce) (optional)

In a 2-quart saucepan, mix milk, sugar, egg whites, and tapioca and let stand for 5 minutes. Bring mixture just to a boil over medium heat, stirring constantly.

Remove from heat and stir in vanilla and nutmeg. Transfer pudding to a medium bowl. Place plastic wrap directly on surface and let pudding stand at room temperature for 20 minutes. Stir and pour into 4 individual serving dishes. Sprinkle with almonds. Serve warm or chilled.

**NUTRIENT ANALYSIS**

Calories 159

Protein 8 g

Carbohydrate 31 g

Total Fat 0 g

Saturated Fat 0 g

Polyunsaturated Fat 0 g

Monounsaturated Fat 0 g

Cholesterol 3 mg

Sodium 114 mg

# ORANGE FLUFF

*Serves 6*

*This airy dessert features the fresh taste of orange juice and aromatic oils from the grated orange rind. Use whatever fresh fruit is in season to adorn each serving.*

¼ cup cold water

1 envelope unflavored gelatin (1 tablespoon)

½ cup sugar

½ cup boiling water

1 cup fresh or frozen orange juice (3 to 4 medium oranges or 8 ounces frozen)

½ cup nonfat or low-fat frozen whipped topping, thawed

1 tablespoon finely grated orange rind

2 kiwifruit, 2 peaches, or 6 fresh strawberries, sliced (optional)

6 small fresh mint sprigs (optional)

Place cold water in a small bowl. Sprinkle gelatin over water. Let stand for 2 to 3 minutes.

In another small bowl, dissolve sugar in boiling water.

Add gelatin mixture; stir until dissolved.

Add orange juice.

Place bowl in refrigerator or over ice water and allow to chill, stirring occasionally, until mixture thickens, 8 to 10 minutes.

Add whipped topping and beat vigorously with a hand beater. Continue beating for 8 to 10 minutes, or until mixture is fluffy and doubles in volume.

Fold in orange rind.

Spoon mixture into a serving bowl or individual glasses and refrigerate until set. Garnish with sliced fruit and mint before serving.

**NUTRIENT ANALYSIS**

Calories 95

Protein 1 g

Carbohydrate 23 g

Total Fat 0 g

Saturated Fat 0 g

Polyunsaturated Fat 0 g

Monounsaturated Fat 0 g

Cholesterol 0 mg

Sodium 6 mg

# BANANAS FOSTER PLUS

*Serves 4*

*This 1950s specialty of Brennan's restaurant in New Orleans has been updated for the 1990s cook with a pretty trio of fruit and significantly less fat.*

2 tablespoons light margarine (⅛ cup)

3 tablespoons light brown sugar

¼ teaspoon ground cinnamon

⅛ teaspoon ground nutmeg

2 medium bananas, sliced ½ inch thick

2 kiwifruit, peeled and sliced ½ inch thick

1 medium peach or nectarine, pitted and sliced ½ inch thick, or ½ cup canned juice-pack sliced peaches (about 4 ounces), drained

1 tablespoon dark rum or ¼ teaspoon rum extract

2 cups nonfat or low-fat vanilla frozen yogurt or ice milk (1 pint)

In a medium skillet over medium heat, melt margarine.

Stir in brown sugar, cinnamon, and nutmeg. Cook and stir for 3 to 5 minutes, or until sugar melts.

Add bananas, kiwifruit, and peach. Cook, stirring gently, for about 1 minute or until heated through.

Stir in rum. Cook, stirring gently, for 1 minute. Serve warm with frozen yogurt.

## NUTRIENT ANALYSIS

Calories  257

Protein  4 g

Carbohydrate  55 g

Total Fat  3 g

Saturated Fat  1 g

Polyunsaturated Fat  1 g

Monounsaturated Fat  1 g

Cholesterol  1 mg

Sodium  126 mg

# CHERRIES JUBILEE

*Serves 4*

*What an elegant finale to a dinner party!*

16-ounce can dark, sweet, pitted cherries

¼ cup unsweetened apple juice

1 tablespoon cornstarch

2 tablespoons brandy or rum

2 cups nonfat or low-fat vanilla ice milk or nonfat or
    low-fat frozen yogurt (1 pint)

Drain syrup from cherries and mix syrup with apple juice.

In a small bowl, mix cornstarch and 2 tablespoons of juice until no lumps remain.

In a small saucepan over high heat, bring remaining juice mixture to a boil. Reduce heat to medium.

Add cornstarch mixture, stirring constantly. Let mixture return to a boil and cook for about 1 minute, or until thickened.

Add brandy and stir in cherries. Using a long-handled match, carefully ignite the *fumes*.

Place a ½-cup scoop of ice milk in 4 small bowls. When flames have extinguished, pour hot cherries over each. Serve immediately.

**NUTRIENT ANALYSIS**

Calories 211

Protein 5 g

Carbohydrate 42 g

Total Fat 1 g

Saturated Fat 1 g

Polyunsaturated Fat 0 g

Monounsaturated Fat 0 g

Cholesterol 2 mg

Sodium 88 mg

# MELON WITH SHERBET

*Serves 6*

*Serve this dessert in pretty glasses with frosted rims.*

1 small honeydew melon, cut in half and seeded

4 oranges or 2 cups fresh strawberries (10 to 12 ounces)

2 tablespoons powdered sugar, sifted

Lime juice, lemon juice, or water

12 ounces rainbow sherbet (about 1½ cups)

6 sprigs of fresh mint

With a melon baller, scoop out flesh of melon. Section oranges or slice strawberries. Combine fruit in a large bowl, cover, and refrigerate.

Place powdered sugar in a pie pan. Dampen rims of 6 dessert glasses with lime juice, then dip rims in powdered sugar.

Divide fruit mixture among glasses, top each with a scoop of sherbet, and garnish with a mint sprig. Serve immediately.

**COOK'S TIP:**

Instead of powdered sugar, use any color of dry gelatin dessert powder on the rims of the glasses.

**NUTRIENT ANALYSIS**

Calories 157

Protein 2 g

Carbohydrate 37 g

Total Fat 1 g

Saturated Fat 1 g

Polyunsaturated Fat 0 g

Monounsaturated Fat 0 g

Cholesterol 3 mg

Sodium 37 mg

# STRAWBERRIES ROMANOFF

*Serves 6*

*This great dessert can also be served as a breakfast treat; just leave out the liqueur and top with crunchy whole-grain cereal. For flavor variety, try substituting other fresh fruit and complementary liqueurs.*

### SAUCE

1 cup Yogurt Cheese (see page 155)

¼ cup firmly packed light brown sugar

2 tablespoons orange or strawberry liqueur (optional)

1 teaspoon vanilla extract

½ teaspoon ground cinnamon


2 pints fresh strawberries, hulled and cut into bite-size pieces (about 1½ pounds)

2 tablespoons finely chopped pecan pieces, dry-roasted (optional)

In a small bowl, whisk together sauce ingredients until fully mixed. Cover and refrigerate for at least 1 hour, or until sauce is slightly firm.

Spoon berries into 4 dessert dishes. Top each serving with ¼ cup sauce and a sprinkling of nuts. Serve immediately.

## NUTRIENT ANALYSIS

Calories 174

Protein 8 g

Carbohydrate 35 g

Total Fat 1 g

Saturated Fat 0 g

Polyunsaturated Fat 0 g

Monounsaturated Fat 0 g

Cholesterol 2 mg

Sodium 101 mg

# YOGURT-FRUIT CUP

*Serves 6*

*This offers a new twist to a back-to-basics favorite. You'll like the fragrant touch of cardamom.*

16-ounce can sliced peaches or pears, canned in their own juice

16-ounce container nonfat or low-fat vanilla yogurt

2 tablespoons finely chopped almonds, preferably dry-roasted

½ teaspoon ground cardamom

Drain fruit and divide among 6 small dessert bowls.

Top with yogurt and nuts and sprinkle lightly with cardamom. Serve immediately.

---

**NUTRIENT ANALYSIS**

Calories 79
Protein 4 g
Carbohydrate 13 g
Total Fat 2 g
Saturated Fat 0 g
Polyunsaturated Fat 0 g
Monounsaturated Fat 1 g
Cholesterol 2 mg
Sodium 32 mg

---

# MANGO BRÛLÉE
# WITH PINE NUTS

*Serves 4*

**COOK'S TIP:**
If fresh fruit is out of
season, you can use
frozen unsweetened fruit
that's been thawed, fruit
in a jar, or fruit canned
in natural juice.

*Easy, elegant, and fast, too, this very special dessert requires only four ingredients.*

2 cups cubed fresh mango, papaya, or peaches (about 3
    mangoes, 2 medium papayas, or 4 medium peaches)

⅔ cup nonfat or low-fat sour cream

2 tablespoons pine nuts

2 tablespoons light brown sugar

Preheat broiler.

Place fruit in the bottom of a 9-inch pie pan.

Stir sour cream and dollop over fruit. Use the back of a spoon to spread sour cream evenly.

Sprinkle with pine nuts and brown sugar.

Broil 4 to 6 inches from the heat for 1 to 2 minutes, or until sugar melts and pine nuts toast (watch nuts closely to avoid burning). Serve immediately.

**NUTRIENT ANALYSIS**

Calories 128
Protein 4 g
Carbohydrate 25 g
Total Fat 3 g
Saturated Fat 0 g
Polyunsaturated Fat 1 g
Monounsaturated Fat 1 g
Cholesterol 1 mg
Sodium 47 mg

# VERY BERRY SORBET

*Serves 2*

*To freeze or not to freeze, that is the question. With this slightly tart dessert, either answer is correct. Try both ways and see which you prefer.*

1½ cups frozen unsweetened blackberries, slightly thawed (6 to 8 ounces)

2 teaspoons water

1 teaspoon frozen orange juice concentrate

1 teaspoon brandy or cognac (optional)

Fresh mint sprigs (optional)

In a blender or food processor, process all ingredients except mint until smooth, scraping sides as needed.

Sorbet can be served immediately or frozen. If sorbet is frozen, remove it from freezer about 15 minutes before serving to defrost until soft enough to serve. Garnish with mint sprigs.

**NUTRIENT ANALYSIS**

Calories 60
Protein 1 g
Carbohydrate 15 g
Total Fat 0 g
Saturated Fat 0 g
Polyunsaturated Fat 0 g
Monounsaturated Fat 0 g
Cholesterol 0 mg
Sodium 0 mg

# STRAWBERRY MARGARITA ICE

*Serves 6*

**COOK'S TIP:**

If you leave the straw-berry mixture in the freezer until it becomes frozen solid, let it stand at room temperature for about 15 minutes before breaking it into chunks and beating with an electric mixer.

*This frosty dessert reflects the Southwest's love for a slushy drink called a frozen margarita. You can adjust the level of sugar in this recipe depending on the sweetness of your strawberries and how tart you like your margaritas.*

2 cups fresh or frozen unsweetened strawberries, thawed (10 to 12 ounces)

⅔ cup fresh lime juice (6 to 8 medium limes)

½ to ⅔ cup sugar

1 tablespoon tequila or fresh lime juice

1 tablespoon orange liqueur or fresh orange juice

In a blender or food processor, combine all ingredients. Process until smooth.

Transfer mixture to a 9 × 5 × 3-inch loaf pan. Cover and freeze for about 4 hours or until firm but not frozen solid.

Place a large bowl in refrigerator to chill.

When mixture is firm, break it into chunks. Transfer to the chilled bowl. Beat with an electric mixer until smooth but not melted. Serve immediately or return mixture to loaf pan, cover, and freeze until serving time.

To serve when frozen, scrape across the surface with a spoon and mound shavings in dessert dishes.

**NUTRIENT ANALYSIS**

Calories 108
Protein 0 g
Carbohydrate 25 g
Total Fat 0 g
Saturated Fat 0 g
Polyunsaturated Fat 0 g
Monounsaturated Fat 0 g
Cholesterol 0 mg
Sodium 7 mg

# BAKED APPLES

*Serves 4*

*Each apple is stuffed with dried fruit that's been plumped in a flavorful mixture of wine and apple juice. The aroma of cinnamon will permeate the air as these apples bake.*

¼ cup port

¼ cup frozen unsweetened apple juice concentrate, thawed

¼ cup raisins or dried cranberries, blueberries, or tart cherries

¼ teaspoon ground cinnamon

4 baking apples, such as Rome Beauty, Jonathan, or McIntosh

Preheat oven to 350° F.

In a small saucepan over high heat, bring wine and juice concentrate to a boil. Turn heat off and add raisins and cinnamon. Stir, cover, and let sit for 15 minutes.

Meanwhile, core apples, but don't cut through the bottoms. If necessary, slice a small section from the bottom of each apple so that it does not fall over. With a paring knife, score around the apple, about ½ inch from the bottom. Peel from top down to scored line to prevent splitting.

Place apples in a glass baking dish so they are not touching. Fill centers with the juice-soaked raisins, spooning remaining juice evenly over apples. Pour water in the dish to a depth of ⅓ inch. Cover dish with aluminum foil. Bake for 20 minutes. Remove foil and bake for 20 minutes. Serve warm.

## NUTRIENT ANALYSIS

Calories 154

Protein 1 g

Carbohydrate 39 g

Total Fat 1 g

Saturated Fat 0 g

Polyunsaturated Fat 0 g

Monounsaturated Fat 0 g

Cholesterol 0 mg

Sodium 6 mg

# APPENDIXES

# YOU ARE WHAT YOU EAT: HOW DIET AFFECTS YOUR BLOOD CHOLESTEROL LEVEL

## WHAT RAISES YOUR BLOOD CHOLESTEROL?

When it comes to how you eat, three main factors raise your blood cholesterol level. These are saturated and trans fats, cholesterol, and obesity.

### SATURATED AND TRANS FATS

All fats are composed mainly of triglycerides. These, in turn, are composed of "fatty acids." These fatty acids fall into four categories: saturated, trans, monounsaturated, and polyunsaturated. Of these, only the saturated and trans fatty acids raise blood cholesterol. In this book, we're using the popular terms "saturated fat" and "trans fat" as shorthand for the more accurate terms "saturated fatty acid" and "trans fatty acid."

Foods high in saturated fat come from both animals and plants. Animal-based foods containing lots of saturated fat include butter, beef tallow, lard, and poultry fat. Seafood contains a small amount. Plant-based oils containing saturated fat include coconut oil, palm kernel oil, palm oil, and cocoa butter.

Trans fat is found in foods such as margarine, french fries, doughnuts, crackers, and commercially baked cookies.

### CHOLESTEROL IN YOUR BLOOD

For the average person, research shows, eating 1 gram of saturated fat increases blood cholesterol by about 1 milligram per deciliter of blood (mg/dl). This response varies from person to person. Some people are unusually sensitive to saturated fat, and their blood cholesterol increases dramatically when they eat it. Others show less striking increases.

Of the several kinds of saturated fat, some raise blood cholesterol more than others. Butterfat, coconut oil, palm oil, and palm kernel oil raise blood cholesterol the most. Cocoa butter and meat fats, such as beef tallow and lard, raise blood cholesterol less, but they still raise it too much.

Trans fats, which result from the process used to make hydrogenated fats and oils, also raise blood cholesterol levels.

## Cholesterol in Your Food

Another substance that can raise the cholesterol in your blood is the cholesterol found in many of the foods you eat. It's important to distinguish between the cholesterol in foods and the cholesterol in your blood. The two are not the same.

Cholesterol in foods comes exclusively from animal products. The richest sources are egg yolks and organ meats. Some cholesterol is found in all meats, poultry, seafood, and animal fats, such as butter and lard. For most Americans, cholesterol in the diet comes from eggs, meats, and animal fats.

How dietary cholesterol affects blood cholesterol is a controversial and disputed subject. Many research studies show that a high-cholesterol diet raises the blood cholesterol level—but the amount of that increase varies from person to person. Also, even an individual's response can vary from one time to another. On the average, for every 250 milligrams of cholesterol you normally eat in foods, your blood cholesterol rises by about 10 mg/dl. Most of this increase occurs in the low-density lipoprotein (LDL) cholesterol, the type of cholesterol most likely to build up in your arteries. (For a more-detailed discussion of the types of cholesterol and their significance, see appendix F, page 344.)

## Obesity

Another way that diet can raise your blood cholesterol is if you gain too much weight. Taking in more calories than your body burns in activity can lead to obesity. Medical studies show that when an obese person has high blood cholesterol, it's usually found in both LDL cholesterol and VLDL cholesterol (very low density cholesterol, which also tends to build up in the arteries). In contrast, the level of HDL, or "good," cholesterol is usually low.

Take a look at figure 1. It shows how eating too much saturated fat and cholesterol and too many calories raises blood cholesterol. The left panel shows how the body reduces the amounts of LDL and VLDL in the blood. Here's how it works: Both VLDL remnants and LDLs are removed primarily by LDL receptors in the liver. These receptors, special proteins located on the surface of liver cells, are extremely important for reducing LDL, or "bad," cholesterol. They work by binding both VLDL remnants and LDLs and pulling them out of the blood.

The right panel of figure 1 shows how this LDL and VLDL removal process is changed by a cholesterol-raising diet. When a diet is rich in cholesterol, the excess cholesterol makes its way into the liver. As the liver receives more dietary cholesterol, it partially quits producing LDL receptors, which slows down the removal of LDL cholesterol from the blood.

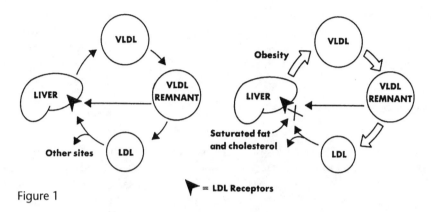

Figure 1

Also, saturated fats seem to help the cholesterol you eat make fewer LDL receptors. That's how both saturated fat and cholesterol in your diet decrease LDL and VLDL removal and increase the blood's LDL cholesterol level.

At the same time, obesity overloads the liver with calories, causing it to make more VLDLs. Excess VLDLs are then broken down into LDLs. When an obese person eats a diet high in saturated fat and cholesterol, the LDL-cholesterol level of the blood usually rises dramatically. Sadly, this combination of obesity and a high-saturated-fat, high-cholesterol diet is common in this country. In some people, it leads to a borderline cholesterol problem; in others, to a serious one.

## WHAT LOWERS YOUR BLOOD CHOLESTEROL?

Although some nutrients, including some fats, raise the blood cholesterol level, some other nutrients have no effect on it, and still others reduce it. Nutrients that help reduce blood cholesterol levels include polyunsaturated fat and monounsaturated fat. Carbohydrates can help replace fat in the diet. By substituting these nutrients for foods containing saturated fat and cholesterol, you can help decrease your blood cholesterol level.

## POLYUNSATURATED FAT

Polyunsaturated fat is one of two types. One type is composed of omega-6 fatty acids, found in many vegetable oils, such as safflower, sunflower, soybean, and corn. The other type is composed of omega-3 fatty acids, which are found in large amounts in some fish and fish oils.

In the American diet, polyunsaturated fat of all kinds accounts for about 6 to 7 percent of our total calories. Most polyunsaturated fat is the omega-6 type; very little is the omega-3 type. When saturated fat is replaced with polyunsaturated omega-6 fatty acids, total blood cholesterol and LDL-cholesterol levels fall. There's not much evidence so far that omega-3 fatty acids will cause this.

## MONOUNSATURATED FAT

Monounsaturated fat is found mostly in olive oil, canola (rapeseed) oil, and high-monounsaturated-fat forms of sunflower and safflower oil. For many years, monounsaturated fat was thought to be neutral, neither raising nor lowering blood cholesterol. Thanks to research, we now know that monounsaturated fat does, in fact, lower LDL cholesterol as much as polyunsaturated fat when used in place of saturated fat.

## CARBOHYDRATES

Carbohydrates are one of three types: simple sugars, such as those in cake and candy; digestible complex carbohydrates, otherwise known as starches; or indigestible complex carbohydrates, which we call fiber.

We know that some types of fiber, particularly the soluble kind, may lower blood cholesterol. Examples of these are pectins, psyllium, and certain gums. One such gum is beta-glucon, present in oat products and beans. Eating between 15 and 25 grams of soluble fiber per day has been reported to slightly lower blood cholesterol levels. (If you suddenly begin to eat lots of soluble fiber, you may have some gastrointestinal side effects, such as gas, but they usually disappear when your new diet becomes a habit.) The major sources of digestible complex carbohydrates and fiber are plant foods, such as vegetables, fruits, legumes, and grains.

# SHOPPING THE LOW-FAT, LOW-CHOLESTEROL WAY

Grocery store aisles are full of temptation. Artery-clogging, high-fat foods call out from almost every shelf. That's why you need a game plan in the grocery store. It will help you fill your cart with foods that are taste-tempting but low in fat and cholesterol.

Luckily, that's easy these days. Food manufacturers have created non-fat and low-fat versions of almost everything. From dairy products to baked goods, frozen entrées to salad dressings, you'll find alternatives that make breakfast bliss, lunch luscious, and dinner delectable. And your heart will love you for it.

In this appendix, we'll explore how to find these foods. It's easier than you think. All you have to do is read the package label.

## THE FAT IS ON THE LABEL

The U.S. Food and Drug Administration (FDA) has mandated that all U.S. food manufacturers must put a nutrition label on their products. This label must clearly state how much total fat, saturated fat, cholesterol, sodium, carbohydrate, fiber, sugar, and protein each serving contains. It also must cite serving size and the number of calories per serving.

Look closely at the sample nutrition label on the next page. You'll see that it first lists the serving size and the number of servings per container. Remember that if you eat double the serving size listed, you need to double the amount of fats, cholesterol, and other nutrients in your calculations, too.

### FATS AND SODIUM

Look carefully at the grams of total fat, saturated fat, and cholesterol. You can get an idea of the amount of fat in each food by looking at the number of total calories in a serving, then at the number of calories from fat. Make sure the calories from fat are just a small part of the total calories. As for saturated fat and cholesterol, the lower the better.

You'll also want to pay close attention to the amount of sodium listed. Be sure to keep your total intake to no more than 2,400 milligrams a day.

## Nutrition Facts

Serving Size ½ cup (114g)
Servings Per Container 4

**Amount Per Serving**

**Calories** 90          Calories from Fat 30

|  | % Daily Value* |
|---|---|
| **Total Fat** 3g | **5%** |
| Saturated Fat 0g | **0%** |
| **Cholesterol** 0mg | **0%** |
| **Sodium** 300mg | **13%** |
| **Total Carbohydrate** 13g | **4%** |
| Dietary Fiber 3g | **12%** |
| Sugars 3g | |
| **Protein** 3g | |

| Vitamin A | 80% | • | Vitamin C | 60% |
|---|---|---|---|---|
| Calcium | 4% | • | Iron | 4% |

* Percent Daily Values are based on a 2,000 calorie diet. Your daily values may be higher or lower depending on your calorie needs:

|  |  | Calories | 2,000 | 2,500 |
|---|---|---|---|---|
| Total Fat | Less than | | 65g | 80g |
| Sat Fat | Less than | | 20g | 25g |
| Cholesterol | Less than | | 300mg | 300mg |
| Sodium | Less than | | 2,400mg | 2,400mg |
| Total Carbohydrate | | | 300g | 375g |
| Fiber | | | 25g | 30g |

Calories per gram:
Fat 9  •  Carbohydrate 4  •  Protein 4

*More nutrients may be listed on some labels.*

## CARBOHYDRATES AND PROTEIN

When you cut down on fat, you'll want to make up for the calories you aren't consuming. Increasing your intake of complex carbohydrates, such as vegetables, fruits, legumes, and grain products, is a good solution. When you look at carbohydrates, also check out the dietary fiber. Both soluble and insoluble fiber can help reduce the risk of heart disease and cancer, so aim for high-fiber carbohydrates. Examples are beans, peas, whole-grain foods, vegetables, and fruits.

Finally, there's protein. As we've said before, many Americans eat more protein than they need. It's best to eat a daily total of 5 to 6 ounces of lean meat, poultry, and seafood. Keep protein to only about 15 percent of your total calories.

## DAILY VALUES

On the right-hand side of the nutrition label, you'll see percentages. These are called "daily values," and they're listed for people who eat 2,000 calories each day. If you eat more than one serving of this food, your daily value will be higher; if you eat less, your daily value will be lower.

Using the product our sample label describes, if you eat 2,000 calories a day, the amount of fat it contains would be just 5 percent of the total you can eat for the day. Just below the chart, you'll see that vitamins and minerals are also listed. In this example, the product would furnish 80 percent of the vitamin A you need that day.

## COMPARING LABEL INFORMATION

The answer to finding low-fat, low-cholesterol foods is to compare product labels. For example, take a look at the tables below. One compares whole milk to nonfat milk; the other compares butter to margarine. It's easy to see which products have the most saturated fat and which will help your heart.

### COMPARING WHOLE AND FAT-FREE MILK

| Nutrition Information Per Serving | Whole Milk | Fat-Free Milk |
| --- | --- | --- |
| Serving size | 1 cup | 1 cup |
| Calories | 150 | 86 |
| Protein | 8 g | 8 g |
| Carbohydrates | 11 g | 12 g |
| Fat | 8 g | Less than 1 g |
| Polyunsaturated | Less than 1 g | 0 g |
| Saturated | 5 g | Less than 1 g |
| Cholesterol | 33 mg | 4 mg |

### COMPARING BUTTER AND MARGARINE

| Nutrition Information Per Serving | Butter, Stick | Margarine, Tub |
| --- | --- | --- |
| Serving size | 1 tbsp | 1 tbsp |
| Calories | 101 | 101 |
| Protein | 0.1 g | 0.1 g |
| Carbohydrates | 0.1 g | 0.1 g |
| Fat | 11.4 g | 11.4 g |
| Polyunsaturated | 0.4 g | 3.9 g |
| Saturated | 7.1 g | 1.8 g |
| Cholesterol | 31 mg | 0 mg |

Note: The amount of monounsaturated fat is unlisted but can be calculated approximately by subtracting polyunsaturated and saturated fats from total fat.

The nutrition labels on packaged foods give you all the information you need so you can put together scrumptious meals that will help you lower your cholesterol level. All you have to do is read 'em!

## WHAT'S IN A NAME?

Plenty, because the FDA has also issued strict guidelines for the descriptors food manufacturers are allowed to put on their packages. For example, if you see the words "low fat" on a package, by law that means that the product contains 3 or fewer grams of fat per serving. Thanks to the FDA, you can count on it.

At the same time, you have to be careful. Low fat does not necessarily mean low calorie. Many people have gained weight suddenly because they weren't aware of that. In fact, while your heart will enjoy the low-fat food, your waistline may be getting the same calories as in the high-fat version.

If you see the words "low calorie" on a package, it means the product contains no more than 40 calories per serving. "Reduced calorie" means the product has at least one third fewer calories than the standard version of the product. Whether you're reducing your blood cholesterol level, watching your weight, or both, it pays to read food labels carefully.

Take a look at the following key words you might read on food packages. Knowing what they actually mean will help you choose the foods that will help your heart.

| Key Words | What They Mean |
|---|---|
| Calorie free | Fewer than 5 calories per serving |
| Light (lite) | One third fewer calories or no more than one half the fat of the higher-calorie, higher-fat version; or no more than one half the sodium of the higher-sodium version |
| Fat free | Less than 0.5 gram of fat per serving |
| Low fat | 3 grams of fat (or less) per serving |
| Reduced or less fat | At least 25 percent less fat per serving than the higher-fat version |
| Lean | Less than 10 grams of fat, 4 grams of saturated fat, and 95 milligrams of cholesterol per serving |
| Extra lean | Less than 5 grams of fat, 2 grams of saturated fat, and 95 milligrams of cholesterol per serving |
| Low in saturated fat | 1 gram saturated fat (or less) per serving and not more than 15 percent of calories from saturated fatty acids |

| | |
|---|---|
| Cholesterol free | Less than 2 milligrams of cholesterol and 2 grams (or less) of saturated fat per serving |
| Low cholesterol | 20 milligrams of cholesterol (or less) and 2 grams of saturated fat (or less) per serving |
| Reduced cholesterol | At least 25 percent less cholesterol than the higher-cholesterol version and 2 grams (or less) of saturated fat per serving |
| Sodium free (no sodium) | Less than 5 milligrams of sodium per serving and no sodium chloride (NaCl) in ingredients |
| Very low sodium | 35 milligrams of sodium (or less) per serving |
| Low sodium | 140 milligrams of sodium (or less) per serving |
| Reduced or less sodium | At least 25 percent less sodium per serving than the higher-sodium version |
| Sugar free | Less than 0.5 gram of sugar per serving |
| High fiber | 5 grams of fiber (or more) per serving |
| Good source of fiber | 2.5 to 4.9 grams of fiber per serving |

You don't have to try to remember all these! *Notice, however, that the key words follow the same pattern for each nutrient:*

- "Free" has the least amount.
- "Very low" and "low" have a little more.
- "Reduced" or "less" always means that the food has 25 percent less of that nutrient than the reference (or standard) version of the food.

Food packages might also sport certain health claims related to heart disease and cancer. You can believe those, too, now that the FDA has spelled out in concrete terms exactly what the food must offer in order to make these claims. Take a look at the following health claims chart.

| To Make Health Claims About . . . | The Food Must Be . . . |
|---|---|
| Heart disease and fats | Low in fat, saturated fat, and cholesterol |
| Heart disease and fruits, vegetables, and grain products | A fruit, vegetable, or grain product that is low in fat, saturated fat, and cholesterol and contains at least 0.6 gram of soluble fiber per serving |
| Blood pressure and sodium | Low in sodium |
| Cancer and fat | Fat free or low in fat |

# ARE YOU WHAT YOU EAT?

As long as you're reading food labels, take a minute to look at the ingredients. They're listed in order by weight. The ingredient in the greatest amount is listed first. The ingredient in the least amount is listed last. Sometimes what you see can surprise you. For example, in many cereals, the first ingredient listed is sugar. That is, the cereal has more sugar than wheat, oats, or other grains!

When you're looking for hidden saturated fat and cholesterol in foods, keep your eyes peeled for the ingredients listed in the chart below. For example, when you see "palm or palm kernel oil" listed on baked goods labels, you know you're getting lots of saturated fat. You even have to beware of the term "vegetable oil" because that *could* mean coconut, palm, or palm kernel oil. Instead, look for a specific polyunsaturated or monounsaturated vegetable oil, such as corn oil or canola oil, to be listed.

## SOURCES OF SATURATED FAT AND CHOLESTEROL

| | | |
|---|---|---|
| Animal fat | Cream | Palm kernel oil* |
| Bacon fat | Egg and egg yolk solids | Palm oil* |
| Beef fat | Ham fat | Pork fat |
| Butter | Hardened fat or oil | Turkey fat |
| Chicken fat | Hydrogenated vegetable oil* | Vegetable oil† |
| Cocoa butter* | Lamb fat | Vegetable shortening* |
| Coconut* | Lard | Whole-milk solids |
| Coconut oil* | Meat fat | |

*Sources of saturated fat only.
†Could be coconut, palm, or palm kernel oil.

Now that we know how to find what we need on grocery shelves, let's go shopping!

## SHOPPING FOR A HEALTHY HEART

To stock the kitchen, start with a grocery list that covers all the food groups. Aim for a variety of nonfat or low-fat, no- or low-cholesterol foods for breakfast, lunch, dinner, and snacks. We've come up with some tried-and-true shopping tips that will cut time, money, and fat from your diet!

## PLANNING

- Start by planning your weekly menus. If you're running short on time, plan just the entrées. Make a list *before* you go shopping. This helps cut down on impulse buying of items that may not fit into your new eating plan. Use the "Daily Food Guide" below to help you plan your meals.

- Never go shopping on an empty stomach. Hunger may tempt you to reach for the wrong foods.

- Buy specials or sale items only if they fit into your food plan for the week and into your overall cholesterol-lowering program. Otherwise, they may go to waste. Or to waist.

- You can cut costs by trying store brands in place of your usual brand-name products, but compare the ingredients lists and nutrition labels to make sure you're getting what you expect.

- Food manufacturers have created a host of new products that are low in fat, cholesterol, and sodium. However, you must read the nutrition labels. Just because a food is low in fat doesn't mean it's low in calories or sodium.

## SODIUM SEARCH

- Check ingredients lists for salt and other high-sodium additives. Be alert to any food label that has the word "sodium" on it.

- "Sodium free" on a label means that the item has less than 5 milligrams of sodium per serving. "Very low sodium" means less than 35 milligrams of sodium per serving.

- "Low sodium" means 140 or fewer milligrams per serving or 140 or fewer milligrams in 100 grams of food in a meal or main dish. "Reduced sodium" means the product has at least 25 percent less sodium than the regular food or a similar food.

- "Unsalted," "no salt added," or "without added salt" means that the product is made without the salt that is normally used, but the product still contains the sodium that naturally occurs in the food.

The discussion starting on page 322 covers each food group you'll want in your eating plan: meats, poultry, and seafood; dairy and eggs; fats and oils; vegetables and fruits; breads, cereals, pastas, rice and other grains, and dried peas and beans; and even sweets and snacks. You'll find lots of tips about what kind of food to buy and the serving sizes to plan for. Grab a shopping cart and let's get going!

# DAILY FOOD GUIDE

| Food Group | Number of Servings | Serving Size |
|---|---|---|
| Lean meat, poultry, and seafood | ≤6 ounces a day on Step I Diet<br>≤5 ounces a day on Step II Diet (leanest cuts only) | |
| Nonfat/low-fat dairy foods | 2 to 3 | 1 cup fat-free milk<br>1 cup nonfat or low-fat yogurt<br>1 ounce fat-free or low-fat cheese with 3 or fewer grams of fat per serving |
| Eggs | ≤4 yolks a week on Step I Diet*<br>≤2 yolks a week on Step II Diet* | |
| Fats and oils | ≤6 to 8† | 1 teaspoon soft margarine or vegetable oil<br>1 tablespoon salad dressing<br>1 ounce nuts |
| Fruits | 2 to 4 | 1 piece fruit<br>½ cup diced fruit<br>¾ cup fruit juice |
| Vegetables | 3 to 5 | 1 cup leafy or raw<br>½ cup cooked<br>¾ cup juice |
| Breads, cereals, pasta, rice, dried peas and beans, grains, and potatoes | 6 to 11 | 1 slice bread<br>½ bun, bagel, or muffin<br>1 ounce dry cereal<br>½ cup cooked cereal, dried peas or beans, potatoes, or rice or other grains<br>½ cup tofu |
| Sweets and snacks | Now and then | |

* Includes food preparation.
† Includes salad dressings and nuts.
≤means less than or equal to.

## MEATS, POULTRY, AND SEAFOOD

When planning your menu, remember that the recommended amount of protein is up to 6 ounces a day for the Step I Diet and up to 5 ounces a day for the Step II Diet. When it comes to meats, the leaner the better. Choose USDA select, which is the lowest in saturated fat. Just follow these fat-cutting tips when shopping for entrées.

# Meats

- "Prime" grades of meat are heavily marbled, making them high in saturated fat. "Choice" grades are less fatty than prime but are still high in saturated fat. Choose "select" grades instead—they're lower in fat.

- Look for the words "lean," "extra lean," and "light" on beef, lamb, pork, and processed meats. "Lean" means the product has fewer than 10 grams of fat, 4 grams of saturated fat, and 95 milligrams of cholesterol in a serving. "Extra lean" means the product has fewer than 5 grams of fat, 2 grams of saturated fat, and 95 milligrams of cholesterol in a serving. The term "light" means the product has been changed to have half the fat or one third fewer calories than the regular product; the sodium in a low-calorie, low-fat food has been cut by 50 percent; or a meal or main dish is low fat or low calorie.

- Organ meats, such as liver, brains, kidney, and sweetbreads, are extremely high in cholesterol, so eat them sparingly.

- Choose lean cuts of beef, such as eye of the round, top round, tenderloin, sirloin, or flank.

- Select lean pork, such as tenderloin, loin chops, sirloin, center-cut ham (fresh and cured), and Canadian bacon.

- All cuts of veal except breast and ground or cubed cutlets are lean. Examples of lean veal are chops and roast.

- The leanest cut of lamb is the leg or shank.

- Some wild game, such as venison, rabbit, squirrel, and pheasant, is very lean; duck and goose are not.

- Limit processed meats, such as bacon, bologna, salami, hot dogs, and sausage. They're high in saturated fat and total fat. Reduced-fat, low-fat, perhaps even nonfat versions of these meats are available, but watch out for high sodium.

# Poultry

- Chicken, Cornish hens, and turkey are good choices for entrées. Since much of the fat in poultry is in the skin, removing it greatly reduces the fat content. Remember that the white meat is lower in saturated fat than the dark meat. Avoid goose, duck, and processed poultry products, which are high in saturated fat.

- Try fresh ground turkey or chicken made from white meat. If the package doesn't say "white meat," "light meat," or "breast," it may include the skin and dark meat, so it will be higher in fat.

- Hot dogs—chicken, turkey, beef, or pork—are now available in nonfat and lean varieties. Compare labels to find the brands that are lowest in fat, saturated fat, and sodium.

## SEAFOOD

- Fish is always a good choice because most varieties are lower in saturated fat and cholesterol than are meats and poultry.
- Tuna canned in water or rinsed is another good choice.
- Try uncreamed or smoked herring, as well as sardines canned in tomato sauce or rinsed.
- Shellfish varies in cholesterol content. Some, such as squid and shrimp, are fairly high in cholesterol. Others, including scallops, mussels, and clams, are low. Shellfish have little saturated fat and total fat. You can eat shellfish as part of a cholesterol-lowering diet, but make sure you stay within the limits of your dietary cholesterol for each day.

### MEAT, POULTRY, AND SEAFOOD: A COMPARISON

| Food Type (3 oz cooked) | Saturated Fat (g) | Dietary Cholesterol (mg) | Total Fat (g) | Calories |
|---|---|---|---|---|
| Beef, top round, broiled | 3 | 73 | 8 | 185 |
| Beef, whole rib, broiled | 10 | 72 | 26 | 313 |
| Chicken, light meat without skin, roasted | 1 | 64 | 4 | 130 |
| Chicken, light meat with skin, roasted | 3 | 71 | 19 | 189 |
| Ground turkey (breast meat only) | <1 | 35 | <2 | 130 |
| Ground turkey (meat and skin), cooked | 3 | 87 | 11 | 200 |
| Cod, baked | <1 | 47 | <1 | 89 |
| Mackerel | 4 | 64 | 15 | 223 |

< means less than.

# DAIRY AND EGGS

You have lots to choose from in the dairy case, thanks to food manufacturers that are giving us nonfat and low-fat versions of everything! As for eggs, you can do anything with egg substitute that you can do with cholesterol-laden yolks or whole eggs.

# Dairy

- Choose nonfat or low-fat dairy products such as fat-free or 1 percent low-fat milk, nonfat or low-fat yogurt, nonfat dry milk, nonfat or low-fat cottage cheese, and fat-free or low-fat evaporated milk. Plus, don't forget buttermilk! Despite its name and rich taste, buttermilk is very low in fat, since it's made from cultured fat-free milk.

- Look for fat-free, reduced-fat, low-fat, light, or part-skim cheeses; nonfat, low-fat, or dry curd cottage cheese; farmer cheese; nonfat or part-skim mozzarella or ricotta; or dry cheese such as Parmesan or sapsago. In addition, imitation cheeses with 2 to 5 grams of fat per ounce are okay. Creamy cheeses, such as Brie or processed cheese spreads, are high in saturated fats. Go easy on those.

### POULTRY, BEEF, AND CHEESE: A COMPARISON

| Food (per serving) | Saturated Fat (g) | Cholesterol (mg) | Total Fat (g) |
|---|---|---|---|
| Chicken, without skin, white meat, roasted (3 oz) | 1 | 64 | 4 |
| Beef, top round, broiled (3 oz) | 3 | 73 | 8 |
| Natural Cheddar (1 oz) | 6 | 30 | 9 |

Note: If you're on the Step II Diet, select only nonfat dairy products and cheese with 2 or fewer grams of fat per ounce.

- For dessert, choose nonfat or low-fat yogurt, frozen yogurt, ice milk, or ice cream.

- Typical cream substitutes—nondairy coffee creamers, sour cream substitutes, and whipped toppings—often contain coconut, palm, or palm kernel oil and are high in saturated fat. Instead, try nonfat or low-fat sour cream or cream cheese blends. Instead of nondairy creamers, choose fat-free evaporated milk.

# Eggs

- Egg yolks are high in cholesterol. Each one contains about 213 milligrams. That's why you'll want to limit the yolks, including the ones you get in baked goods and processed foods (see pages 18–19 for a list).

- On the other hand, egg whites contain no cholesterol. Feel free to eat all the egg whites you want. You can also substitute two whites for a whole egg in recipes. Egg substitutes work well, too.

# FATS AND OILS

When you buy fats and oils, look for those that are unsaturated. It's easy when you keep the following tips in mind.

- Buy margarine instead of butter. Always look for a margarine that has unsaturated liquid vegetable oil listed as the first ingredient. Choose tub or liquid margarine or vegetable oil spreads. The softer the margarine, the more unsaturated it is.

- Because diet or nonfat margarine contains water, it's not easy to use for baking. It works well for cooking and for flavoring vegetables and casseroles, however.

- Stay away from lard, fatback, and solid shortenings. They're high in saturated fat. Use liquid vegetable oils instead.

- When shopping for unsaturated vegetable oil, choose safflower, corn, sunflower, soybean, olive, or canola. Use peanut oil for a flavor change only.

- Nonstick vegetable sprays—plain or flavored—are great to use in place of butter or oil on equipment such as pans, baking sheets, and casserole dishes.

- Buy nonfat or light mayonnaise instead of the regular kind, which is high in fat and cholesterol.

- We're including nuts in the fat section because most nuts and any variety of seeds, olives, peanut butter, and avocado contain lots of fat. The good news is that, except in coconuts, it's mostly unsaturated fat. On the other hand, if you're watching your weight, you'll want to go easy on nuts because they're extremely high in calories.

- Beware of chocolate, coconut, coconut oil, palm kernel oil, and palm oil. They contain more saturated than unsaturated fat. When choosing manufactured food items containing these ingredients, look on the label to find out the kinds of fat included.

- The foods you buy should contain more polyunsaturated than saturated fat. Currently, nutrition labels don't have to list monounsaturated fat. You can figure out about how much monounsaturated fat a product contains by subtracting the amounts of polyunsaturated fat and saturated fat from the total fat.

## BREADS, CEREALS, PASTAS, RICE AND OTHER GRAINS, AND DRIED PEAS AND BEANS

Good news! Most foods in this category are high in fiber and low in fat and calories. Plus, they don't contain cholesterol. On the other hand, some commercially baked products contain large amounts of saturated fat. Croissants, muffins, biscuits, butter rolls, and doughnuts are among these products. Look for whole-grain products because they contain even more fiber than others.

- Here's where reading labels is a must. Many baked goods are made with whole milk and dried egg yolks. Steer clear!
- Check cracker labels for fats and oils. Scandinavian-style rye crackers and other whole-grain crackers are often made without fats or oils and with little or no salt.
- Try buying brown rice, bulgur wheat, millet, and other whole grains to cook in low-sodium seasoned broth for a side dish. They're high in fiber, relatively low in calories, and economical.
- Buy pasta, rice, dried beans or peas, and lentils to use as entrées or substitute for meats in casseroles, stews, and soups. They're excellent protein sources and very economical.
- Check the ingredients lists on packaged cereals. Most of these are low in saturated fat, but many contain large quantities of sugar, some contain salt, and a few even contain fat. Be particularly cautious about so-called natural cereals and granolas, which may contain all three, including coconut or coconut oil.
- Look for reduced-salt versions of canned soups and canned vegetables. You can find them either in the diet section or on the shelves with their "regular" counterparts.
- Look for canned or dehydrated varieties of soup with no more than 3 grams of fat, 2 grams of saturated fat, and 20 milligrams of cholesterol per cup. Be sure to check the nutrition label—you may get sticker shock over the amount of sodium in many of these soups.

## VEGETABLES AND FRUITS

Here's where you can really have fun filling up your grocery cart. Fresh vegetables and fruits are the perfect heart-healthy foods because, except for avocados and olives, they contain little or no fat and they're naturally delicious. Plus, they're packed with vitamins and minerals.

When you buy fresh fruits and vegetables to prepare at home, you can cook them with low-fat ingredients. However, when you buy processed fruits and vegetables, be on the lookout for fat and sodium, which often are added in large quantities. When shopping for processed foods, keep the following things in mind.

- Vegetables prepared with butter, cream, or cheese can be high in fat.
- Fried vegetables have several times more fat and calories than vegetables prepared without fat.
- Fruits that are fresh or canned in water are lower in calories than fruits canned in juice or in syrup. Drain fruits canned in syrup.

## SWEETS AND SNACKS

What would life be without the occasional snack? Luckily, we can have healthy hearts and tasty snacks, too. Before you reach for any snack food, though, figure out how it fits into your cholesterol-lowering eating plan.

- Want a cookie? You'll be glad to know that dozens of commercially prepared cookies are low in fat. For example, Newton-type cookies, graham crackers, animal crackers, and gingersnaps have always been low-fat favorites. Now, thanks to savvy food manufacturers, nonfat and low-fat cookies come in a host of delectable varieties. Check labels to find them. As a rule, they should contain no more than 3 grams of fat, 1 gram of saturated fat, and 20 milligrams of cholesterol per ounce.
- You'll want to make desserts (cakes, pies, cookies, and puddings) at home with acceptable margarine or oil, fat-free or reduced-fat milk, and egg substitute or egg whites.
- Classic snacks, such as most chips and rich crackers, are high in saturated fat. However, you can find chips cooked in unsaturated oil and others that are baked and are lower in fat or fat free. Choose only those labeled as having more polyunsaturated than saturated fats.
- For dessert, try angel food cake topped with fruit puree or fresh fruit slices.
- You also can find fat-free or low-fat brownies, cakes, cheesecakes, cupcakes, and pastries. The packages should be clearly marked as fat free or low fat.
- Don't forget gelatin desserts—they're naturally fat free.

- Any help-your-heart dessert list should include nonfat or low-fat frozen yogurt, fruit ices, ice milk, sherbet, and sorbet.

## THE BEST THINGS IN LIFE ARE FAT FREE

A serving of any of the foods and drinks listed below contains fewer than 20 calories and no fat.

**Drinks**

Low-sodium bouillon or broth without fat*
Carbonated drinks, sugar free[†]
Carbonated water
Club soda*
Cocoa powder, unsweetened
Coffee or tea
Drink mixes, sugar free[†]
Tonic water, sugar free[†]

**Fruits**

Cranberries, unsweetened
Rhubarb, unsweetened

**Condiments**

Flavored peppers, salt-free herb blends, and spice blends
Flavored vinegars

**Sweet Substitutes[†]**

Candy, hard, sugar free
Gelatin, sugar free
Gum, sugar free
Jam or jelly, all fruit

*High in sodium. Look for seltzers or soda with no salt added.
[†] Sugar-free foods are listed for the benefit of those following a diabetic diet.

# COOKING FOR A HEALTHY HEART

Now that you have a refrigerator full of fresh low-fat foods, don't torpedo your cholesterol-lowering efforts by cooking these foods in lots of fat. Instead, take a minute now to learn some delicious ways to prepare foods that are light on fat but heavy on flavor.

On the following pages, we'll explain how you can save an astounding amount of fat by grilling, baking, roasting, or sautéing instead of deep-fat frying or panfrying. You'll find that these lower-fat cooking methods can be faster, easier, and tastier than their higher-fat counterparts! Best of all, the more healthful methods let you eat well while lowering your cholesterol.

## LOW-FAT, HIGH-FLAVOR COOKING METHODS

**Baking.**   Add a little liquid to poultry, seafood, and meat, then bake the food in covered cookware. The moisture from the liquid makes this method particularly good for fish or chicken breasts, which tend to be a little dry.

**Braising or Stewing.**   If you're braising or stewing meat or poultry, begin a day ahead. Prepare the dish, then refrigerate it overnight. The next day, the chilled fat will have congealed, allowing you to remove it easily before reheating the food. This cooking method uses a little more liquid than baking does, and it can be done in a covered container on top of the stove or in the oven. Braising is also an excellent way to cook vegetables.

**Grilling or Broiling.**   When you cook meat or poultry on a rack, the fat drips away, but the flavor remains. Grilling or broiling is also a good way to cook fish steaks or whole fish. For extra flavor, try marinating food before putting it over the coals or under the broiler. Vegetables and even fruit and bread also taste great browned over an open flame.

**Microwave Cooking.**   Fast and easy microwave cooking requires no added fat. That's because foods don't tend to stick in the moist heat of microwaving. In fact, you can drain the fat off food as it cooks by microwaving the food between two paper towels.

If you want to adapt a recipe for microwaving, cut the cooking time to one fourth or one third of the conventional time. If that isn't enough, gradually increase the cooking time. You might also look for a microwave recipe similar to the one you're trying to adapt. Keep the following hints in mind when microwave cooking.

- Choose foods that cook well in moist heat: chicken, fish, ground meat, vegetables, sauces, and soups.
- Pieces that are about equal in size and shape will cook more uniformly.
- Reduce the liquid used in cooking beverages, soups, vegetables, fruits, and main dishes by about one third because less liquid evaporates in microwave cooking.
- Choose a microwave-safe container slightly larger than the dish required for cooking the recipe in a conventional oven.
- Use 100 percent power (high) for soups, beverages, fruits, vegetables, fish, ground meat, and poultry. Use 70 percent power (medium-high) for simmering stews and 50 percent power (medium) for baking breads, cakes, and muffins and for cooking less-tender cuts of meat.
- To create a crusty look on baked items, coat pans with an acceptable vegetable oil and add crumbs.
- Add nonfat or low-fat cheese and other toppings near the end of cooking to keep the top of your food from becoming tough or soggy.
- Don't coat meat with flour if you'll be adding liquid for cooking. The coating becomes soggy.
- Use quick-cooking instead of long-grain rice.

**Poaching.**   To poach chicken or seafood, immerse it in a pan of simmering liquid on the stove. This cooking method is particularly tasty when you serve the food with a sauce made of pureed vegetables and herbs.

**Roasting.**   Start by placing a rack in your roasting pan so the meat or poultry doesn't sit in its own fat drippings. Be sure to roast at a moderate temperature, about 350° F, to avoid searing, which seals in the fat. Baste with fat-free liquids, such as wine, fruit juice, or low-sodium broth.

**Sautéing.**   Seafood, poultry, and vegetable dishes can be sautéed in an open skillet with little or no fat. The high temperature and motion keep food from sticking. Use nonstick cookware or nonstick vegetable spray, a small amount of low-sodium broth or wine, or a tiny bit of polyunsaturated oil rubbed on the pan with a paper towel.

**Steaming.** When you cook food in a basket over simmering water, the natural flavor, color, and nutritional value of the food remain intact. Try adding herbs to the steaming water or replacing the water with broth to add even more flavor to the finished dish.

**Stir-Frying.** Based on the same principle as sautéing, stir-frying is best done in a wok, although a large frying pan will also work. The high temperature and the constant movement of the food keep it from sticking and burning. Try stir-frying vegetables and diced poultry or seafood with just a tiny bit of oil.

## RECIPE SUBSTITUTIONS

Do you have several favorite recipes you hate to give up with your cholesterol-lowering diet? Don't worry! You can salvage many of them simply by making a few easy substitutions.

| When Your Recipe Calls For . . . | Use . . . |
| --- | --- |
| Sour cream | Nonfat or low-fat sour cream; nonfat or low-fat yogurt; nonfat or low-fat cottage cheese plus nonfat or low-fat yogurt for flavor; nonfat or low-fat ricotta cheese (thinned with nonfat or low-fat yogurt or low-fat buttermilk, if desired); one can of chilled fat-free evaporated milk whipped with 1 teaspoon of lemon juice; Yogurt Cheese (see recipe on page 155). |
| Whipped cream | Nonfat or low-fat frozen nondairy topping (thawed); Creamy Dessert Topping (see recipe on page 243); whipped fat-free evaporated milk (must be well chilled or it won't whip). |
| Butter | Unsaturated margarine or oil (1 tablespoon of butter = 1 tablespoon of margarine or $\frac{3}{4}$ tablespoon of oil). |
| Whole milk or cream | Fat-free milk. |
| Cream cheese | Nonfat or low-fat cream cheese. |
| Eggs | Cholesterol-free egg substitutes; 2 egg whites for 1 egg. |
| Unsweetened baking chocolate | Unsweetened cocoa or carob powder blended with unsaturated oil or margarine (one 1-ounce square of chocolate = 3 tablespoons of cocoa or carob plus 1 tablespoon of unsaturated oil or margarine). Because carob is sweeter than cocoa, reduce the sugar in the recipe by one fourth. |

# MORE HELP-YOUR-HEART COOKING TIPS

The tips in the chart above aren't the only tools at your fingertips. Here are more little ways to trim cholesterol, fat, salt, and calories from your dishes—without trimming taste. These tips will help you help your heart.

## MEATS, POULTRY, AND SEAFOOD

- Trim all visible fat before cooking meat or poultry.

- After you roast meat or poultry, refrigerate the drippings. Once chilled, the fat will rise to the top and harden. You can remove the fat easily and discard it, saving the liquid to use in stews, sauces, and soups.

- If you're using leftover marinade in a sauce or for basting, you'll need to take precautions to kill any harmful bacteria that the raw food might have transmitted. Boiling the marinade for at least 5 minutes will do the trick, as will not basting the food during the final 15 minutes of cooking time.

- Buy only the leanest ground meat and poultry (no more than 15 percent fat). After browning, put the ground meat or poultry into a strainer or colander and rinse under hot water to remove even more fat. Ground meat is generally higher in fat than nonground meat. Even the leanest ground beef contains more fat than is recommended for those on the Step II Diet. Instead of buying prepackaged ground beef, have your butcher grind a sirloin steak for you. Be sure to have him or her remove all visible fat and clean the grinder to remove any fat from previous grindings.

- When figuring serving sizes, remember that meat loses about 25 percent of its weight during cooking. (For example, 4 ounces of raw meat will weigh about 3 ounces when cooked.)

- Unless you're roasting a chicken, skin it and remove all visible fat before cooking. The skin will be easier to remove if you use paper towels or a clean cloth. (Be sure to scrub the cutting surface and utensils well with hot, sudsy water after preparing poultry for cooking.) If you're roasting a chicken, leave the skin on to prevent the meat from drying out. Remove the skin before serving the chicken.

- Cook turkeys that are *not* self-basting. Self-basting turkeys are high in saturated fat.

- Baste meats and poultry with fat-free ingredients, such as wine, fruit juice, or defatted beef or chicken broth.

- The rule of thumb for cooking fresh fish is 10 minutes for every inch of thickness. Add 5 minutes if the fish is wrapped in foil. Frozen fish requires 20 minutes per inch of thickness, plus 10 minutes if it's wrapped in foil. Cooking time may vary, depending on the cooking method used. Fish is done when the flesh is opaque and flakes easily when tested with a fork.
- Buy tuna packed in water and sardines packed in tomato sauce instead of oil.

## VEGETABLES

- To retain their natural juices, wrap food in foil before grilling or baking. Or try wrapping food in edible pouches made of steamed lettuce or cabbage leaves.
- Cook vegetables just long enough to make them tender-crisp. Overcooked vegetables lose both flavor and important nutrients.
- Clean mushrooms with a damp cloth or a quick rinse in cold water. (If you soak mushrooms, they'll get soggy.)
- Cut down on cholesterol by using more vegetables and less poultry, seafood, or meats in soups, stews, and casseroles. Finely chopped vegetables are great for stretching ground poultry or meat.
- Use fat-free margarine spray or nonfat or reduced-fat soft margarine instead of butter or stick margarine to flavor vegetables.
- Use small amounts of lean meats instead of salt pork or fatback to flavor vegetables.
- Substitute chopped vegetables for some of the bread when you make stuffing.

## SOUPS, SAUCES, AND GRAVIES

- After making soups and sauces, refrigerate them and skim the hardened fat off the top.
- Thicken soups, stews, or sauces with pureed cooked vegetables.
- Another nonfat way to thicken food is to blend a tablespoon of cornstarch, flour, or ground leftover rice with a cup of room-temperature low-sodium broth by shaking the two in a jar with a tight-fitting lid. Add the blended liquid to the soup, sauce, or gravy and simmer until thickened.
- Reduced-fat tofu that's been processed in a blender or a food processor is creamy and works wonderfully as a thickener.

## MISCELLANEOUS

- Since many recipes include more sugar than necessary, you can usually reduce the amount of sugar by one fourth to one third.
- Reduce or omit salt in baking recipes that don't use yeast.
- Substitute herbs, spices, and salt-free seasonings for salt as you cook and at the table.
- Substitute onion or garlic flakes or powder for onion salt and garlic salt.
- Add a drop of lemon juice to the water you cook pasta in, and eliminate the salt and oil.
- Substitute brown rice for white rice to add whole-grain roughage.
- Use a blend of whole-wheat flour and all-purpose flour in recipes that call for regular flour.
- Use wheat germ, bran, and whole-wheat bread crumbs in place of buttered crumbs to top casseroles.
- Cut down on fat in creamy salad dressing by mixing the dressing with plain nonfat or low-fat yogurt or sour cream.
- Prepare scrambled eggs or omelets using egg substitute or only one egg yolk per portion. Add a few extra egg whites to the mixing bowl to make more generous servings.
- Instead of nuts in salads and casseroles, try water chestnuts or wheat berry sprouts.
- Use margarine instead of shortening in cakes that require creaming.
- If a packaged cake mix or other baking mix offers directions for a lower-fat version, give that a try. Also, your grocery probably has a variety of fat-free and low-fat mixes.
- Use fat-free evaporated milk for cream when making whipped topping. (The evaporated milk won't whip unless it's well chilled first.)

# APPENDIX D

# HOW TO STAY WITH YOUR NEW EATING PLAN

We're all creatures of habit, and habits are acquired *slowly*. That's why it's difficult to alter your eating patterns overnight. When people make rapid changes, it's likely that they'll just as quickly revert to their old ways. For that reason, it works best to ease into your new eating routine gradually.

For example, if you never eat breakfast, don't start forcing yourself to do so right away. If you like having lunch in the cafeteria, you don't have to bring lunch from home; just start making more careful selections. If you take your time, you will form new, positive eating habits that eventually will become just as firmly established as your old ones.

Meanwhile, we've included the following hints for changing your way of eating and reaching your goal of lowering your blood cholesterol. Many of the same strategies can work if your goal is to lose weight.

## WHAT MOTIVATES YOU? WHY DO YOU EAT?

As you start your new way of eating, it's important to examine your old eating habits and to understand your behaviors, attitudes, and motivations. You will need some personal reflection and perhaps a frank discussion with members of your family. Your doctor may recommend that you consult with a registered dietitian, who'll probably suggest that you keep a written record of your eating habits for at least a few days. As you reflect on these habits, look for signs of subconscious behaviors. For instance, do you use high-fat "comfort" foods to relieve anxiety or depression or give in to social pressure from family or friends to eat foods that are wrong for you? What you learn from your answers can be eye-opening—and can help you change your eating behaviors.

When you start a new way of eating, your family's support—or lack of it—can have a major effect. Sometimes your family and social environment won't allow you easy access to the foods you need. Sometimes your family won't back your efforts to change the way you eat. To enlist their support, you may want to explain how important your new way of eating is to your health. If you consult a registered dietitian or a licensed nutritionist, take your spouse or other family members along so they'll understand exactly what your eating plan requires. Ideally, your whole family should know about the dangers of high blood cholesterol and adopt a cholesterol-lowering eating plan, too. Even if they won't join you in your new way of eating, do encourage them to support your efforts.

## HOW TO WIN BIG BY EATING LESS FAT

You may find that your biggest obstacles to low-fat eating are your own thoughts and habits. Try the following suggestions on for size.

### THE STRAIGHT SKINNY ON LOW-FAT EATING

- Be your own cheerleader. Be proud of yourself when you succeed at new habits and make good choices. Argue with yourself when temptation appears.
- Analyze your environment and eliminate those things that stimulate you to eat foods high in fat.
- Store high-fat foods out of sight—or better yet, don't buy them in the first place.
- Get rid of tempting foods until you can handle having them around.
- Eat in a designated place and sit down. Eating on the run or while standing in front of the refrigerator or pantry contributes to eating the wrong things.
- Find friends, neighbors, and coworkers who support and encourage your new lifestyle changes.
- Trim the fat from your diet gradually.
- Plan your meals ahead of time. Social engagements, holidays, and business luncheons will always happen. So will depressing or upsetting episodes in life. You can always find an excuse for not getting more exercise. Instead of letting these temptations control you, plan the kind of life you really want, and live it every day.
- Although you ultimately want lifelong changes, appreciate the smaller goals along the way. If you can't bring your cholesterol to below 200, but you did manage to drop it to 220 mg/dl, celebrate that—and keep going.
- Set realistic goals. It will take time to get your cholesterol to the level you want it.
- Depriving yourself of special treats only makes you crave them. Plan

to enjoy a small treat once or twice a week. Yes, treats are possible on a cholesterol-lowering diet.

- If you need support for your new eating plan, find it. Consider consulting a registered dietitian.

## EXERCISE YOUR OPTIONS

Check with your doctor before beginning an exercise program. If he or she says you can exercise in moderation, it will help your overall health, including your efforts to reduce cholesterol. Here are some ideas.

- Add a daily walk to your schedule. Start slowly and gradually build up to 30 minutes or longer. Use the time to relax, make plans, and enjoy life. If you would rather swim or ride a bicycle, by all means do so. It's important to choose activities you enjoy.

- Look for ways to put more activity into your life. Walk to the store or post office, or park farther away from your office or home. Take the stairs instead of the elevator. Turn off the TV and do yard work or go dancing.

- To make your outdoor exercise safer and more enjoyable, wear good exercise shoes, comfortable clothing, and a hat in hot weather. Be sure to drink plenty of water. Avoid exercising outdoors in very cold, very hot, or humid weather. In hot weather, walk in the early morning or after the temperature drops in the evening.

You *can* reduce your cholesterol level. It requires commitment and hard work, and it isn't always easy. However, once you reach your goal and learn to adopt a lifestyle that will keep you at your best level, you'll forget you ever had a problem with high fat.

## HOW TO KEEP IT LOW

After you reduce your cholesterol level, you face your most important challenge—keeping it low. You'll be around high-fat foods at most social events, so you'll be tempted by old habits. Sticking with a daily exercise habit also takes commitment.

## LAPSES, RELAPSES, AND COLLAPSES

Start by realizing that you will face lapses, relapses, and collapses on the way to a safe cholesterol level. A *lapse* is a slight error or return to your fat-eating habits, the first instance of backsliding. For example, you may have a bad day and eat several high-fat foods or maybe you skip a week of exercise. Your response? Get back on track as soon as you can. This will save you from a *relapse,* which is returning to your former habits by eating high-fat foods for several days in a row or skipping exercise for weeks. Once again, this is your signal to stop, take stock, and begin your new eating and exercise habits afresh. This will save you from a *collapse,* which occurs if you are unable to reverse the negative trend, and you go back to old ways of unhealthful eating and not exercising.

The critical thing to realize is that a lapse or even a relapse *should not be seen as a failure.* Instead, see it as a challenge to overcome, a wake-up call. Setbacks are a natural part of the process. Simply use the following proven countermeasures to help handle these times.

## URGES AND HIGH-RISK SITUATIONS

It's important to be able to tell the difference between hunger (gnawing in your stomach and light-headedness) and urges (mental cravings for comfort foods). Hunger or low blood sugar tells you it's time to eat, either a meal or perhaps a small piece of fruit or glass of fat-free milk. Urges are another matter. Examples include eating a high-fat snack to reward yourself after a stressful incident. Try to handle these urges with the following techniques.

- *Delayed gratification.* Delayed gratification is a behavioral tool that you can successfully use to stop your impulsive grabbing for high-fat food. It is a lesson in tolerance. When you feel the urge to eat something you shouldn't, set a timer for 15 minutes and wait or find something else to do before eating it. This will give you time to rethink your desire for this particular food and perhaps substitute something more healthful.

- *ABC theory.* Learn how to respond to life's stresses with a behavior other than eating high-fat foods. The theory works like this: If A happens (you have an argument with your spouse, for example), you always do B (leave the argument with hard feelings), and this always causes C (you respond by eating ice cream). How can you change this? Change A or B so that you don't have a reason to do C, or find a release for your frustrations other than high-fat foods, such as jogging, going for a walk, or meditating.

# When Healthful, Natural Eating Is a Habit

By now you know that eating healthfully doesn't require starvation or self-deprivation. Instead, it's a way of life in which you can look forward to enjoying mealtimes and social occasions, not just enduring them.

## Tips for Staying at Your Best Cholesterol Level Forever

- Accept the idea that wise eating doesn't mean eating tasteless foods—it just means eating delicious, low-fat foods cooked with creativity.
- Stock up on good, fresh foods that make you look forward to meals. Make a shopping list, and always shop after a meal instead of on an empty stomach.
- Plan your meals, and don't leave your eating habits to chance. Before meals and parties, decide what you can do to make the occasion easier to handle. For instance, offer to bring a vegetable appetizer or a fruit dessert.
- When confronted with a high-fat meal at a friend's house or other social occasion, use your head. Life wouldn't be much fun without some special occasions. It's okay to splurge sometimes, but don't eat everything in sight. If the dinner is lasagna, green beans, tossed salad, garlic bread, and a special dessert, don't panic. You can pick and choose what to eat. One way to handle the situation is to eat a medium serving of lasagna and salad and a large serving of green beans. Then choose bread or dessert. Another way is to eat a little of everything.
- It's usually better to eat a little bit of a high-fat food you crave than to avoid it for so long that you gorge when you finally decide to indulge yourself. Eat a small amount, and leave it at that. If you don't trust yourself with just a small amount, don't eat any at all.

## The Best You Can Be

When you learn and accomplish these techniques, your days of being concerned about your cholesterol will be over. You can enjoy good health and not worry. The techniques we've offered here are the tools you need to stay at your best cholesterol level forever. This new lifestyle will always work for you. Why? Because *you're* in control.

# TIPS FOR DINING OUT

If you're like most other Americans, often you don't make dinner—you make reservations.

You love to let someone else do the cooking. However, you worry about the effect of restaurant food on your heart. Well, cheer up. You can find low-fat, low-cholesterol meals at your local restaurant. All you have to know is how to eat out with your heart in mind. Take a look at the following tips for dining out.

## BEFORE YOU ORDER

- If you're familiar with the menu, decide what you'll order before you enter the restaurant. That will help you avoid the temptation of ordering something that won't pamper your heart.
- If you're trying a new place, take some time to study the menu. This will help you avoid making split-second—and often regrettable—decisions.
- If your companions don't mind, have the waiter remove unnecessary temptations, such as butter.
- Don't be shy. Ask the waiter about ingredients or preparation methods for the dishes you're not familiar with. You deserve to know what you're eating.

## MAKE A FEW SIMPLE REQUESTS

- Ask the waiter to substitute low-fat foods for high-fat ones. For example, ask for steamed vegetables in place of French fries or a fresh fruit salad in place of mayonnaise-laden coleslaw.
- If virtually everything on the menu is high in fat, ask the waiter whether the chef could prepare a fruit or vegetable platter for you. Most chefs are eager to please.
- Order all dressings and sauces on the side so you can control your portions.
- Ask the waiter to have your food prepared without butter or cream sauces.
- Order vegetable side dishes. Be sure to ask the waiter to leave off any sauces or butter.

- If you love potatoes, order them baked, boiled, or roasted—not fried. Then ask the waiter to leave off the butter and sour cream. Try salsa or pepper and chives instead.
- For dessert, check your menu to see whether the restaurant offers its own low-fat dishes. If not, order fresh fruit or sorbet.

## TIME TO EAT!

- Order first. You'll be less likely to be swayed by your dining partner's choices.
- Rather than fried appetizers or cream soups, begin your meal with broth-based soups, such as minestrone or gazpacho.
- Salad bars can be friend or foe, depending on what you select. Stay away from high-fat items, such as grated cheese, cream dressings, chopped eggs, and croutons.
- Try a squeeze of lemon instead of dressing on your salad.
- Choose seafood, chicken, or lean meat. Avoid fatty meats.
- Fried entrées are out. Broiled, baked, grilled, steamed, or poached entrées are in.
- If you order a chicken dish, don't eat the skin. That's where almost all the fat is!
- If you order meat, remove all visible fat.

## EATING ETHNIC

### Asian

- Choose a steamed main dish, or try a stir-fried chicken or seafood and vegetable dish. Be sure to ask for steamed instead of fried rice.
- Ask the chef to use a minimal amount of oil, and leave out the soy sauce, MSG, and salt.
- Choose entrées with lots of vegetables.
- If your dining partner agrees, ask the waiter to remove the crispy fried noodles sometimes served as an appetizer.
- Instead of tempura-style vegetables, ask for steamed or stir-fried vegetables.

### Italian

- Opt for red marinara or marsala sauce instead of white cream sauce.
- Try a seafood selection or meatless pasta in place of an entrée with sausage or meatballs.

- If you order pizza, choose one with a thin crust. Opt for topping ingredients such as spinach, mushrooms, broccoli, and roasted peppers instead of sausage or pepperoni.
- Ask for plain Italian bread instead of buttery garlic bread.
- Go easy on the grated Parmesan cheese—just a little for flavor.
- For dessert, choose an Italian ice.

## Mexican

- Ask your waiter not to bring fried tortilla chips to the table.
- Ask him or her to hold the sour cream and guacamole from the entrées. Use salsa, pico de gallo, cilantro, and jalapeño peppers instead for flavor.
- Ask for a tomato-based sauce instead of a creamy or cheesy sauce.
- If you order a taco salad, don't eat the fried shell.
- Choose corn rather than flour tortillas.
- Instead of the ever-present refried beans, ask for charra or borracho beans instead.
- Chicken fajitas or chicken or beef enchiladas with red sauce or salsa, for example, are more heart-healthy than chimichangas or burritos.

You can make similar choices wherever you eat and whatever cuisine is featured, whether it's German or Thai, Pacific Rim or Indian. Use your head to make wise choices for your heart.

# HOW YOUR BODY HANDLES CHOLESTEROL

If you've been diagnosed with high blood cholesterol, you probably want to know exactly what your body does with all that cholesterol. The information that follows will explain how cholesterol is carried in your blood, how it's eliminated from your body, and how it can get deposited on your artery walls.

The cholesterol and other fats in your blood are carried throughout your body by tiny particles called lipoproteins. Some of these lipoproteins are harmful, some are innocuous, and some are even beneficial. The harmful lipoproteins carry cholesterol into the walls of your small arteries, allowing it to build up. That condition is called atherosclerosis. Heavy atherosclerotic buildup can cause the blood flow to become blocked, resulting in heart attack or stroke. Conversely, other lipoproteins may actually remove excess cholesterol from the arteries. That's why it's important to know which is which.

## LOW-DENSITY LIPOPROTEINS (LDLs)

In most people, the majority of blood cholesterol is carried in low-density lipoproteins, or LDLs. The "bad guy" of lipoproteins, LDL is the kind that enters artery walls and leads to atherosclerosis. Your doctor can judge your risk of heart attack more accurately by determining the amount of cholesterol carried by your LDLs. This is referred to as LDL cholesterol.

If your LDL cholesterol is more than 160 milligrams per deciliter of blood (mg/dl), it's considered high risk. If your LDL level is between 130 and 160, it's borderline high risk. Ideally, your LDL cholesterol is below 130.

Total blood cholesterol can indicate your level of risk. If it's 200 mg/dl or over, your doctor will probably measure your LDL cholesterol level, which is a more accurate indicator of heart disease.

## HIGH-DENSITY LIPOPROTEINS (HDLs)

Typically, one third to one fourth of the cholesterol in your blood is carried in high-density lipoproteins, or HDLs. HDL is the "good guy" among lipoproteins because a high HDL level seems to protect against heart attack. (You want high amounts of HDLs because they are the good guys and low amounts of LDLs because they're the bad guys.)

We're not sure exactly how HDL works, but some experts believe that it removes excess cholesterol from the arteries, thus preventing the buildup of cholesterol in the artery wall. That's how a high level of HDL cholesterol reduces your risk of heart attack and a low level increases it.

HDL cholesterol levels for men usually range from 40 to 50 mg/dl. For women, levels of 50 to 60 mg/dl are normal. If your blood level is below 35 mg/dl, your HDL cholesterol is abnormally low and is a major cardiac risk factor for you.

Low HDL cholesterol levels can be caused by many factors. The most common are cigarette smoking, obesity, and lack of exercise. Fortunately, all can be corrected, resulting in an increased HDL level and a reduced risk of heart attack.

Another factor is triglycerides. People who have a high level of triglycerides in their blood often have lower levels of HDL cholesterol, which may be why most people with high triglycerides are at increased risk for heart attack.

Some drugs used to treat high blood pressure (for example, beta-blockers) also lower HDLs. Male sex hormones (androgens), progesterone, and anabolic steroids all lower HDL levels. People who take anabolic steroids to build muscles may be setting themselves up for heart attacks later in life. Female sex hormones (estrogens) raise HDL cholesterol. This difference between male and female sex hormones may be one reason why men are more likely than women of the same age to have heart attacks.

## VERY LOW DENSITY LIPOPROTEINS (VLDLs)

Another lipoprotein that carries blood cholesterol is very low density lipoprotein, VLDL for short. VLDLs also carry most of the blood triglycerides. Chemically, triglycerides are what most people know as fat. In fact, most body fat occurs in the form of triglycerides. (Fats such as butter, margarine, and vegetable oil are triglycerides, too.)

Normally, triglycerides are removed from VLDLs during circulation to be used as energy by the muscles. After the triglycerides are removed, the remaining lipoprotein particles are called VLDL remnants, which break down further to produce LDLs. Thus, VLDLs eventually become cholesterol-rich LDLs.

Scientists are divided on whether VLDLs are bad guys in the sense of contributing to the buildup of cholesterol-laden plaque in the arteries.

Many investigators believe that VLDLs themselves can enter the coronary arteries and deposit cholesterol. If those people are right, VLDL cholesterol may contribute to atherosclerosis in the same way that LDL cholesterol does.

Your blood triglyceride level is an indirect measure of VLDL cholesterol. A simple way to estimate your VLDL cholesterol is to divide the blood triglyceride by five. If your blood triglyceride level is high, it could reflect a higher risk of heart attack by indicating an elevated VLDL cholesterol. More than one fourth of all patients who've had heart attacks have triglyceride levels that are abnormally high (over 250). Medical experts aren't certain whether that relationship is because of abnormally high VLDL cholesterol levels or reduced levels of HDL cholesterol, which also often result from elevated triglyceride levels. The fact is, both may contribute to atherosclerosis.

Of course, blood triglyceride levels can be high for any number of reasons, including overweight, high alcohol consumption, diabetes, and various inherited disorders of triglyceride metabolism.

# DRUGS: WHEN DIET ALONE WON'T WORK

For some people, diet won't lower blood cholesterol enough. For example, 1 in 500 people has familial hypercholesterolemia, a genetic condition typically causing blood cholesterol levels to be over 300 milligrams per deciliter (mg/dl) and often as high as 500. For this or a related condition, your doctor may prescribe drug therapy immediately.

If you don't have coronary heart disease, your physician may want you to try to lower your cholesterol through diet before considering drug treatment. If changing your diet doesn't lower your low-density lipoprotein (LDL) cholesterol level enough, drugs may be an appropriate alternative. A change in diet should always go along with drug treatment to maximize the effect.

In the past few years, there has been growing evidence that cholesterol-lowering drugs will reduce the risk of future heart attack in people who have already experienced coronary heart disease. Thus, if you have had a heart attack (myocardial infarction), angina pectoris, coronary artery surgery, or coronary angioplasty, it is very likely that your physician will prescribe a cholesterol-lowering drug. Again, however, you can achieve additional benefit by changing your eating plan.

The types of drugs used to lower cholesterol are varied and work in a number of different ways.

## BILE ACID BINDING DRUGS

Cholestyramine was used in the Coronary Primary Prevention Trial to prove the connection between lowering blood cholesterol and preventing heart attack.

Bile acid binding drugs stay within the intestinal tract and are not absorbed into the body. They act by binding the bile acids, which are breakdown products of cholesterol. This binding action leads to more excretion of bile acids and therefore to a more rapid breakdown of cholesterol in the liver. This in turn causes the liver to make more LDL receptors, thus allowing it to remove more cholesterol.

The three bile acid binding drugs and their trade names are

- Colestipol (Colestid)
- Cholestyramine (Questran)
- Colesevelam (Welchol)

The bile acid binding drugs sometimes cause gastrointestinal side effects, such as constipation, bloating, intestinal gas, feelings of stomach fullness, and nausea. Constipation is a consequence of the bile acid's binding process because, left in their natural state, bile acids are natural laxatives. A good way to control the constipation is to add more fiber to your diet with bran cereals or with fiber laxatives containing psyllium. Also, your physician may recommend a stool softener. You shouldn't use regular laxatives because prolonged use may produce side effects.

Many patients have some trouble taking bile acid binding drugs at first. If you're one of them, don't give up. Eventually, you'll adjust. Start at very low doses, then increase them slowly. Although these drugs are somewhat inconvenient to take, they've proved to be both safe and effective for preventing heart attacks.

## NICOTINIC ACID

This is an inexpensive drug that's been used for many years to treat high blood cholesterol. In a major clinical trial, the Coronary Drug Project, patients who had suffered heart attacks took nicotinic acid or a placebo. Nicotinic acid was found to significantly reduce the recurrence rate of heart attack. Moreover, after 15 years, fewer deaths had occurred among the nicotinic acid group.

Nicotinic acid works by reducing the formation of lipoproteins in the liver. In doing so, it lowers blood triglycerides, VLDL cholesterol, and LDL cholesterol; by lowering triglycerides, it also raises HDL cholesterol. Nicotinic acid is the most effective drug available for raising HDL cholesterol levels.

The major problem with nicotinic acid is its troublesome side effects. One is a flushing of the skin, especially on the face. This happens several minutes after the patient takes the drug. Itching and skin rash can also result. Gastrointestinal problems can make the drug a poor choice for people who are prone to peptic ulcers. At the very least, this drug necessitates periodic monitoring through certain types of blood test. Other side effects can occur, too. For some people, the drug proves mildly toxic to the liver and has to be discontinued. It may also raise the blood uric acid level and possibly lead to gout; if you have gout, you probably should not take nicotinic acid. Additionally, nicotinic acid could make a diabetic condition worse.

Nicotinic acid comes in regular, sustained-release, and extended-release forms. The sustained-release pills are less likely to cause flushing than the regular tablets but more likely to cause liver problems. The newer extended-release tablets cause fewer side effects than either of the earlier ones. This form is available only by prescription.

If your doctor has prescribed nicotinic acid, be sure to avoid confusing it with the vitamin nicotinamide, which is not effective for lowering cholesterol.

## STATINS

Statins are powerful cholesterol-lowering drugs. They've been available for treating high blood cholesterol for the past two decades. The six statins now on the market, along with their trade names, are as follows:

- Lovastatin (Mevacor)
- Pravastatin (Pravachol)
- Simvastatin (Zocor)
- Fluvastatin (Lescol)
- Atorvastatin (Lipitor)
- Cerivastatin (Baycol)

Statins work by interfering with the formation of cholesterol in the liver, forcing the liver to produce more LDL receptors to take LDL cholesterol out of the bloodstream. The result is a major reduction in blood cholesterol, often by 25 to 35 percent. This is a much greater reduction than with other drugs and requires only relatively small doses. Because of their high effectiveness and low dose requirement, statins are extremely attractive drugs for treating high blood cholesterol. They are currently the most widely used drugs for this purpose.

Serious side effects have been very rare. A few people get a high blood level of certain liver enzymes because the enzymes leak out of the liver cells. This change may reflect mild toxicity to the liver but can be reversed rapidly when the drug is stopped. In rare instances, statins are toxic to muscles. If you take a statin and develop sore muscles, report it immediately to your physician. Failure to stop the medication may result in muscle and kidney damage.

# FIBRATES

The fibrates are useful triglyceride-lowering drugs, especially for people with very high triglycerides. For these people, fibrates are also good at raising HDL cholesterol. Fibrates aren't particularly good for reducing high cholesterol levels. The three fibrates (and their brand names) currently available in the United States are

- Gemfibrozil (Lopid)
- Clofibrate (Atromid-S)
- Fenofibrate (Tricor)

In the Helsinki Heart Study, a large clinical trial, gemfibrozil reduced the risk of heart attacks among patients with high blood cholesterol. However, its benefit was limited to people who also had high triglycerides.

Patients taking fibrates should be aware of certain side effects. The drug increases the risk of developing gallstones. It sometimes causes gastrointestinal discomfort or diarrhea. Some patients experience muscle pain similar to that caused by the statins.

# ESTROGENS

Although estrogen replacement therapy has not been shown to prevent heart disease, it does lower the LDL cholesterol level and raises the HDL cholesterol level. These beneficial effects on cholesterol may be viewed as a beneficial side effect of estrogen prescribed for other reasons, such as relief of menopausal symptoms or prevention of osteoporosis. The best way for a woman to prevent heart disease is to control her risk factors.

# OTHER HEART ATTACK RISK FACTORS

High blood cholesterol is one of several factors that can increase your risk of heart attack or stroke. Research has identified major risk factors as well as contributing risk factors. The more risk factors a person has, the greater the chance of developing heart disease. That's why it's important to eliminate or minimize these risks whenever possible.

## MAJOR RISK FACTORS THAT CAN'T BE CHANGED

**Heredity.**   The tendency toward heart disease seems to run in families. If your parent or sibling has had heart disease, your chance of having it increases. Race is also a factor. African-Americans have moderate high blood pressure twice as often as whites and severe hypertension three times as often. As a result, their risk of heart disease is greater.

**Being Male.**   Men have a greater risk of heart attack than women earlier in life. Men tend to have higher levels of low-density lipoprotein (LDL) cholesterol and lower levels of high-density lipoprotein (HDL) cholesterol than women. However, women's death rate from heart disease increases after menopause.

**Increasing Age.**   Most people who die of heart attack are age 65 or older. At older ages, women who have heart attacks are twice as likely as men to die from them within a few weeks.

## MAJOR RISK FACTORS THAT CAN BE CHANGED

**Cigarette/Tobacco Smoke.**   A smoker's risk of heart attack is more than twice that of a nonsmoker. Smokers also have two to four times the risk of sudden cardiac death. Your risk of heart disease also increases if you simply breathe in secondhand smoke at home or in the workplace. When a person quits smoking, no matter how long or how much he or she smoked, the risk of heart disease drops rapidly. Three years after quitting, the risk of death from heart disease and stroke for a person who smoked a pack a day or less is almost the same as for a person who never smoked.

**High Blood Pressure.**   High blood pressure has no symptoms, which is why it's called the "silent killer." High blood pressure increases the risk of stroke, heart attack, kidney failure, and congestive heart failure. Have your blood pressure checked regularly. If it's 140/90 or above, your doctor can help you control it through proper diet, losing weight, exercising regularly, cutting down on sodium, and medication, if necessary.

**Physical Inactivity.**   Regular, vigorous physical activity protects against heart disease. It raises HDL cholesterol and, in some people, reduces LDL cholesterol and blood pressure. The American Heart Association recommends 30 to 60 minutes of vigorous activity, such as jogging, swimming, or playing basketball, three to four times per week.

Recent research also indicates that even moderate levels of low-intensity physical activity, such as walking, dancing, and doing housework, can be beneficial. Aim for a total of at least 30 minutes a day on most days.

If you decide to begin an exercise program, remember to consult your physician first, especially if you're middle-aged or older and haven't exercised for a long time.

**Diabetes.**   The 3 million Americans who have adult diabetes are major candidates for heart attack. In fact, heart attack is the number-one killer of diabetic patients. Since the risk factors of having diabetes and being overweight often go hand in hand, it's especially important for diabetic patients to watch their diet and maintain proper weight.

**Obesity.**   People who are overweight or obese are more likely than those who aren't to develop heart disease and stroke even if they have no other risk factors. Excess weight causes a reduction in HDL cholesterol and may increase LDL cholesterol. It also predisposes people to high blood pressure and diabetes.

Recent evidence indicates that how your weight is distributed on your body may be a clue to your risk of heart disease. If a man's waist measures 40 inches or more, he has a significantly greater risk of heart disease. For women, the waist measurement should not be 35 inches or more. Take a look at the table on the next page to find the proper weight range for your sex and height. If you're one of the millions of overweight Americans, it's possible to lose weight and maintain a desirable weight for life through exercise and diet (see appendix D, page 336).

## DESIRABLE BODY WEIGHT RANGES

| Height Without Shoes | Weight Without Clothes Men (lb) | Women (lb) |
|---|---|---|
| 4'10" | — | 92–121 |
| 4'11" | — | 95–124 |
| 5'0" | — | 98–127 |
| 5'1" | 105–134 | 101–130 |
| 5'2" | 108–137 | 104–134 |
| 5'3" | 111–141 | 107–138 |
| 5'4" | 114–145 | 110–142 |
| 5'5" | 117–149 | 114–146 |
| 5'6" | 121–154 | 118–150 |
| 5'7" | 125–159 | 122–154 |
| 5'8" | 129–163 | 126–159 |
| 5'9" | 133–167 | 130–164 |
| 5'10" | 137–172 | 134–169 |
| 5'11" | 141–177 | — |
| 6'0" | 145–182 | — |
| 6'1" | 149–187 | — |
| 6'2" | 153–192 | — |
| 6'3" | 157–197 | — |

Source: Adapted from the 1959 Metropolitan Desirable Weight Table.
Note: For women 18 to 25 years old, subtract one pound for each year under 25.

## CONTRIBUTING FACTORS

**Stress.** Social and professional stress may provoke other risk factors (for example, a rise in blood pressure or blood cholesterol), lead to excessive smoking or eating, or, perhaps, induce coronary thrombosis. However, stress levels are difficult to measure, and responses to stress vary markedly. Try to find healthful ways to handle stress.

**Hormonal Factors.** Sex hormones seem to play a role in heart disease. Men have more heart attacks than women who haven't been through menopause, but after menopause a woman's risk increases. Female hormones tend to raise the good cholesterol and lower the total blood cholesterol; male hormones do the opposite. If you've experienced menopause and you're considering estrogen replacement therapy, confer with your doctor about your individual benefits and risks.

**Birth-Control Pills.** If you're taking oral contraceptives and you have risk factors for heart disease, you have an increased risk for developing blood clots and having a heart attack. This is especially true if you're over 35. Don't smoke, and be sure to get annual check-ups for blood pressure, triglycerides, and glucose to make sure they stay within the desirable range.

**Excessive Alcohol.** Too much alcohol can lead to many harmful results. It can raise blood pressure, cause heart failure, and lead to stroke. If you don't drink, don't start. If you do drink, the American Heart Association recommends no more than one drink a day for women and no more than two drinks a day for men.

# INDEX

acceptable margarine, 15, 21–22, 24, 326
acceptable oils, 15, 21, 24, 326
acidic foods, cook's tip on, 28
alfalfa sprouts:
  cook's tip on, 194
  quinoa in vegetable nests, 194–95
almond(s):
  -cocoa meringue kisses, 291
  green beans almondine, 208
  sautéed zucchini, 235
  stuffed fish fillets, 92
ancho-honey dressing, jícama and grapefruit salad with, 64–65
appetizers, 26–41
  canapés with roasted garlic, artichoke, and chèvre spread, 40
  chicken triangles, 38–39
  chili peppers, stuffed, 31
  crab spring rolls with peanut dipping sauce, 34–35
  hummus, 30
  melon balls with turkey and ham, 41
  nectarine-plum chutney, 28
  stuffed mushrooms, 36
  toasted ravioli with Italian salsa, 32–33
  zesty potato skins, 37
  zucchini spread, 29
apple(s):
  baked, 307
  -berry topping, gingerbread pancakes with, 262–63
  cook's tip on, 284
  nectarine-plum chutney, 28
  -raisin sauce, 245
  -rhubarb crisp, 284
  spiced cider, 272

apple juice:
  marinated vegetable salad, 70
  sautéed carrots, 215
  warm mushroom salad, 63
apricots, salad with creamy mustard vinaigrette, 60
arrowroot, cook's tip on, 79
artichoke:
  creamy vinaigrette, 80
  eggplant parmigiana, 200–201
  -horseradish sauce, grilled cod with, 98–99
  roasted garlic, and chèvre spread, canapés with, 40
Asian broth, poached fish in, 96–97
Asian grilled chicken, 136
Asian restaurants, dining out, 342
asparagus:
  -chicken à la king with roasted peppers, 140–41
  penne and cannellini bean casserole with sun-dried tomatoes, 186–87
avocado-tomatillo puree, 82–83

baked beans, Boston, with chipotle peppers, 206–7
bakery goods, 21
baking, low-fat, 330
baklava, 289
bananas Foster plus, 299
barley and cranberry bean stew with sage, 192–93
bars, gingerbread, 292–93
basil, Thai chicken with vegetables and, 128–29
bean(s):
  black, and spinach enchiladas, 196–97

bean(s) (*cont'd*):

black, gingered salsa, mesquite-grilled red snapper with, 100–101

Boston baked, with chipotle peppers, 206–7

cannellini, and penne casserole with sun-dried tomatoes, 186–87

chili, 168–69

cranberry, and barley stew with sage, 192–93

cranberry, cook's tip on, 192

dried, shopping for, 327

green, almondine, 208

green, cook's tip on, 208

ground beef ragout, 164–65

kidney, crispy tortilla salad, 73

kidney, substitutions for, 192

lima, Brunswick stew, 131

red, and lamb, 171

refried, 209

vegetarian sauce, 184–85

beef, 19

braised eye of round roast with brown gravy, 150–51

broth, *see* beef broth

bulgur and ground beef casserole, 162–63

chili, 168–69

comparison chart, 325

cook's tip on, 153

and corn bread pie, Mexican, 166–67

ground beef ragout, 164–65

marinated steak, 153

meat loaf with roasted vegetables, 157

peppery, with blue cheese sauce, 152

shepherd's pie, 160–61

sloppy joes, 156

stroganoff, 154–55

Swedish meat loaf with dill sauce, 158–59

-vegetable burgers, 170

beef broth, 56

braised eye of round roast with brown gravy, 150–51

Mexican beef and corn bread pie, 166–67

stroganoff, 154–55

Swedish meat loaf with dill sauce, 158–59

beets:

cook's tips on, 210

in orange sauce, 210

berry(ies):

-apple topping, gingerbread pancakes with, 262–63

chocolate custard cake with, 278–79

chocolate shortcake, 276–77

margarita ice, 306

-orange froth, 271

-peach cobbler, 282–83

Romanoff, 302

sauce, 244

sorbet, 305

beverages, 22, 268–73

chocolate cappuccino, 273

orange juice cooler, 270

orange-strawberry froth, 271

spiced apple cider, 272

biscuits, buttermilk, 258

black-eyed peas:

dried, cook's tip on, 69

lemon-curried salad, 69

Southern-style, 219

blue cheese sauce, peppery beef with, 152

bok choy:

cook's tip on, 190

soba lo mein with sugar snap peas and, 190

Boston baked beans with chipotle peppers, 206–7

Boston citrus salad, 62

bouquet garni, cook's tip on, 272

braising, low-fat, 330

bread crumbs, seasoned, 267

breads and breakfast dishes, 246–67

buttermilk biscuits, 258

cardamom-lemon muffins, 261

cook's tips on breads, 250, 252, 261

gingerbread pancakes with apple-berry topping, 262–63

honey-nut bread, 254

oat bran muffins, 259

oatmeal-fruit muffins, 260

potato bread, 252–53

savory dill bread, 248–49

seasoned bread crumbs, 267

cheese (*cont'd*):
    grilled vegetable quesadillas,
        198–99
    -herb chicken medallions,
        122
    spinach and black bean enchi-
        ladas, 196–97
    -spinach strudel, 230–31
    spinach-stuffed pizza, 188–89
    turkey and vegetable calzone,
        146–47
    yogurt, 155
    *see also specific cheeses*
cheesecake:
    mocha, 294–95
    vanilla, 294–95
cherries jubilee, 300
cherry tomatoes, *see* tomato
chèvre:
    artichoke, and roasted garlic
        spread, canapés with, 40
    *see also* goat cheese
chicken:
    Asian grilled, 136
    -asparagus à la king with roasted
        peppers, 140–41
    breasts stuffed with ricotta and
        goat cheese, 120–21
    broth, *see* chicken broth
    Brunswick stew, 131
    cheese-herb medallions, 122
    cordon bleu, 123
    crispy oven-fried, 137
    fajitas, 132–33
    garlic fillets in balsamic vinegar,
        124–25
    hearty stew, 130
    herbed salad, 77
    meat loaf with roasted vegeta-
        bles, 157
    with mustard and herbs, 126
    ragout, 138–39
    Swedish meat loaf with dill
        sauce, 158–59
    Thai, with basil and vegetables,
        128–29
    triangles, 38–39
    -vegetable stir-fry, 127
chicken broth, 55
    asparagus-chicken à la king with
        roasted peppers, 140–41

    braised brussels sprouts with
        pimiento and water chest-
        nuts, 212–13
    Brunswick stew, 131
    chicken ragout, 138–39
    cioppino, 116–17
    cook's tip on, 56
    corn bread dressing, 216
    country-style vegetable soup, 46
    creamy wild rice and wheat
        berry soup, 52
    fish in a package, 94–95
    golden rice, 229
    ham and rice salad, 78
    lamb and red beans, 171
    lentil-spinach soup, 50
    light and lemony spinach soup,
        51
    poached fish in Asian broth,
        96–97
    pork with savory sauce, 173
    pork and tofu stir-fry, 174–75
    red and green pilaf, 228
    roast Cornish hens, 144
    seafood and lemon risotto,
        114–15
    tomato, orange, and tarragon
        soup, 44
    tomato soup, 45
    vegetable stir-fry, 237
chick-peas:
    hummus, 30
    marinated vegetable salad, 70
chili, 168–69
chili peppers:
    ancho-honey salad dressing,
        64–65
    canned, cook's tip on, 209
    stuffed, 31
    warning about, 31
chocolate:
    cappuccino, 273
    cocoa-almond meringue kisses,
        291
    custard cake with raspberries,
        278–79
    mocha cheesecake, 294–95
    soufflé with vanilla sauce, 296
    strawberry shortcake, 276–77
    sugar-dusted mocha brownies,
        290

cholesterol, 5–22, 311–54
  diets for lowering levels of, 9–15
  and HDLs, 344–45
  how to keep it low, 338–40
  how your body handles, 3,
    44–46
  and LDLs, 344
  levels of, 6–7
  lowering of, 313–14
  saturated fats and, 311
  and shopping, 315–29
  staying at best level of, 340
  and VLDLs, 345–46
  in your blood, 311
  in your food, 312
chowder, clam and potato, with
  fresh herbs, 53
chutney, nectarine-plum, 28
cider, spiced apple, 272
cilantro-corn pesto, pork with,
  176–77
cioppino, 116–17
citrus Boston salad, 62
clams:
  cioppino, 116–17
  and potato chowder with fresh
    herbs, 53
cobbler, peach-raspberry, 282–83
cocoa-almond meringue kisses,
  291
cocoa powder, cook's tip on, 296
cod, grilled, with artichoke-horseradish sauce, 98–99
cooking for a healthy heart, 330–35
  baking, 330
  braising, 330
  broiling, 330
  gravies, 334
  grilling, 330
  meats, 333
  microwave, 330–31
  miscellaneous tips, 335
  poaching, 331
  poultry, 333
  recipe substitutions, 332
  roasting, 331
  sautéing, 331
  seafood, 333–34
  soups and sauces, 334
  steaming, 332
  stewing, 330

stir-frying, 332
  vegetables, 334
cook's tips:
  acidic foods, 28
  alfalfa sprouts, 194
  apples, 284
  arrowroot substitute for corn-
    starch, 79
  baking bread, 250, 252
  baking potatoes, 220
  baklava, freezing of, 289
  beef broth, 56
  beef cuts, 153
  beets, 210
  boiling potatoes, 227
  bok choy, 190
  bouquet garni, 272
  broth, 55, 56, 216
  brussels sprouts, 212
  canned chili peppers, 209
  celery added to soup, 46
  cheesecake, 294
  chicken broth, 56
  chipotle peppers, 206
  cioppino, frozen, 116
  cocoa powder, 296
  cranberry beans, 192
  cutting dried fruit, 260
  decorative topping, 290
  defatting broth, 216
  dried black-eyed peas, 69
  dried herbs and spices, 122
  dry gelatin powder, 301
  dry-roasting nuts, 29
  fish sauce, 128
  flavored vinegar, 86
  flour substitution, 261
  fresh greens, 48
  frozen fruit, 306
  fruit substitution, 304
  gingerroot, 47
  grated orange rind, 44
  green beans, 208
  ground beef, 160
  hot peppers, 168
  jasmine rice, 128
  jícama, 65
  leftover fresh herbs, 33
  leftover pesto, 176
  mangoes, cutting, 54
  muffin pans, 92

tapioca pudding, 297
very berry sorbet, 305
yogurt-fruit cup, 303
deviled eggs, 68
diet:
ABC theory of, 339
and cholesterol, 8, 12–15, 311–14
dining out, 341–43
and drugs, 347–50
and exercise, 338
how to stay with, 336–40
less fat in, 337–38
and motivation, 336–37
urges, 339
dill bread, savory, 248–49
dill sauce, Swedish meat loaf with,
158–59
dining out, 341–43
dipping sauce:
honey mustard, 41
peanut, crab spring rolls with,
34–35
dressing (salad), *see* salads and
salad dressings
dressing (stuffing), corn bread, 216
drugs, 347–50
bile acid binding, 347–48
estrogens, 350
fibrates, 350
nicotinic acid, 348–49
statins, 349

e ggplant:
parmigiana, 200–201
ratatouille, 236
eggs, 18–19
deviled, 68
shopping for, 324–25
Spanish-style scrambled, 266
for spinach salad, 61
enchiladas, spinach and black
bean, 196–97
exercise, 338

f ajitas, chicken, 132–33
fat-free foods, chart, 329
fats, 12–16, 17–22
in cooking, 330–35

on food labels, 315
lowering, 336–43
monounsaturated, 15–16, 21,
314
polyunsaturated, 15, 21, 314
removing from broths, 216
saturated, 5, 8, 15, 21, 311–13
trans, 15, 311
shopping healthfully for, 315–29
feta cheese:
-spinach strudel, 230–31
vinaigrette with Dijon mustard,
79
*see also* goat cheese
fish:
broiled steaks, 105
bulgur-stuffed rainbow trout,
90–91
cioppino, 116–17
cooking tips, 334
grilled catfish with mustard-
lemon sauce, 102–3
grilled cod with artichoke-
horseradish sauce, 98–99
halibut kebabs, 106
mesquite-grilled red snapper
with gingered black bean
salsa, 100–101
with mustard sauce over
steamed spinach, 93
in a package, 94–95
poached, in Asian broth, 96–97
poached, and fish broth, 104
stew, 107
stuffed fillets, 92
tuna-pasta casserole, 108–9
tuna salad pita sandwiches, 110
*see also* seafood
fish sauce, cook's tip on, 128
flavored vinegar, 86–87
flour, cook's tip on, 261
fluff, orange, 298
food labels, 315–20
carbohydrates and protein, 316
comparing information on,
317–18
daily values, 317
fats and sodium, 315
ingredients listed on, 320
names and descriptors on,
318–19
nutrition facts on, 316

French bread, whole-wheat, 250–51
fruits, 20
    cooking tips, 334
    dried, cook's tip on cutting, 260
    fresh, salad with poppy seed and
        yogurt dressing, 67
    frozen, cook's tip on, 306
    -oatmeal muffins, 260
    shopping for, 327–28
    substitutions, cook's tip on, 304
    summertime soup, 54
    vinegar, 86–87
    -yogurt cup, 303
    *see also specific fruits*

g arlic:
    chicken fillets in balsamic vine-
        gar, 124–25
    and greens gumbo, 48–49
    roasted, artichoke, and chèvre
        spread, canapés with, 40
    roasted, cook's tip on, 40
    sauce, steamed red potatoes
        with, 227
gazpacho salad dressing, 84
gelatin, dry, cook's tip on, 301
gingerbread bars, 292–93
gingerbread pancakes with apple-
    berry topping, 262–63
gingered black bean salsa, 100–101
gingerroot, cook's tip on, 47
gingersnap and graham cracker
    crust, 288
goat cheese:
    artichoke, and roasted garlic
        spread, canapés with, 40
    chicken breasts stuffed with
        ricotta and, 120–21
    -spinach strudel, 230–31
    vinaigrette with Dijon mustard,
        79
golden rice, 229
graham cracker and gingersnap
    crust, 288
grains, 20, 327
grapefruit:
    Boston citrus salad, 62
    and jícama salad with
        ancho-honey dressing,
        64–65

gravy:
    brown, braised eye of round
        roast with, 150–51
    cooking tips, 334
green and red pilaf, 228
greens:
    cook's tip on, 48
    and garlic gumbo, 48–49
    grilled portobello mushrooms
        with couscous and, 180–81
    sautéed, 217
    *see also* salads and salad dress-
        ings; *specific greens*
green tomatoes, oven-fried with
    poppy seeds, 233
grilled foods:
    Asian chicken, 136
    catfish with mustard-lemon
        sauce, 102–3
    cod with artichoke-horseradish
        sauce, 98–99
    halibut kebabs, 106
    low-fat cooking tips, 330
    portobello mushrooms with
        couscous and greens,
        180–81
    red snapper with gingered black
        bean salsa, 100–101
    vegetable quesadillas, 198–99
ground beef:
    and bulgur casserole, 162–63
    chili, 168–69
    cook's tip on, 160
    and corn bread pie, Mexican,
        166–67
    low-fat cooking tips, 333
    meat loaf with roasted vegeta-
        bles, 157
    ragout, 164–65
    shepherd's pie, 160–61
    sloppy joes, 156
    Swedish meat loaf with dill
        sauce, 158–59
    -vegetable burgers, 170
gumbo, greens and garlic, 48–49

h alibut kebabs, 106
ham:
    chicken cordon bleu, 123
    greens and garlic gumbo, 48

melon balls with turkey and, 41
and rice salad, 78
Southern-style black-eyed peas,
219
split pea soup, 47
HDLs (high-density lipoproteins),
6–7, 344–45
healthy heart:
cooking for, 330–35
shopping for, 320–29
heart attack risk factors, 351–54
herbs:
baby potatoes, 224
bouquet garni, 272
-cheese chicken medallions, 122
chicken with mustard and, 126
chicken salad, 77
cook's tips on, 33, 122, 272
creamy salad dressing, 81
fresh, clam and potato chowder
with, 53
Italian salsa, 32–33
for salad dressing, 61
twice-baked potatoes and,
222–23
vinegar, 86–87
*see also specific herbs*
home-fried potatoes, 225
honey:
-ancho dressing, jícama and
grapefruit salad with, 64–65
Asian grilled chicken, 136
baklava, 289
carrots, 214
mustard dipping sauce, 41
-nut bread, 254
horseradish-artichoke sauce, grilled
cod with, 98–99
hummus, 30

I ce, strawberry margarita, 306
ice cream, 17–18
ingredients:
on food labels, 320
substitutions of, 24, 332
Italian restaurants, dining out,
342–43
Italian salsa, toasted ravioli with,
32–33

j alapeño peppers:
mesquite-grilled red snapper
with gingered black bean
salsa, 100–101
salsa, 242
stuffed, 31
tomatillo-avocado puree, 82–83
jambalaya rice, 134–35
jasmine rice, cook's tip on, 128
jícama:
cook's tip on, 65
and grapefruit salad with ancho-
honey dressing, 64–65
jubilee, cherries, 300

k ebabs, halibut, 106
kisses, cocoa-almond meringue, 291

l amb, 19
and red beans, 171
LDLs (low-density lipoproteins), 8,
344
legumes, 20
lemon:
-cardamom muffins, 261
-curried black-eyed pea salad, 69
-mustard sauce, grilled catfish
with, 102–3
poppy seed cake, 280–81
and seafood risotto, 114–15
spinach soup, 51
lentil:
spicy curry, 191
-spinach soup, 50
lo mein, soba with bok choy and
sugar snap peas, 190

m acaroni:
beef stroganoff, 154–55
and salmon salad, 74–75
mango(es):
brûlée, with pine nuts, 304
cutting, cook's tip on, 54
summertime soup, 54
margarita strawberry ice, 306

meats, 19–20, 148–77
    loaf with roasted vegetables, 157
    low-fat cooking tips, 333
    organ, 19
    processed, 19
    shopping for, 322–23
    Swedish loaf with dill sauce,
        158–59
    *see also specific meats*
melon:
    balls with turkey and ham, 41
    -cucumber salad with raspberry
        vinegar, 66
    with sherbet, 301
    summertime soup, 54
meringue kisses, cocoa-almond,
    291
meringue shells, 286–87
mesquite-grilled red snapper with
    gingered black bean salsa,
    100–101
Mexican beef and corn bread pie,
    166–67
Mexican restaurants, dining out,
    343
microwave cooking, 330–31
milk, 17
mint:
    tabbouleh, 72
    -tomato raita, 241
mocha:
    cheesecake, 294–95
    chocolate cappuccino, 273
    sugar-dusted brownies, 290
muffin pans, cook's tip on, 92
muffins:
    cardamom-lemon, 261
    oat bran, 259
    oatmeal-fruit, 260
mushroom(s):
    beef stroganoff, 154–55
    chicken ragout, 138–39
    fresh, cook's tip on, 145
    grilled portobello with couscous
        and greens, 180–81
    stuffed, 36
    stuffed fish fillets, 92
    vegetarian sauce, 184–85
    warm salad, 63
mustard:
    baked crabmeat, 111
    chicken with herbs and, 126

cook's tip on, 112
creamy vinaigrette, salad with,
    60
feta cheese vinaigrette with,
    79
honey dipping sauce, 41
-lemon sauce, grilled catfish
    with, 102–3
sauce, fish over steamed spinach
    with, 93

nectarine-plum chutney, 28
nutrient analyses, 23–24
nutrition facts on food labels, 316
nuts, 21
    baklava, 289
    cocoa-almond meringue kisses,
        291
    corn-cilantro pesto, 176–77
    dry-roasting, 29
    green beans almondine, 208
    -honey bread, 254
    peanut dipping sauce, 34–35
    pine, mango brûlée with, 304
    praline butternut squash, 232
    sautéed zucchini, 235
    stuffed fish fillets, 92
    stuffed mushrooms, 36
    zucchini spread, 29

Oat bran muffins, 259
oatmeal-fruit muffins, 260
obesity, 312–13, 353–54
oils:
    hydrogenated, 21–22
    sesame, 35
    shopping for, 326
olives, black, for zesty potato skins,
    37
onion, cook's tip on, 164
orange:
    Boston citrus salad, 62
    fluff, 298
    fresh fruit salad with poppy
        seed and yogurt salad dress-
        ing, 67
    grated rind of, cook's tip on,
        44

juice cooler, 270
sauce, beets in, 210
-strawberry froth, 271
tomato, and tarragon soup, 44
organ meats, 19

P ancake, pan-fried pasta, with
vegetables, 218
pancakes, gingerbread, with apple-
berry topping, 262–63
Parmesan cheese, -peppercorn
ranch dressing, 85
parmigiana, eggplant, 200–201
parsnips, cranberry bean and barley
stew with sage, 192–93
pasta:
beef stroganoff, 154–55
pan-fried pancake with vegetables, 218
penne and cannellini bean
casserole with sun-dried
tomatoes, 186–87
primavera, 182–83
and salmon salad, 74–75
seafood salad, 76
shopping for, 327
soba lo mein with bok choy and
sugar snap peas, 190
-tuna casserole, 108–9
turkey tetrazzini, 145
whole-wheat, with vegetarian
sauce, 184–85
peach(es):
-raspberry cobbler, 282–83
summertime soup, 54
peanut dipping sauce, crab spring
rolls with, 34–35
peas:
black-eyed, see black-eyed peas
chicken ragout, 138–39
dried, shopping for, 327
ham and rice salad, 78
hearty chicken stew, 130
red and green pilaf, 228
seafood pasta salad, 76
shepherd's pie, 160–61
snow, see snow peas
split, soup, 47
sugar snap, soba lo mein with
bok choy and, 190

pecans:
baklava, 289
corn-cilantro pesto, 176–77
praline butternut squash, 232
zucchini spread, 29
penne and cannellini bean casserole with sun-dried tomatoes,
186–87
peppercorn(s):
cook's tip on, 85
-Parmesan ranch salad dressing,
85
peppers:
ancho-honey salad dressing,
64–65
canned, cook's tip on, 209
chicken-vegetable stir-fry,
127
chili, stuffed, 31
chipotle, Boston baked beans
with, 206–7
herbed chicken salad as stuffing
for, 77
hot, cook's tip on, 168
hot, warning about, 31
how to roast, 140
Italian salsa, 32–33
ratatouille, 236
roasted, asparagus-chicken à la
king with, 140–41
roasted bell, cook's tip on, 73
salsa, 242
tomatillo-avocado puree,
82–83
vegetarian sauce, 184–85
pesto, corn-cilantro, pork with,
176–77
phyllo dough:
baklava, 289
chicken triangles, 38–39
cook's tip on, 231
spinach-cheese strudel, 230–31
pie crust, gingersnap and graham
cracker, 288
pies:
Mexican beef and corn bread,
166–67
pumpkin, 285
shepherd's, 160–61
pilaf:
golden rice, 229
red and green, 228

pimiento and water chestnuts,
    braised brussels sprouts with,
    212–13
pineapple:
    chicken-vegetable stir-fry, 127
    praline butternut squash, 232
pine nuts, mango brûlée with, 304
pita:
    canapés with roasted garlic, arti-
        choke, and chèvre spread, 40
    tuna salad sandwiches, 110
pizza:
    dough, 188–89
    spinach-stuffed, 188–89
    turkey and vegetable calzone,
        146–47
plum-nectarine chutney, 28
poaching, low-fat cooking tips, 331
poppy seed(s):
    cook's tip on, 280
    lemon cake, 280–81
    oven-fried green tomatoes with,
        233
    and yogurt dressing, fresh fruit
        salad with, 67
pork, 19
    with corn-cilantro pesto, 176–77
    with savory sauce, 173
    spicy baked chops, 172
    tenderloin, cook's tip on, 176
    and tofu stir-fry, 174–75
portobello mushrooms, grilled,
    with couscous and greens,
    180–81
potato(es):
    baked, with vegetable topping,
        220–21
    bread, 252–53
    and clam chowder with fresh
        herbs, 53
    cook's tips on, 220, 227
    country-style vegetable soup,
        46
    fish stew, 107
    hearty chicken stew, 130
    herbed baby, 224
    home-fried, 225
    meat loaf with roasted vegeta-
        bles, 157
    salad, 71
    scalloped, 226

shepherd's pie, 160–61
steamed red, with garlic sauce,
    227
tomato, orange, and tarragon
    soup, 44
twice-baked, and herbs, 222–23
zesty skins, 37
poultry, 20, 118–47
    comparison chart, 325
    low-fat cooking tips, 333
    shopping for, 322, 323–24
    skinning, cook's tip on, 137
    see also chicken; Cornish hens;
        turkey
praline butternut squash, 232
primavera, pasta, 182–83
protein, 316
pudding, tapioca, 297
pumpkin pie, 285

q uesadillas, grilled vegetable,
    198–99
quinoa in vegetable nests, 194–95

r adishes:
    cucumber-melon salad with
        raspberry vinegar, 66
    ham and rice salad, 78
    potato salad, 71
    seafood pasta salad, 76
ragouts:
    chicken, 138–39
    ground beef, 164–65
raisin(s):
    -apple sauce, 245
    nectarine-plum chutney, 28
raitas:
    cucumber, 240
    tomato-mint, 241
ranch salad dressing, Parmesan-
    peppercorn, 85
raspberries:
    chocolate custard cake with,
        278–79
    -peach cobbler, 282–83
raspberry vinegar, cucumber-melon
    salad with, 66

sugar snap peas, soba lo mein with
bok choy and, 190
summertime soup, 54
sun-dried tomatoes, penne and
cannellini bean casserole
with, 186–87
sunflower seeds, toasting of, 60
Swedish meat loaf with dill sauce,
158–59
sweet potato, cranberry bean and
barley stew with sage,
192–93
sweets:
shopping for, 328–29
*see also* desserts

tabbouleh, 72
tahini, cook's tip on, 30
tandoori Cornish hens, 142–43
tapioca pudding, 297
tarragon, tomato, and orange soup,
44
tetrazzini, turkey, 145
Thai chicken with basil and vegetables, 128–29
tofu:
cook's tips on, 68, 174
creamy mustard vinaigrette, 60
deviled eggs, 68
eggplant parmigiana, 200–201
and pork stir-fry, 174–75
tomatillo-avocado puree, 82–83
tomato(es):
Brunswick stew, 131
bulgur and ground beef casserole, 162–63
Cajun tortilla wrap, 134–35
cherry, canapés with roasted
garlic, artichoke, and chèvre
spread, 40
cherry, pork and tofu stir-fry,
174–75
cherry, sautéed, 234
cherry, spinach salad, 61
crispy tortilla salad, 73
fish stew, 107
green, oven-fried with poppy
seeds, 233
ground beef ragout, 164–65
hearty chicken stew, 130

herbed chicken salad as stuffing
for, 77
Italian salsa, 32–33
Mexican beef and corn bread
pie, 166–67
-mint raita, 241
orange, and tarragon soup, 44
salmon and pasta salad, 74–75
salsa, 242
sauce, 176–77
seafood pasta salad, 76
soup, 45
sun-dried, penne and cannellini
bean casserole with, 186–87
tabbouleh, 72
vegetable broth, 57
vegetarian sauce, 184–85
toppings:
apple-berry, gingerbread pancakes with, 262–63
creamy dessert, 243
decorative, cook's tip on, 290
vegetable, baked potatoes with,
220–21
tortillas:
breakfast wrap, 264–65
Cajun wrap, 134–35
chicken fajitas, 132–33
crispy salad, 73
grilled vegetable quesadillas,
198–99
spinach and black bean enchiladas, 196–97
triangles, chicken, 38–39
trout, rainbow, bulgur-stuffed, 90–91
tuna:
-pasta casserole, 108–9
salad pita sandwiches, 110
turkey:
melon balls with ham and, 41
tetrazzini, 145
and vegetable calzone, 146–47
*see also* chicken recipes
turmeric, cook's tip on, 142
turnip, clam and potato chowder
with fresh herbs, 53

Vanilla:
cheesecake, 294–95
sauce, chocolate soufflé with, 296

veal, 19
vegetable(s), 20, 204–37
    -beef burgers, 170
    broth, *see* vegetable broth
    -chicken stir-fry, 127
    country-style soup, 46
    gazpacho salad dressing, 84
    grilled, quesadillas, 198–99
    low-fat cooking tips, 334
    marinated, salad, 70
    pan-fried pasta pancake with, 218
    quinoa in nests of, 194–95
    ratatouille, 236
    roasted, meat loaf with, 157
    shopping for, 327–28
    stir-fry, 237
    Thai chicken with basil and,
        128–29
    topping, baked potatoes with,
        220–21
    and turkey calzone, 146–47
    *see also specific vegetables*
vegetable broth, 57
    cranberry bean and barley stew
        with sage, 192–93
    green beans almondine, 208
    grilled portobello mushrooms
        with couscous and greens,
        180–81
    penne and cannellini bean
        casserole with sun-dried
        tomatoes, 186–87
    soba lo mein with bok choy and
        sugar snap peas, 190
    soybean sauté, 202–3
vegetarian dishes, 178–203
    cranberry bean and barley stew
        with sage, 192–93
    eggplant parmigiana, 200–201
    grilled portobello mushrooms
        with couscous and greens,
        180–81
    grilled vegetable quesadillas,
        198–99
    pasta primavera, 182–83
    penne and cannellini bean
        casserole with sun-dried
        tomatoes, 186–87
    quinoa in vegetable nests,
        194–95
    soba lo mein with bok choy and
        sugar snap peas, 190

soybean sauté, 202–3
spicy lentil curry, 191
spinach and black bean enchi-
    ladas, 196–97
spinach-stuffed pizza, 188–89
whole-wheat pasta with sauce,
    184–85
venison stroganoff, 154–55
vinaigrettes:
    creamy artichoke, 80
    creamy mustard, salad with, 60
    feta cheese, with Dijon mustard,
        79
vinegar:
    balsamic, garlic chicken fillets
        in, 124–25
    cook's tip on, 86
    herbed or fruit, 86–87
    raspberry, cucumber-melon
        salad with, 66
VLDLs (very low density lipopro-
    teins), 345–46


# Walnuts:
    stuffed mushrooms, 36
    zucchini spread, 29
water chestnuts and pimiento,
    braised brussels sprouts with,
    212–13
weight, and heart attacks, 353–54
wheat berries:
    cook's tip on, 52
    and wild rice soup, creamy,
        52
whole-wheat flour, substitute for,
    261
whole-wheat French bread, 250–51
whole-wheat pasta with vegetarian
    sauce, 184–85
wild rice and wheat berry soup,
    creamy, 52
wine:
    beef stroganoff, 154–55
    chicken ragout, 138–39
    cioppino, 116–17
    fish in a package, 94–95
    ground beef ragout, 164–65
    marinated steak, 153
    peppery beef with blue cheese
        sauce, 152

wine (*cont'd*):
  poached fish in Asian broth, 96–97
  pork and tofu stir-fry, 174–75
  seafood and lemon risotto, 114–15
  turkey tetrazzini, 145
  vegetarian sauce, 184–85
  warm mushroom salad, 63

Yeast bread, cook's tip on, 250
yogurt:
  cheese, 155
  creamy dessert topping, 243
  creamy herb salad dressing, 81
  cucumber raita, 240
  fruit cup, 303
  herbed chicken salad, 77

mustard sauce, 93
and poppy seed dressing, fresh fruit salad with, 67
potato salad, 71
summertime soup, 54
tandoori Cornish hens, 142–43
tomato-mint raita, 241
tuna-pasta casserole, 108–9

Zucchini:
  bread, 255
  country-style vegetable soup, 46
  herbed chicken salad as stuffing for, 77
  pasta primavera, 182–83
  ratatouille, 236
  sautéed, 235
  spread, 29